CAMBRIDGE SURVEYS OF ECONOMIC LITERATURE

MARKET STRUCTURE AND INNOVATION

CAMBRIDGE SURVEYS OF ECONOMIC LITERATURE

The literature of economics is expanding rapidly and many subjects have
changed out of recognition within the space of a few years. Perceiving the
state of knowledge in fast-developing subjects is difficult for students and
time-consuming for professional economists. This series of books is intended
to help with this problem. Each book will be quite brief, giving a clear
structure to and balanced overview of the topic and written at a level
intelligible to the senior undergraduate. They will therefore be useful for
teaching, but will also provide a mature yet compact presentation of the
subject for economists wishing to update their knowledge outside their own
specialism.

Other books in the series
E. Roy Weintraub: Microfoundations: The compatibility of
microeconomics and macroeconomics
Dennis C. Mueller: Public choice
Robert Clark and Joseph Spengler: The economics of
individual and population aging
Edwin Burmeister: Capital theory and dynamics
Mark Blaug: The methodology of economics or how
economists explain
Robert Ferber and Werner Z. Hirsch: Social experimentation
and economic policy

Market structure and innovation

MORTON I. KAMIEN

and

NANCY L. SCHWARTZ

J. L. Kellogg Graduate School of Management
Northwestern University

CAMBRIDGE UNIVERSITY PRESS
CAMBRIDGE
LONDON   NEW YORK   NEW ROCHELLE
MELBOURNE   SYDNEY

Published by the Press Syndicate of the University of Cambridge
The Pitt Building, Trumpington Street, Cambridge CB2 1RP
32 East 57th Street, New York, NY 10022, USA
296 Beaconsfield Parade, Middle Park, Melbourne 3206, Australia

First published 1982

Printed in the United States of America

Library of Congress Cataloging in Publication Data
Kamien, Morton.
Market structure and innovation.
(Cambridge surveys of economic literature)
Bibliography: p.
Includes index.
1. Technological innovations. 2. Industrial organiza-
tion (Economic theory)   I. Schwartz, Nancy Lou.
II. Title.   III. Series.
HC79.T4K3   338   81-12254
ISBN 0 521 22190 0   hard covers   AACR2
ISBN 0 521 29385 5   paperback

CONTENTS

v

Contents vii

PREFACE

We have long been intrigued by technical advance both because of its substantive role in shaping virtually every facet of our lives and because of the conceptual challenges in explaining it as an economic phenomenon. The economics of market structure and innovation involves almost all the difficulties excluded from the standard analysis of competitive equilibrium – nonconvexities, externalities, public goods, uncertainty, and nonprice competition. Thus to provide a comprehensive economic theory of market structure and innovation, one must try to resolve these difficulties oneself or await their resolution by others. Unfortunately, either strategy takes a long time and in the interim we are asked as economists to give whatever guidance possible on how to shape the course and pace of technical advance.

The absence of a complete theory of market structure and innovation is matched by our incomplete knowledge of the facts regarding this subject. Indeed, these are simultaneous problems. This theme, incomplete theory and incomplete factual information, is of course common to many branches of economics. The purpose of this book is to present what economists currently do know both theoretically and empirically about the relationship between market structure and innovation. Much of the theory in Chapters 4 and 5 is new, representing significant integration, extension, and generalization of previously published materials.

How much we still do not know will also become apparent in the course of this presentation. Hopefully, it will stimulate further interest and progress as well.

This volume is intended for anyone interested in the economics of technical advance, especially for students of microeconomics and industrial organization, both undergraduate and graduate. Businesspeople engaged in innovative activity may also find it of interest. A certain background in economics and mathematics is useful, say, an intermediate microeconomics course and an elementary calculus course, for full appreciation of the material. Perhaps what is primarily required is a level of economic and mathematical "maturity," which is so elusive.

This book can be used as a text for an advanced undergraduate or graduate course on the economics of technical advance or as a supplement to courses in applied microeconomics or industrial organization. We have attempted to minimize the amount of mathematics in the main text without sacrificing the details of the hypotheses, because these details indicate the limitations of the theories and form the basis for generalization to more realistic theories. Derivations of major results are presented in appendixes.

We wish to acknowledge the helpful comments and suggestions of our Northwestern University colleagues: Ronald Braeutigam, Mike Scherer, and Nancy Stokey, as well as those of Richard Nelson of Yale, Almarin Phillips of the University of Pennsylvania, Tim McGuire of Carnegie-Mellon, Gary Fethke and Sam Wu of the University of Iowa, and Nathan Rosenberg of Stanford. The two anonymous reviewers of the first draft of this edition were especially helpful. Thanks are also due Colin Day, our editor, for sharing his wisdom and providing encouragement and gentle nudging when needed. We owe a special debt to Mark Perlman for his role in the publication of our article, "Market Structure and Innovation: A Survey," *Journal of Economic Literature,* 1975, from which this text evolved. All these people assisted in making it a better book; any shortcomings, of course, are ours.

We have benefited from financial support by the National Science

Foundation, IBM, and The Center for Advanced Study in Managerial Economics and Decision Sciences. Ann Crost and Rita Terry provided the excellent typing. We are also grateful to Lenore and Randall Kamien who showed considerable patience during the preparation of *Market Structure and Innovation*.

M. I. K.
N. L. S.

1

The emergence of an economics of technical advance

It hardly seems necessary these days to point out the importance of technical advance. We look to it to rescue us from the consequences of exhausting essential natural resources; abate inflation through productivity increases; improve our balance of payments deficit; eliminate famine; and cure cancer, heart disease, and a variety of other ailments. Our faith in technical advance is bolstered by achievements such as the atomic bomb, electronic computers, the landing of a man on the moon, heart transplants, and test-tube babies. We no longer ask if something is possible, but how soon it can be done and at what price.

Serendipity in technical advance brought us, among other things, penicillin, cellophane, current electricity, vulcanized rubber, X-rays, radioactivity, and practical photography. Still technical advance has come to be regarded largely as a purposeful activity, subject to guidance in pace and direction. It is also recognized that research is carried out for a variety of reasons, including self-expression, altruism, and prestige. Further, creativity cannot be elicited on request. Yet our focus in this book is on research that takes money to do and for which money is the reward. The opportunity to raise money for innovation and to realize a profit from it depends importantly on the economic environment in which it is performed. We are concerned with the relationship between market

1

structure and innovation in the economic environment of the modern market economy.

By market structure we shall mean any one of the possible configurations of sellers – many small, many small and a few large, only a few large – of which perfect competition and monopoly are the polar cases. By innovation we shall mean all those activities, from basic research to invention to development and commercialization, that give rise to a new product or means of production. We shall not distinguish among (1) basic research – generation of new knowledge without any specific use in mind, (2) invention – application of scientific knowledge to achieve a specific end, including construction of a prototype model, and (3) development – refinement of the prototype into a final product or process. Although such a serial taxonomy may be useful for certain purposes, in reality these activities are often carried out in parallel with interactions and feedback among the various stages. Moreover, as will become apparent, current measurement techniques and data do not really allow such fine distinctions.

Likewise, we shall not distinguish between process innovations and product innovations. Process innovations are technical advances that reduce the cost of producing existing products, whereas product innovations involve development of new or improved products. Equivalently, the former may be defined as upward shifts in the production function, and the latter, as creation of new production functions. Product innovations reduce the cost of satisfying existing needs. In actuality, the classification of innovations depends on the perspective. For example, a new computer is a product innovation from the standpoint of its manufacturers but is a cost-reducing innovation for its users, say, commercial banks.

The course of technical advance influences market structure, in part, through altering the methods of production. The development of the steam-powered engine favored large manufacturing facilities and a concomitant reduction in the number of firms in a market, whereas the development of an electric-powered motor tends to have had the reverse effect. Introduction of new products by industry entrants may increase the competitiveness in the market, but frequent new product development by a large firm may drive out smaller firms and discourage entry of others. The bulk of the research reported in this text, however, deals with the impact of market structure upon innovation. Empirical research reveals that an intermediate market structure, one that is neither perfectly competitive nor perfectly monopolistic, is usually most conducive to technical advance. A closely related result, especially because firm size and monopoly power are often linked, perhaps erroneously, is that inventive activity rises more than proportionately with firm size up to some point and slows thereafter. The rest of this book is devoted to explaining how these results and others were reached, from the initial hypotheses to the empirical tests. The new theories that have evolved are also exposited.

Early observations on technical advance

Intense study of technical advance as an economic phenomenon is a relatively recent event, beginning at about the end of World War II. Even now many economics texts treat technology as a given characteristic of the environment that is determined outside the economic system. They do occasionally include a reference, or even a chapter, on technology as an endogenous economic variable. Yet recognition of the role of economic gain in the achievement of technical advance can be traced back at least to the "father" of modern philosophy, René Descartes:

> As for myself, I am persuaded that if I had been taught in my youth all the truths of which I have since sought demonstrations, and if I could have learned them without difficulty, I might never have learned any others, or at least, I would never have acquired the habit and ability that I believe I possess, always to *find truths in proportion to the efforts I made to find them* ...
>
> It is true that as far as the related experiments are concerned, one man is not enough to do them all, but he could not usefully employ other hands than his own, unless those of workers or other persons whom he could pay. *Such people would do, in the hope of gain, which*

is a very effective motive, precisely what they are told.
As for these volunteers who might offer to do it out of
curiosity or the desire to learn, besides that ordinarily
they are stronger in promises than in performance and
they make nothing but beautiful proposals of which
none ever succeeds, they would infallibly expect to be
paid by the explanation of some difficulties, or at least
in compliments and useless conversation, which would
necessarily consume so much time needed for investigation that the assistance would be a net loss (Descartes,
1956, pp. 46–7, emphasis added).

Indeed, the translator, Lafleur, suggests that the *Discourse on
Method* was a proposal for funding of Descartes's researches
(Descartes, 1956, p. xvi).

According to Rescher (1978, p. xii):

It was Leibniz who first clearly conceived of science as a
productive enterprise. Throughout much of his many-
sided activity he was concerned to put science on a busi-
nesslike basis. He sought to organize and systematize
scientific work (in his academy projects), to secure its
financial support (in his démarches upon princes), and to
inventory systematically its stock-in-trade (in his projects
of encyclopedism and of a *scientia universalis*).

Despite the 150-year precedence of Descartes's statement over
Adam Smith's *Wealth of Nations* (1937), recognition of technical
advance as an economic activity evolved slowly. Smith recognized
the role of technical advance in economic progress – it would have
been difficult for such a keen observer of the Industrial Revolution
not to – and he indicated how the division of labor would yield, as a
by-product, improvements in the methods of production as each
worker grew more expert at his task. These advances were of a run-
of-the-mill variety; Smith saw the major ones coming from men of
independent means, seeking truth for its own sake. Thus although
Smith identified the two ingredients that make technical advance an
economic activity – namely, it is done to gain an advantage, such
as easing one's work, and it requires the investment of money,

available to men of independent means – he failed to combine them into a theory of technical advance as a deliberate economic process.

Malthus and Ricardo were also concerned with the impact of technical advance, especially in the form of improved machinery, on the displacement of labor but regarded it as exogenous to the economic system. In John Stuart Mill's conceptualization of the "stationary state," a situation in which all the economic variables are fixed relative to each other, the classical economists' vision of the economy was brought into sharp focus. Economies were tending toward this stationary state equilibrium, with technical advances creating transient disturbances. (The mechanistic model of planetary motion of Copernicus–Galileo–Newton is likely to have inspired this view of the economic system.) This view has had a profound effect on the development of economic theory, particularly in its preoccupation with the properties of static general equilibrium under perfect competition. The concept of the stationary state was reinforced by Walras and other mathematical economists who found it convenient to posit stationary supply and demand functions in their study of general equilibrium. Also, the supposition of complete knowledge of all elements of the environment associated with perfect competition is most plausible in a stationary state; see Stigler (1957).

The classical economists' failure to recognize technical advance as a continuing process also led them, especially Malthus, to foresee the stationary state darkly. Indeed, Carlyle dubbed economics the "dismal" science. It is perhaps ironic that today, with technical advance an expected phenomenon, these fears have resurfaced. Only now, according to the Club of Rome's report, *The Limits to Growth* (Meadows et al., 1972), our future is threatened by exhaustion of essential natural resources and suffocation – through contamination of the atmosphere – as well as by starvation. Adding in Rescher's thesis that maintenance of linear growth in scientific knowledge requires exponential growth in expenditures, which cannot be maintained forever, we have again a bleak outlook on our long-range future. Rescher (1978), like the classical economists, overlooks the possibility that the product of technical advance may release more than the required resources for continued growth in scientific knowledge.

The replacement of the vision of an economic system tending to a stationary state with the vision of continual evolution can be traced to Marx's *Capital* (1919). He analogized an economic system to a biological entity that is ever changing instead of to a chemical reaction that is tending to an equilibrium. Further, he argued that capitalists' profits, realized through the exploitation of labor, were reinvested in capital equipment not only to offset depreciation or increase its amount but also to keep pace with its continuous improvement. Competition from other capitalists exerted pressure to keep abreast of the latest technology. In this assertion there is the glimmer of the theory of competition through innovation subsequently developed by Schumpeter, as will be described shortly. Marx, however, appeared to view technical advance as a change in the environment that capitalists welcomed but reacted to rather than initiated.

The classical economists cannot, however, be faulted too strongly for failing to recognize technical advance as a deliberate economic activity, for they, like their successors, were much better at reflecting the current economic environment than divining the future. They saw that technical advance frequently depended on the right person being in the right place at the right time. For example, the electrical properties of metals, the basis for the eventual development of batteries, were discovered by an anatomist, Galvani, while dissecting frogs. Watt's development of the steam engine began with his attempt to repair an earlier engine of Newcomen. It was only after Watt's steam engine that the science of thermodynamics came into being. Likewise, Bessemer's steel-making process preceded its scientific foundation. The image of the inventor of that genre is perhaps best epitomized by Edison, testing some two thousand filaments in the course of developing the electric light bulb. Indeed, a recent biography of Edison by Robert Conot, commemorating the centennial of the incandescent light, is entitled *A Streak of Luck*. Accounts of other inventors of this era are presented in the biographical notices of the John Fritz medalists.

It was not until 1876, according to Beer (1964), that competition among manufacturers of dyes compelled Farbenfabriken vorm, Friedrich Bayer & Co. of Elberfeld in Westphalia, to hire professional chemists and establish the first industrial research laboratory. Edison and Bell were setting up their laboratories around this time, too. Subsequently, such laboratories were established by Arthur D. Little (1866), Eastman Kodak (1893), B. F. Goodrich (1895), General Electric (1900), and AT&T (1925). Thus technical advance came to be institutionalized as part of the quest for profits. Indeed, recently, International Rockwell claimed that it's the place, presumably above all others, "Where science gets down to business."

By 1915, on the occasion of Brown University's 115th anniversary, the eminent Harvard economist Frank Taussig after going on about the inventive and financial activities of Bell, Edison, Fulton, Morse and Watt, opined: "To sum up: the direction in which the contriver turns his bent is immensely affected by the prospect of gain for himself. Now, gain and profit come from supplying people with what they want; and the influence of individual interest on the direction of the inventors' activity turns it toward the promotion of the general welfare" (Taussig, 1915, pp. 50–1).

In 1932 Hicks argued in *The Theory of Wages* that technological advance be divided into two components, autonomous and induced. According to Hicks, a substantial amount of technical advance was induced by producers' attempts to reduce their need for relatively expensive factors of production. This of course means producers can take an active rather than a passive role in determining their technology. The induced innovation hypothesis set in motion further theoretical work by Fellner (1961), Salter (1960), Kennedy (1964), Samuelson (1965), Kamien and Schwartz (1968, 1970), and empirical testing by Brown (1966), Binswanger and Ruttan (1978), and others.

Schumpeter and beyond

It was Schumpeter, however, who in three books, *The Theory of Economic Development* (1961), *Business Cycles* (1964), and *Capitalism, Socialism and Democracy* (1975), portrayed most fully the active role played by economic agents in technical advance. [A comparison of Marx's and Schumpeter's views on this subject is presented by Elliott (1980)]. In the first two books the central role is played by the entrepreneur, defined as the person who creates new combinations – the one who sees how to fulfill currently unsatisfied needs or perceives a more efficient means of doing what is already being done. Either of these acts may, but need not, involve invention. In some cases it may only involve a new application of an existing technology. For example, the development of digital watches may be viewed more as an act of entrepreneurship than invention. Thus in Schumpeter's definition the act of invention and the act of entrepreneurship are separate, as are the inventor and the entrepreneur. An inventor need not be an entrepreneur and an entrepreneur need not be an inventor. It is the act of entrepreneurship, however, that brings an invention to its fruition.

Entrepreneurship is rewarded with extraordinary profit. It is the profit for being first. The successful new product or new method of production calls forth imitation that eventually erodes the extraordinary profit. If imitation is immediate, then entrepreneurial profit does not exist and there is no incentive to engage in this activity. This of course means that there is a basic incompatibility between entepreneural activity and perfect competition, for perfect competition implies immediate elimination of excess profits through imitation. The main theme of Schumpeter's theory is that in the conflict between entrepreneural activity and perfect competition, the latter should be sacrificed.

The portrayal of technical progress most associated with Schumpeter appears in the third book, especially Chapter VII, entitled "The Process of Creative Destruction." Here Schumpeter's focus shifted somewhat from celebration of the entrepreneur to defense of the existing capitalistic system, with its very large firms and monopolistic or oligopolistic markets, against critics who bemoaned the passing of the era of perfect competition. Schumpeter's defense of the present system was two pronged. First, he denied that a golden age of perfect competition ever actually existed. Further, he noted that despite its absence, substantial progress in economic well-being had occurred. Second, he argued that even if the conditions for perfect competition could be achieved, it would be undesirable. That is, although perfect competition could assure efficient allocation of resources at every point in time, it would stifle the type of activity that would allocate resources most efficiently over time. As Schumpeter (1975, p. 83) put it: "A system... that at *every* point in time fully utilizes its possibilities to its best advantage may yet in the long run be inferior to a system that does so at *no* given point in time, because the latter's failure to do so may be a condition for the level or speed of long-run performance." This argument rests heavily on the supposition that the economy is not in or tending toward a stationary state, because in a stationary state immediate optimization is synonymous with long-run optimization. Schumpeter of course denied that the economy was tending to a stationary state, but, as Marx, he envisioned an ever changing economic environment.

Beyond his defense of an imperfectly competitive market system, Schumpeter attacked the concept of perfect competition as irrelevant because it focused entirely on price competition, as the following passage illustrates:

> But in capitalist reality as distinguished from its textbook picture, it is not that kind of competition which counts but the competition from the new commodity, the new technology, the new source of supply, the new type of organization (the largest-scale unit of control for instance) – competition which commands a decisive cost or quality advantage and which strikes not at the margins of the profits and the outputs of the existing firms but at their foundations and their very lives (Schumpeter, 1975, p. 84).

This process of creative destruction is more important than price competition and in fact justifies, according to Schumpeter, certain monopolistic practices and the realization of monopoly profits. That is, in the course of introducing a new product or process a firm has to engage in monopolistic practices designed to retard imitation in order to reap the profits from its investment. Its extraordinary profits will eventually be eroded anyway and society will benefit from the introduction of the new product or process. Moreover, the extraordinary profits realized by the innovating firm will be a source of funds for the next round of innovation.

The process of creative destruction implies that almost all monopoly positions are temporary because of their vulnerability to competition through innovation. Illustrations of the process are numerous. Ball-point pens replace fountain pens (when was the last time you gave a Parker 51 as a Bar Mitzvah present?), jet-engined aircraft replace piston-engined (Boeing grows relative to Douglas), pocket calculators replace slide rules (whatever happened to Keuffel and Esser?), and electronic watches replace mechanical ones.

From a policy standpoint this meant to Schumpeter that antitrust enforcement should take a more tolerant view toward monopolistic practices, as indicated in the following passage:

> Thus it is not sufficient to argue that because perfect competition is impossible under modern industrial conditions – or because it always has been impossible – the large-scale establishment or unit of control must be accepted as a necessary evil inseparable from the economic progress which it is prevented from sabotaging by the force inherent in its productive apparatus. What we have got to accept is that it has come to be the most powerful engine of that progress and in particular of the long-run expansion of total output not only in spite of, but to a considerable extent through, this strategy which looks so restrictive when viewed in the individual case and from the individual point of time. In this respect, perfect competition is not only impossible, but inferior, and has no title to being set up as a model of ideal efficiency. *It is hence a mistake to base the theory of government regulation of industry on the principle that big business should be made to work as the respective industry would in perfect competition* (Schumpeter, 1975, p. 106).

In *Capitalism, Socialism, and Democracy,* Schumpeter placed more emphasis on the role of the large firm than on the entrepreneur, on economic progress, than he did in the previous two books. Perhaps he thought by then that innovation had become institutionalized. Galbraith (1952) pushed this point even further in *American Capitalism,* in which he claimed that the era of the cheap invention was over and that the remaining costly inventions could only be undertaken with resources of the magnitude commanded by large firms:

> There is no more pleasant fiction than that technical
> change is the product of the matchless ingenuity of the
> small man forced by competition to employ his wits to
> better his neighbor. Unhappily, it is a fiction. Technical
> development has long since become the preserve of the
> scientist and the engineer. Most of the cheap and simple
> inventions have, to put it bluntly, been made. Not only
> is development now sophisticated and costly but it must
> be on a sufficient scale so that successes and failures will
> in some measure average out... Because development is
> costly, it follows that it can be carried on only by a firm
> that has the resources associated with considerable size
> (Galbraith, 1952, pp. 91–2).

Galbraith also reinforced Schumpeter's claim of the primacy of competition through innovation over price competition, claiming that firms in oligopolistic industries realized the mutually destructive nature of price competition and therefore tacitly refrained from it. Competition through innovation, he argued, was unrestrained because it was more difficult to control tacitly and because the very convention against price competition would prolong the response to it.

Thus by 1952 the stage was set for the emergence of an economic theory of technical advance. The curtain was raised by a complementary set of events. After World War II, when many colonies of the great powers achieved independence, economic growth and development became a hot topic, which, eventually, led to seeking the sources of past economic growth. The prevailing view attributed growth to the increase in capital per worker. As industry became more mechanized, output per worker grew. But independent studies by Abramovitz (1956) and Solow (1957) claimed that the conventional wisdom was mistaken. Abramovitz found that after accounting for increases in the capital–labor ratio, there remained substantial unexplained growth. Solow's claim was perhaps the most dramatic – 90 percent of the doubling of per capita output in the U.S. nonfarm sector in the forty-year period 1909–49 was the result of technical advance and only 10 percent was the result of the increase in the capital–labor ratio. Subsequent studies of the U.S. industrial sector led to similar results, as did studies of other economies; see Brown (1966) and Lave (1966). These studies were subjected to a variety of criticisms: The concept of an aggregate production function is suspect, inadequate adjustment was made for changes in the quality of capital or labor through time, and economies of scale were not taken into account as a source of increased productivity. Yet after refinements of these studies by Edward F. Denison (1962) (who claimed that about half of the increased productivity attributed to technical advance was due to the improved education of labor), Zvi Griliches (1973), John W. Kendrick (1977), and others, technical advance continued to be regarded as a major source of economic growth.

Since then, the confluence of recognizing technical advance as an economic activity and its identification as a major source of growth has subjected it to intense study. Many questions have been addressed. What is the nature of the process by which economic resources are transformed into technological advances? What are the inputs and outputs of this process? Does this process exhibit increasing, constant, or decreasing returns to scale? Does it involve significant spillover effects? What is the nature of the market for technical advances? Will the competitive marketplace allocate resources so that the mix and timing of technological advances will be efficient? Is there a market structure that is most favorable to technological advance? If so, is it sustainable? What is the effect of technological advance on market structure? Is government allocation of resources to technological advance necessary? Desirable? Efficient? What is the effect of government regulation of industry on the pace of technical advance? Is there a divergence between the private and social benefits to technical advance, and if so, of what magnitude? What determines the rate at which new technology is adopted?

Apart from these essentially microeconomic questions, there are a host of macroeconomic questions. What is the role of technical advance in business cycles? Is it a source of instability or a defense against economic stagnation? How does it affect the distribution of income between labor and capital? Does it raise or lower the skill levels necessary for employment at the minimum wage? How are international payments and trade patterns affected? Does technical advance tend to widen or narrow the gap between the rich countries and the poor ones? What socioeconomic conditions are necessary for the successful adoption of new technologies? Is it more advantageous to import technical advances or to develop them domestically?

All these questions and others have been addressed in the past years. Our attention in this book is confined largely to the microeconomic questions, especially as they bear on the relationship between market structure and innovation.

Collective versus market direction

Before proceeding to the specifics of the relationship between market structure and innovation, a few words on the importance of this issue are in order. It could be argued that since technical advance has come to be recognized as an economic activity, its pace and direction should be left to the marketplace, with perhaps a few rules imposed by government to prevent certain forms of behavior. According to Taussig, it will be recalled, inventors, as other creative people, will promote the common good if they are financially rewarded. This of course is part of the view handed down by the classical economists that individuals in seeking their own selfish interests will in fact serve the general welfare, all of which will be orchestrated by the famous "invisible hand." Some economists maintain that there is little, if anything, to be said beyond this. But others claim that the nature of innovative activity is such that self-seeking behavior in this sphere is incompatible with the general welfare.

The conflict between individual and collective welfare can be illustrated by considering the interests of an inventor of a new method of production. He* uses this method to manufacture a product at well below the prevailing cost of other sellers, realizing an extraordinary profit from his superior method of production as long as it is unknown to rivals. But as soon as it becomes widely known and employed, his cost advantage disappears and along with it, his extraordinary profit. Thus his interest is to keep the invention a secret as long as possible. From society's standpoint, however, early disclosure, perhaps immediate, would be most beneficial, because then all society, not just the inventor, could benefit from this superior method of production. Indeed, in principle, society as a whole could compensate the inventor for the disclosure of his secret, so that he would be as well off as if he kept it, and still come out ahead. However, in the absence of a mechanism for effecting this transfer, and such a mechanism is difficult if not impossible to devise, the inventor's and society's interests will be at odds. Moreover, if for some reason the inventor cannot anticipate keeping his new process secret, at least for a time, he will have no incentive to invest in its development in the first place and society will surely be worse off.

A similar conflict occurs when the invention involves a new product. Here the inventor realizes an extraordinary profit as long as there are no good imitations of his product. In the absence of close substitutes he has a certain amount of monopoly power or control of price. But as in the new-means-of-production case, society as a whole could in principle compensate his loss of monopoly profits, while permitting competitive production and pricing, and still be better off. Again, unless such a transfer is actually made, society and the individual are at odds. We can, of course, bar monopoly by law but this only discourages invention of the new product.

Clearly, when the well-being of some members of society can be improved without diminishing the welfare of others, resources are

*"He" will be used as abbreviation for "he or she" throughout.

not being utilized efficiently. Only when no such possibility exists is resource allocation efficient, or Pareto Optimal, as it is said. The preceding two illustrations – the new product invention and the new means of production – are not Pareto Optimal and therefore present possibilities for improvement. Yet in trying to achieve Pareto Optimality in these cases, say, through forced disclosure of the secret or barring monopoly, we may eliminate the incentive to invent. This is the crux of the problem: whether to tolerate a loss of efficiency at every moment for the benefit of new products and processes or not to tolerate it and risk discouraging invention. Do we or do we not encourage inventive activity by letting the inventor have his secret or monopoly, with the anticipation that the secret will get out eventually and the monopoly be usurped by others, to the benefit of all? How much of present benefits should be sacrificed for future benefits?

In our patent laws we recognize the necessity of this trade-off. We concede extraordinary profits to the inventor for a time on the assumption that we shall be more than compensated after the invention enters the public domain. The real dilemma occurs in the formulation and enforcement of our antitrust laws, because to the extent that these laws are meant to achieve and maintain efficient allocation of resources in the short run, they may tend to inhibit invention. However, once we pull back from the goal of Pareto Optimality at each instant in time, we confront the question of how far to retreat. Should we repeal our antitrust laws entirely and let markets evolve in their own way or merely temper the laws to take inventive activity into account? The answer to this question rests importantly on the relationship between market structure and innovation.

It is sometimes proposed that the government should be responsible for technical advance, either by doing the research and development or at least by financing it. In this scheme, inventions would be made freely available to all potential users. This proposal would appear to eliminate the trade-off between long- and short-run efficiency posed by privately financed inventive activity. Moreover, it might appear to solve another problem associated with privately generated technical advance, namely, the wrong amount of resources might be devoted to this activity. A potential inventor may not develop an invention because his anticipated return does not justify it. Yet the benefit to society as a whole may warrant its development. Studies by Terleckyji (1977), Leonard (1971), and Mansfield and his co-workers (1977) show a substantial gap, more than double, between the social (55 percent) and private (25 percent) returns to the inventions they considered. Further, the private return to inventive activity is estimated to be about twice as high as the return to other investments in the private sector, on average.

It is also possible that too much resources will be devoted to inventive activity by the private sector. This might occur because either the value of an invention to its developer exceeds its net social value – the inventor counts a favorable redistribution of income as benefit while society does not – or the race among the potential inventors to be first leads to aggregate overinvestment. In other words, the absence of coordination among potential innovators may result in excessive duplication.

Leaving the responsibility for technical advance with the government has its own pitfalls, however, possibly no less severe than total reliance on the private sector. First, it is not clear that the government is better informed about the social value of an invention than a private inventor. Second, it is questionable whether resource allocation through the political process, especially for projects with a distant payoff, is superior to profit-guided allocation, even in the presence of monopoly elements. Third, actual experience appears to show that government-sponsored research cannot succeed without profit incentives. The successes of the Manhattan Project and the Apollo Project may appear to be spectacular counterexamples. But neither of these projects involved commercial products from which a private firm could realistically conceive of profiting.

Stories of government-sponsored research failing to reach fruition in the form of a commercially available new product or process revolve around the unwillingness of firms to engage in their final development and marketing without exclusive rights. For example, unwillingness by the Department of Health, Education, and Welfare to grant exclusive rights, in the form of patents, to private pharmaceutical firms retarded commercial development of an early detection blood test for breast and digestive tract cancer and a test-tube method for testing the effectiveness of different cancer drugs before administering them to a patient. These examples are part of a much bigger picture. The absence of exclusive rights, it is claimed, explains why less than 10 percent of the 28,000 patents owned by the government and available for copying have been licensed by private producers. (In fairness, it must be pointed out that studies performed by Gharrity indicate that between 40 and 80 percent of all patents in the United States have never found use.) Indeed, a General Accounting Office study indicated that not a single pharmaceutical developed with National Institute of Health support ever reached the public because of no exclusive rights. This claim prompted the Department of Health, Education, and Welfare to grant such rights in 1968. In the ten years after that, at least seventy important discoveries were developed by private pharmaceutical manufacturers, including the preceding examples. (Legislation is presently being proposed in the U.S. Senate to allow small companies to retain the patent rights to inventions developed under federal contracts.) Granting of exclusive rights by the government to private firms to market an innovation is of course incompatible with perfect competition and results in an inefficient allocation of resources, at least in the short run. Thus it appears that unless the government goes into the business of actually developing and marketing its inventions, a possibility not seriously advocated by the vast majority of Western economists, the generation of some short-run inefficiency in the course of achieving technical advance cannot be eluded.

Technical advance?

Before proceeding to our major task, a caveat is in order. Thus far we have regarded technical change as an unmitigated benefit to society and will continue to do so. We are aware, however, that this view is not shared by all. Certainly, workers who lost their jobs to a new machine or businesspeople who lost their markets to a new product do not feel this way. Even Lloyds of London, facing enormous insurance claims because of unanticipated advances in computer technology, may not see the virtue of technical progress. (Lloyds insured leasors of computers against their customers breaking leases prematurely. Major advances in computer technology made it worthwhile for the customers to break their leases to acquire new machines and pay a penalty for doing so.) The argument that this is the price of progress can hardly be expected to be persuasive to the bearers of this real loss. Apart from these people, some see technical advance as dehumanizing (as portrayed in Charlie Chaplin's *Modern Times*) and as a threat to our culture (as in George Orwell's *1984*). Television is referred to as the "boob tube." Birth control pills are held to have led to greater promiscuity and immorality, whereas test-tube babies are feared to be the first step toward human engineering. Not too long ago technical advance came to be identified with napalm and defoliants (agent orange) and General Electric, coincidentally, stopped claiming that "Progress is our most important product."

It is undoubtedly true that technical advance has important effects on society, some of which may be irreversible. As to whether they are on net for the "best" is well beyond the scope of this book, and perhaps beyond the purview of economists alone. Measurement of the impact of technical advance in terms of a single number, say, percentage increases in the productivity of labor or output per capita, is audacious to say the least. If anything, however, this measure understates the economic benefits of technical advance because it does not fully account for improvements in the quality of goods and services or reduction in hours worked. Further, it does not reflect improvements in the quality of life afforded by modern conveniences. The services provided by refrigerators, light bulbs, air conditioners, and so on were always available to the rich in one form or another. It is only through technical advance that they have become available to the not-so-rich.

Finally, one may object that to view technical advance as an economic activity may be too cynical. After all, Salk did not develop his polio vaccine for the sake of profit. Many other inventions, too, have resulted from the sheer joy of creativity. The response to this view is best expressed by the following story of Taussig:

> Some twenty years ago a university professor devised a method for measuring with accuracy the content of butter-fat in milk. The device, if patented, would doubtless have yielded him a very handsome income. The inventor gave it freely to the public, saying modestly that to do so was but part of his duty as a servant of the people; and it has come into use the world over. We call his conduct noble; but our very recognition is an admission of its rarity (Taussig, 1915, pp. 49–50).

Organization of the book

In Chapter 2 we present the theoretical basis for a set of hypotheses regarding the economics of technical advance that have been subjected to extensive empirical testing. These hypotheses derive directly from Schumpeter or were formulated in the course of testing those for which he was directly responsible. We have lumped them together, therefore, under the title "Schumpeterian hypotheses." In general, they deal with the relationships among inventive activity and market structure, firm size, the availability of internal financing, "technological opportunity," and "demand-pull." This theoretical basis draws on a wide range of contributions, from Schumpeter's work to Arrow's (1962) famous article on resource allocation to inventive activity and to the immediate work it inspired.

In Chapter 3 we survey the empirical studies related to the Schumpeterian hypotheses. This survey extends our previous one (1975). The central questions addressed in this literature are: (1) Is there a positive relationship between the devotion of resources to research and development and the output of inventions? (2) Does this relationship exhibit increasing, constant, or decreasing returns to scale? (3) Is there a positive, neutral, or negative spillover effect between firm size and the production of inventions? (4) What is the relationship between firm size and the devotion of resources to inventive activity? (5) Between firm size and the output of inventions? (6) Between market structure and the devotion of resources to inventive activity? (7) Between market structure and the output of inventions? (8) What is the role of "technological opportunity" in inventive activity? (9) What is the role of "demand-pull" on inventive activity? (10) What role does the availability of internal financing play in inventive activity?

All these studies are severely hampered by the lack of data that correspond directly to the variables of interest. Thus there is recourse to the use of various surrogates. Also, possibly because of this lack of data, most of them involve single equation models, even if simultaneous equation models would be more appropriate. For example, the intensity of inventive activity and firm size are likely to be mutually determined variables as are market structure and inventive activity. Finally, there is much variation in their "quality," both methodologically and substantively. We have, however, avoided criticism of individual studies and relied instead on similarity of findings among independent studies, when they occurred, to draw conclusions about the issues being addressed.

In Chapter 4 we begin our presentation of more recent developments in the microeconomic theory of technical advance. These developments involve both the mathematical formalization of some of Schumpeter's theories and an attempt to provide a theoretical explanation for some of the empirical findings reported in Chapter 3. They derive largely from the work of Scherer (1967b) and Barzel (1968) and our own work on this subject (Kamien and Schwartz, 1972a, 1974a, 1974b, 1976b, 1978a, 1978b, 1980b). This analysis is focused on the role of competition among potential innovators in the speed of innovation by an individual firm. The questions addressed include: (1) How is the speed of innovation influenced by the intensity of rivalry? (2) By the reward for being first? (3) By the reward from imitation? (4) By the presence of a monopoly profit on a current product or process for which the innovation is a substitute? (5) By the ability to change planned R&D expenditures upon rival preemption? (6) By a change in the ability to complete the innovation upon rival preemption? (7) By the magnitude of the project? (8) By the necessity to finance development entirely from internal resources? (9) Is there an intensity of rivalry at which development of an innovation is most rapid? Under what circumstances is it intermediate between monopoly and perfect competition? (10) Is the individually determined speed of development of an innovation too rapid or too slow compared with the social optimum? The analysis presented in this chapter generalizes the existing literature by relaxing some of the restrictive assumptions previously imposed. In particular, the analysis is conducted in terms of a general probability distribution over the time of rival new product introduction instead of an exponential distribution as had previously been done. Assumptions about the flows of rewards are generalized, too.

In Chapter 5 we continue our presentation of recent contributions to the microeconomics of technical advance. In particular, we draw on the work by Loury (1979), Scherer (1967b), Olivera (1973), Lee and Wilde (1980), Dasgupta and Stiglitz (1980b), Kami (1980), and Reinganum (1980). These contributions focus on the aggregate or industry equilibrium outcome of the individual firm behavior posited in Chapter 4. We have called the methodology used in this literature the game theoretic approach because it relies on the Nash–Cournot concept of equilibrium. That is, each potential innovator determines his level of expenditure on research and development as a best response to every possible choice of research and development expenditure by rivals and assumes that their choices are unresponsive to his. The types of questions discussed are: (1) What is the socially efficient allocation of a given size research budget under different assumptions regarding returns to scale in inventive activity? (2) How does this allocation depend on whether research costs are assumed to be contractual or noncontractual? (3) What is the socially optimal research budget? (4) Does the market equilibrium yield an efficient allocation of resources to inventive activity? (5) Does it yield a socially optimal level of resource allocation to inventive activity? The analysis of these questions is carried out under less restrictive assumptions than those employed in the current previously cited literature.

In Chapter 6 we present a brief summary of economists' current knowledge of the microeconomics of technical advance and a prospectus for the future research directions that are necessary for its advancement.

2

Schumpeterian hypotheses

Two broad hypotheses are associated with Schumpeter: (1) There is a positive relationship between innovation and monopoly power with the concomitant above normal profits. (2) Large firms are more than proportionately more innovative than small firms. The latter hypothesis suggests that General Electric, AT&T, DuPont, Exxon, International Rockwell, General Motors, Searle, IBM, Xerox, and other corporations of comparable size are the major sources of innovation. These two hypotheses are independent because possession of monopoly power does not imply large size, except in relative terms, and conversely, large firm size does not imply monopoly power. Of course large firm size and monopoly power do sometimes occur together.

We attribute these hypotheses to Schumpeter because that is how they are commonly referred to in the literature on the subject. A careful reading of Schumpeter would, however, suggest that he was more responsible for the first hypothesis. Galbraith should receive substantial credit for the second. These hypotheses have undergone considerable refinement, especially in the course of empirical testing. In addition, two new hypotheses have emerged that go beyond what was said by either Schumpeter or Galbraith. The first, called the "technology-push" hypothesis, is most associated with Phillips (1966), although it can also be traced to Nelson (1959). It places major emphasis on the role of underlying scientific knowledge in innovation. The second is referred to as the "demand-pull" hypothesis and is attributed to Schmookler (1966). It emphasizes the role of economic opportunity in innovation. Both these newer hypotheses were inspired by attempts to test the Schumpeterian hypotheses. Finally, Arrow (1962) has provided theoretical explication of some of the problems associated with resource allocation to inventive activity.

Appreciation of the Schumpeterian hypotheses rests on an understanding of the milieu in which they are envisaged. The two most important features of this milieu are competition through innovation and uncertainty. Recall that according to Schumpeter, competition through innovation is more important than price competition because it is the more decisive means of gaining an advantage over competitors. According to Galbraith, it is also more prevalent because of tacit agreement among firms in oligopolistic markets not to engage in price competition. A corollary of this proposition suggested by Lange (1943) and Brozen (1951) is that the absence of price competition generates a bias toward process innovations over product innovations. This is presumably because product innovations would encounter price competition from the products they replace.

Perhaps the most important feature of competition through innovation is that it can come from any quarter. It is not restricted to the firm's acknowledged rivals – the producers of similar products or services – but includes unknown rivals in entirely different lines of business as well since, for example, the functions of mechanical devices can sometimes be performed electronically or even chemically. Likewise, synthetic fibers can replicate the qualities of natural fibers; plastics can be substituted for metals. It is the end product or the services provided that matters to the user. The recent introduction of quartz wristwatches illustrates the phenomenon. The innovations that led to these new wristwatches came from semiconductor manufacturers – Litronix, Hughes Aircraft, and Fairchild Camera and Instruments – not from traditional watch manufacturers, such as Timex, Bulova, Longines, or Seiko. The market share of mechanical watches has declined as have the market shares of those traditional manufacturers that have failed to switch over to the new line.

Potential rivals, known and unknown, present a major source of uncertainty for the firm in this milieu. It faces uncertainty regarding the continued success of its current products; uncertainty about competing innovations; and uncertainty about the profitability of its innovations. Moreover, these uncertainties are interdependent. Continued success of its current products and also the profitability of its own innovations both depend on the nature and timing of competing innovations. The profitability of its innovations depends also on the technical difficulties and the cost of overcoming them. As Schumpeter (1975, p. 85) stated:

> It is hardly necessary to point out that competition of the kind we now have in mind acts not only when in being but also when it is merely an ever-present threat. It disciplines before it attacks. The businessman feels himself to be in a competitive situation even if he is alone in his field or if, though not alone, he holds a position such that investigating government experts fail to see any effective competition between him and any other firms in the same or a neighboring field and in consequence conclude that his talk, under examination, about his competitive sorrows is all make believe.

The presence of uncertainty calls forth activities designed either to reduce it or to mitigate its consequences. For example, uncertainty regarding whether or when a particular objective can be attained through innovation can be reduced by undertaking several alternative research efforts directed toward the given end. Likewise, uncertainty about the profitability of innovative activity can be reduced by undertaking various research efforts directed toward different innovations. Both strategies, however, require diverting resources from the main objective to dealing with the uncertainty. Thus it takes more money to engage in innovative activity with its inherent uncertainties than it would without uncertainty. For this reason, monopoly power and large size are alleged to be advantageous for innovative activity, because they can reduce the uncertainties. The basis for these allegations can best be displayed by considering an idealized situation in which they would be false.

Schumpeter recognized that the act of innovating and the act of bearing risk due to uncertainty were distinct. Indeed, he emphasized that innovational profit was not the reward for risk bearing. It was Arrow (1962), however, who first described an arrangement in which innovation and risk bearing are separate acts. It goes something like this. An inventor announces his availability to develop a new product (or process), the feasibility of which is uncertain. He sets a fee for this service, which is based on his opportunity cost (i.e., the compensation in the next best alternative employment of his service) and offers to sell shares in the project. The proceeds from the sale of shares are used to fund the project, including the inventor's fee. Profits are realized only if the invention is successful and are distributed in proportion to the individual share holdings. Based on their assessments of the probability of success of this project, other competing projects, their taste for risk, and their wealth, individuals purchase shares in this project. The inventor himself may purchase shares in the project. The price of the shares is determined by the condition that, in equilibrium, the expected rate of return to this project is equal to the rate of return in other opportunities. The important feature of this setup, however, is that the inventor bears only as much risk as he wants. He can assume the entire risk of the project by buying all the shares or can take on none of the risk and accept only the guaranteed fee for his service.

The rub in this scheme is that the investors cannot be certain that the inventor will perform the purchased service faithfully. Without costly monitoring, it is difficult to determine whether a failure is due to the infeasibility of the project or to the inventor failing to give it his best effort. They may have greater confidence in the sincerity of his effort if the inventor is forced to buy more of the shares in the project than he wishes, thereby assuming some additional risk. This is the investors' way of insuring against the inventor's shirking or what is referred to as "moral hazard." [This problem occurs in a variety of situations and has come to be studied under the generic label of the "agency paradigm." In our context the inventor is the "agent" and the investors are the "principal"; see Harris and Raviv (1978), Holmstrom (1979), and Shavell (1979)]. It means, however, that the inventor may be forced to hold more shares in the project than he would prefer and therefore be unwilling to undertake the project at all.

Demsetz (1969) has argued that the burden the presence of moral hazard imposes on society, either in the form of excessive risk bearing by the inventor or of costly monitoring, is similar to that incurred by putting locks on cars to avoid theft. The difference, however, is that locks are meant to discourage thievery, which has no social merit, whereas requiring the inventor to bear excessive risk discourages an activity with potential social merit.

The point is that the inventor cannot carry as little of the risk as he desires, for in divesting himself of risk that the invention may fail, he generates a new risk (at least in the minds of investors) that he may shirk in the activities required for success. This, in turn, means that society may not get some inventions that would be forthcoming if the inventor did not need to assume risk. Two remedies to this problem suggest themselves. The first is government, or collective, financing of invention. A virtue of this remedy is that the risk associated with the inventor's shirking is spread among many people. The inventor sells his services to the government and is relieved of the risk of failure. The government assumes the risk and gets the invention if it succeeds. In addition, of course, the government has the advantage of diversification through financing a large number of projects. That is, the probability of all the projects failing is reduced, provided that they are independent, as their number increases. Drawbacks of this scheme relate to identification of inventions that, even if successful, are worthwhile and to the curbing of fraud. That is, although the burden to each individual from an inventor's shirking in any particular project may be small, the total burden over many projects may be substantial.

The second remedy is to turn to the market system and accept departure from the conditions for perfect competition. Here we return to Schumpeter's theme.

Innovation and monopoly power

There are two major sources of interaction between innovation and monopoly power. The first is between innovation and the anticipation of monopoly power and the concomitant monopoly profits. Realizing extraordinary profits is of course the motive (at least from the standpoint of our analysis) for developing an innovation. It is necessary to have some monopoly power for a while to realize this extraordinary profit. This power is the ability to prevent or at least retard imitation of the innovation. It can be achieved by means of a patent, a trademark, or a copyright – all of which are government grants of exclusive rights that confer some monopoly power. Or it can be achieved through erection of barriers to entry by imitators. For example, the innovator may buy up raw materials (beyond his own needs) that are critical in the production of this item so as to deny them to possible imitators. Likewise, he may attempt to gain control over the main channels of distribution of this item for the same reason. He may try to develop a reputation and identity through an advertising campaign; then would-be entrants will similarly need to incur substantial advertising costs to sell their products widely. Finally, he may achieve substantial economies of scale relative to the size of the market by being first. The main point is that the innovator must see some means for realizing an extraordinary profit from his investment in the innovation, in order to be willing to incur the needed costs to bring the innovation to market.

The second source of interaction is between innovation and the possession of monopoly power. There are several facets to this relationship. The first is simply the complement to what was previously said. A firm that has monopoly power with regard to its present products may be able to extend that power to its new products, for example, through its command over channels of distribution or through its unique identity. Establishing uniqueness of its product is important because that reduces the possibility that other products will be regarded as close substitutes. The firm's possession of monopoly power and the associated monopoly profits may also enable it to respond more quickly to innovations of rivals than it would otherwise. Indeed, even the threat that the firm might retaliate quickly may discourage intrusion by rivals into its new product line. Kamien and Schwartz (1972b) have shown that uniqueness of a product together with its producer's ability to improve it in the event of imitation discourages rival innovation. The firm with monopoly power in the sale of its current product may also engage in other practices to assure its new product's profitability. For example, it may tie sales of the existing product to the new product. Although this practice is illegal when carried out directly, it may be achieved indirectly. The buyer may, for instance, be induced to purchase the new product along with the old to take advantage of lower shipping costs associated with large quantities. The upshot is that a firm with the ability to extend monopoly power from its existing product to a new product, thereby capturing monopoly profits, should find innovation more attractive than does one without this ability.

The second source of interaction between possession of monopoly power and innovation is alleged to be through the necessity to finance innovation internally. One reason innovations must be financed largely from internal sources has already been alluded to, namely, the presence of moral hazard associated with developing a new product or process whose feasibility is uncertain. Due to moral hazard, the innovating firm must bear a substantial share of the development costs. A firm realizing extraordinary profits is presumably better able to undertake internal financing than one earning only normal profits. This argument implicitly suggests that stockholders are content with a normal rate of return and that they assign discretion to management over use of above normal profits. The alternative of course is for stockholders to demand payment of the extraordinary profits, which they will then allocate as they see fit. Stockholders who believe that management has superior knowledge of investment opportunities may be eager to leave the discretion to management. This might be especially true with regard to innovation opportunities. A second possible reason for self-financing innovation is that borrowing requires disclosure of information regarding the innovation that may be disadvantageous to the firm.

That is, the information required by potential lenders regarding the feasibility and expected profitability of an innovation may leak out to rivals and reduce or destroy the advantage the firm is attempting to gain. The question of how much information to reveal about an innovation so as to secure outside financing without forfeiting its competitive advantage has been addressed recently by Bhattacharya and Ritter (1979). The restriction on the ability to innovate imposed by the necessity to self-finance is taken up formally in Chapter 4.

A third supposed advantage to possessing monopoly power, closely related to the second, is the ability of the firm with monopoly profits to hire the most innovative people. Entrepreneurial ability, as other characteristics, is not uniformly distributed across the population. There are relatively few people especially talented in this regard. In bidding for their services, firms with greater resources have an advantage over those with fewer resources. The difficulty with this argument is that it implies imperfection in the market for these services. In a perfectly operating market, the price of these services would be bid up to the level equal to their expected marginal contribution to profits. This would tend to eliminate any advantage accruing to the firm with monopoly profits. It is unlikely, however, that the market for entrepreneurial services operates perfectly. Identification of entrepreneurial ability is not easy; it is usually identified by hindsight rather than by foresight, and knowledge about who has it may not be so widespread as is required for perfect operation of this market. Thus the firm with extraordinary resources may be at an advantage by being able to hire a larger number of potential entrepreneurs, hoping to identify those few that actually have this talent.

Although monopoly power may confer the three advantages previously identified to the firm seeking to innovate, it may also have some retarding effects. That is, the firm presently realizing monopoly profits may be less motivated to seek additional profits than the one earning only normal profits. It may, in other words, be less hungry for additional profits than the firm without a monopoly position. Several reasons for this are possible. First, it may begin to regard additional leisure as superior to additional profits.

That is, there may be an X-efficiency effect as described by Leibenstein (1966). Second, it may become more concerned with protecting its current monopoly position than acquiring a new one. Baldwin and Childs (1969) have argued that a firm with monopoly power is in an advantageous position to be a "fast second" in the development of an innovation. Because of its resources and established reputation and channels of distribution, a firm with monopoly power can afford to wait until someone else innovates and imitate it quickly if it appears to be successful. Third, a firm realizing monopoly profits on its current product or process may be slower in replacing it with a superior product or process than a newcomer. That is, the firm realizing monopoly profits on its current product calculates the profit from innovation as the difference between its current profits and the profits it could realize from the new product, whereas the newcomer regards the profits from the new product as the gain. Thus the newcomer always has a greater incentive to innovate than the otherwise identical firm that is realizing a monopoly profit on the current product. This was pointed out by Arrow (1962) for process innovations and by Usher (1964) for product innovations.

Schumpeter also recognized that monopoly power might be disadvantageous to innovation, as the following passage in *Business Cycles* shows:

> Economic evolution or "progress" would differ substantially from the picture we are about to draw, if that form (Trustified Capitalism), of organization prevailed throughout the economic organism. Giant concerns still have to react to each other's innovations, of course, but they do so in other and less predictable ways than firms which are drops in a competitive sea,... Even in the world of giant firms, new ones rise and others fall into the background. Innovations still emerge primarily with the "young" ones, and the "old" ones display as a rule symptoms of what is euphemistically called conservatism (Schumpeter, 1964, p. 71).

Even if it is conceded that having monopoly power is, on net, advantageous for innovative activity, the question remains of how much monopoly power is optimal. In principle, the answer is that the marginal sacrifice in static efficiency resulting from a departure from perfect competition should just equal the marginal social benefit from increased innovative activity. In practice, of course it is difficult to gauge whether such a balance has been achieved. Harberger (1954) has argued that the loss in efficiency from departures from perfect competition are very small as a percent of gross national product (GNP). Other investigators have disputed his findings and reported that their empirical studies show a larger loss. No one has compared these losses with the gains from additional innovation.

Some insight into the trade-off between increased monopoly power and innovation can be gained by studying a simple Cournot oligopoly model with a linear demand function and a constant average cost of production. The loss in allocative efficiency in this model is measured by the loss in consumers' surplus due to a departure from perfect competition, net of the monopoly profits realized by the firms in the industry. This loss is commonly referred to as "dead-weight" loss, which increases as the number of firms in the industry declines. It can be shown, see the appendix, that the elasticity of the dead-weight loss with respect to the number of firms in the industry ranges between minus one (when there is only one firm in the industry) and minus two (approached as the number of firms in the industry approaches infinity). This means that any given percentage decline in the number of firms in the industry, that is, any increase in monopoly power, results in a larger percentage increase in dead-weight loss. Thus suppose innovation took the form of a reduction in the average cost of production and that it led to a decline in the number of firms in the industry and the concomitant increase in monopoly power. Then in order for the innovation to increase "social welfare," the percent cost reduction would have to exceed the percent reduction in the number of firms in the industry.

Innovation and firm size

We turn now to the second major hypothesis identified with Schumpeter. As mentioned earlier, it was more fully developed by Galbraith. Nutter (1956) provided a simple statement of this hypothesis: "just as the prospect of monopolistic position raises the odds in favor of the most risky innovations, so bigness makes possible the most expensive." Moreover, according to Galbraith, innovative activity is becoming increasingly expensive and therefore large firm size is becoming increasingly advantageous. Galbraith's contention that innovation is becoming increasingly costly was shared by the eminent physicist Max Planck, among others. Indeed, Rescher (1978) refers to it as "Planck's Principle of Increasing Effort."

There appears to be little direct evidence to deny or support the contention that innovation is becoming more costly through time. In order to determine the trend, one would have to generate a time series of the real costs of innovation. It may, however, be contended that regardless of what the historical trend has been, large firms have an advantage over small ones because of economies of scale in research and development. There are at least two possible sources for these alleged economies.

The first is that researchers are more productive when they have more colleagues with whom to interact. Colleagues may have new insights or special familiarity with a problem that reduces the effort required to arrive at a solution. Moreover, a large research group may permit division of labor. Each researcher can develop expertise in a particular area and rely on the expertise of colleagues when needed. In addition, a large research group may be better able to exploit special equipment than an individual researcher could. Finally, a large research group may increase the chances of serendipitous discoveries; it is more probable that the unforseen results will be recognized as important when there are more researchers around.

The second possible source of advantage for a large firm over a small one in research and development is in its superior ability to exploit the output of its research efforts. Nelson (1959) has argued that a large firm with an established name and reputation may be in a better position to exploit the development of an unforseen product because it can more easily enter a new market than a firm without these attributes. In addition, there are more opportunities within a large multiproduct firm for diversification of research and development projects so as to realize a higher yield on the resources devoted to this activity. However, in a large organization, unexpected research findings may be more likely to get lost in the shuffle than in a small firm. Researchers may also be less motivated in a large firm than in a small one because in the latter, their compensation may be more directly related to their performance. Some evidence for this negative effect of firm size on innovative activity exists through instances of several employees of a large corporation leaving it to form their own company to exploit an innovation that the corporation would not sponsor. The net effect of firm size on innovative activity is the subject of empirical tests to be discussed in the next chapter.

In addition to the two major hypotheses about the relationship between monopoly power and innovative activity and between firm size and innovative activity, there are two additional broad hypotheses studied by researchers of the microeconomics of technical advance. They are called "technology-push" and "demand-pull," respectively, and can be thought of as emerging from different perspectives regarding the interaction between a firm's operating staff and its research facility.

The "technology-push" hypothesis

In the "technology-push" hypothesis a firm's research staff may be regarded as the initiator of innovations. Advances in basic scientific knowledge are brought to the attention of the parent organization by the research staff for possible commercialization. There are two important implications of this view: (1) A firm with a large research facility will have an advantage over one with a smaller facility because its staff will be able to scan a wider range of the scientific base for possible commercial applications. (2) The pace of innovative activity will depend on advances in the scientific base, implying that in areas where the underlying scientific base is stationary, innovation tends to be slower than in those areas where it is growing. This scenario of the innovation process implies that a firm that is able to finance a large research staff is again favored over one that is not. Such a firm may be better able to exploit the existing scientific base and to add to it, as well, giving it of course a head start over rivals.

A growing scientific base is also alleged to lead to more competition in an industry, because the opportunities for developing a sequence of new and/or improved products or processes are thought to be more plentiful in this circumstance. Scientific instruments, electronics, pharmaceuticals, and chemicals are typically identified as industries with active scientific bases whereas steel, nonferrous metals, railroads, and oil refining are regarded as industries with stagnant scientific bases. These classifications are commonly employed to normalize for differences in the scientific base in empirical tests of the Schumpeterian hypotheses. That is, when relationships between monopoly power or firm size and innovative activity are estimated in different industries, an attempt is made to factor out differences in the scientific bases.

One of the most spectacular examples of the technology-push phenomenon is in the application of lasers. Conceived in the 1950s and built in 1960 without intended use, lasers have since found numerous applications – from surgery to videorecords to the fantasized "death ray." The technology-push hypothesis is further supported by the many contemporaneous discoveries reported by Merton (1973). These coincidences suggest that certain discoveries are almost inevitable in the course of development of a science.

Reliance on the technology-push hypothesis to explain the pace of innovative activity may, however, mask other explanations. For example, the absence of substantial innovative activity in an industry may be the result of lack of competition rather than lack of growth of its scientific base. Moreover, the absence of a growing scientific base may itself be a consequence of a lack of competition. In other words, the scientific base and competitiveness of the industry may be simultaneously determined rather than being sequential. Thus an industry with a growing scientific base and many competing firms may evolve through competition into one with few firms and a decline in both competition and the growth rate of the scientific base. The recent work of Nelson and Winter (1977, 1978), which will be described in Chapter 6, suggests that such an evolution is possible.

The "demand-pull" hypothesis

In the "demand-pull" hypothesis the interaction between a firm's production and marketing staffs and its research staff may be thought of in reverse relation to that assumed in the technology-push hypothesis. That is, in the demand-pull hypothesis initiation of an innovation is seen as coming from the firm's marketing or production people and the response as coming from the research staff. Put another way, a problem is posed by members of the firm that deal directly with its customers or are involved with manufacture of its products and a solution is provided by the research staff. The research staff may call upon any scientific base to come up with a solution and may even propose several solutions based on different technologies. Indeed, it might even engage in scientific research in order to solve the problem. The development of a commercial process for the synthesis of cortisone, after it had been found effective for treatment of severe arthritis, is illustrative; see *Wall Street Journal* Staff (1968). The Upjohn Corporation set up six separate research teams, each pursuing a different approach to the problem. Success came through the "bug process," which was regarded at the outset as highly unlikely to succeed. This process proved competitive with a chemical process for synthesizing cortisone, the beef bile process, developed independently by Merck. There are many other examples of this demand-pull phenomenon. Transistors were developed at Bell Laboratories in response to AT&T's need for smaller and more efficient switches. Celluloid was invented to replace ivory in billiard balls.

The main idea in the demand-pull hypothesis is that invention is a response to profit opportunities. Thus growing industries are thought to generate more inventive activities than declining or stagnating ones. A growing industry usually needs additional capital equipment, which provides a profit opportunity for suppliers with new or improved machines. This in turn creates an incentive for invention along these lines. In a stagnating industry the demand for new equipment is limited to replacement of obsolete or worn-out equipment and therefore creates a smaller incentive for development of new machines. A corollary is that if many technological improvements can be used only through using new equiment – the "embodiment" hypothesis discussed by Jorgenson (1966) – then decline in industrial growth is accompanied by a decline in the productivity growth rate.

The demand-pull hypothesis implies that large firms with large research facilities have an advantage over smaller rivals in innovation. A large multiproduct firm may have more chances to recognize opportunities for profit through innovation. A large research staff may facilitate quicker and more novel solutions to problems posed by other members of the firm.

As an explanation of innovative activity, the demand-pull hypothesis borders on being tautological. Certainly, no innovation is developed to result in a loss. Sometimes innovations are spurred by a firm's efforts to avoid or minimize losses resulting from rivals' innovations, but this too is part of profit-seeking behavior. Moreover, as Mowery and Rosenberg (1979) point out in their excellent critique of empirical tests of this hypothesis, needs may exist and be recognized long before the appearance of an invention to satisfy them. Often they must await advances in basic scientific knowledge before they can be brought to fruition and the profit opportunity realized. This appears to be the present situation regarding elusive inexpensive sources of energy to replace fossil fuels. Further, virtually every invention's antecedents can be traced back to some advance in basic scientific knowledge if one is willing to go back far enough. Thus the technology-push and demand-pull hypotheses may be viewed as complementary rather than as competing explanations of innovation, with the former being more of a long-run theory and the latter, a short-run theory.

Demand-pull and market structure

There is another version of the demand-pull hypothesis that is due to Arrow (1962), although he did not envision it that way. Arrow set out to answer the question of whether the incentive to innovate was greater under perfect competition than under monopoly. He concluded that the incentive was greater under perfect competition. This appears to refute the Schumpeterian contention that at least some monopoly power was necessary for innovative activity. But Arrow's analysis is not a refutation of Schumpeter's because he refers to the structure of the industry *purchasing* the innovation rather than to the structure of the industry *producing* it. In Arrow's analysis the innovator faces no rivals seeking to develop a similar innovation. Analysis of the situation in which the innovator does face innovational rivals began with the work of Scherer (1967b), Barzel (1968), and Kamien and Schwartz (1972a), and will be discussed in Chapters 4 and 5.

Although Arrow's analysis does not confront the question posed by Schumpeter, it does describe the relationship between market structure and the demand-pull for an innovation. Moreover, it initiated a considerable amount of research on this topic. We shall present a slightly modified version of Arrow's model that shows the relationship between demand-pull and market structure as well as exhibits some of the strategic relationships between the innovator and the industry purchasing the innovation.

A critical assumption of this analysis is that the innovation is unique, with no similar or competing innovations. The innovation reduces the constant unit cost of production of an item from its present level c to a lower level c^*. We assume for analytical convenience that the industry that would use the innovation is composed of n identical firms whose behavior is describable by the Cournot oligopoly model and that it faces a linear inverse demand function $P(Q) = a - bQ$, where a and b are positive constants. It can be shown that under these circumstances total industry output is initially

(1) $\qquad Q = n(a - c)/(n + 1)b$

and price is

(2) $\qquad P = (nc + a)/(n + 1)$

To determine his potential profit, the innovator first asks how much profit a monopolist could make were he to face the industry's demand curve and have unit cost c^*. (We assume he alone knows how to produce at unit cost c^*. If any others have the same capability, a monopoly position is untenable.) Let Q_m denote the quantity a monopolist with unit cost c^* would choose and let $P(Q_m)$ be the price he would charge. From (1) and (2) $Q_m = (a - c^*)/2b$ and $P(Q_m) = (a + c^*)/2$. There are two possibilities. First, the monopoly output Q_m may exceed the industry's current output rate Q_0. Then the postinnovation output Q^* is equal to the monopoly output Q_m, and the postinnovation price $P(Q^*) = P(Q_m)$ is lower than the current price $P(Q_0)$. In this case the innovation is said to be *major*. The second possibility is that $Q_m \leq Q_0$. Because it makes little sense (and is untenable) for the postinnovation price to exceed the current price $P(Q_0)$, and for industry output to fall, industry output and price are unchanged by the innovation: $Q^* = Q_0$ and $P^* = P_0$. In this second case the innovation is said to be *minor*. In either event the hypothetical monopolist's profit is denoted $(P(Q^*) - c^*)Q^*$. This is the maximum potential profit from the innovation, short of what could be earned by a discriminating monopolist.

Arrow's test for a drastic innovation is whether it reduces the price of the product below its preinnovation perfectly competitive price. In contrast, our test for a major innovation is whether it reduces price below its current level, whatever the existing market structure (i.e., n) might be. Our definitions of major and minor innovations coincide with what Arrow calls *drastic*, $P(Q^*) = P(Q_m) < c$, and *nondrastic*, $P(Q_m) \geq c = P(Q^*)$, innovations, respectively, only if the industry that uses them is perfectly competitive (n approaches infinity). Otherwise his definitions and ours differ somewhat. A drastic innovation is always a major innovation, but the opposite is not true. On the one hand, our classification seems easier to employ because the benchmark is the current price rather than the price that would prevail under perfect competition. On the other hand, Arrow's classification is more uniform in that it is independent of market structure. In our classification all innovations sold to a monopolist are major. A particular innovation may be major if it were sold to a relatively monopolistic industry and minor if it were sold to a more competitive industry. Our definitions facilitate analysis of the demand-pull hypothesis in a single model encompassing the entire spectrum of market structures.

Moreover, the conclusions are consistent with those obtained by Arrow.

The second issue the inventor confronts is how much of this maximum potential profit he can realize and by what means. One option is to produce the item himself. He could not set a price above the present unit cost c and gain the entire market, because existing producers could lower their price to c and still earn a normal profit. The second option is to license the invention to existing producers, that is, rent them the right to use the lower cost method of production. This option can be exercised only if the licensing arrangement precludes resale of the technique itself. We shall, for the sake of argument, assume that this is so and assume as well that licensing is the only strategy to be pursued by the inventor.

Given that the inventor will license others to use his invention, the questions remain as to how much profit he can realize from his invention and how the financial terms of the license will be set. The existing producers are realizing an aggregate profit of $(P(Q_0) - c)Q_0 = n(a - c)^2/b(n + 1)^2$ (substitute from (1) and (2)) equally divided among them. We shall assume that he is willing to let them retain this profit but not allow them more. If he were to attempt to capture some of the existing profit, the producers would have no incentive to adopt his production process unless he threatened to go into production himself, a possibility that we have ruled out. On the other hand, we also ruled out the possibility that they threaten to develop the invention themselves. We shall comment on the possibility of strategic behavior involving threats and counterthreats by the inventor and the producers later.

Thus the inventor claims the difference between the hypothetical monopoly profit and the current profit of the existing producers, $(P(Q^*) - c^*)Q^* - (P(Q_0) - c)Q_0$, as the reward for his invention. A vehicle for achieving this is to impose a royalty on each unit of output produced with this new process and perhaps to charge a license fee, independent of the number of units produced, as well. If the invention is minor, then $P(Q^*) = P(Q_0)$, $Q^* = Q_0$, and determination of a royalty is straightforward. By setting the unit royalty $r = c - c^*$, the inventor realizes a total reward of

(3) $rQ_0 = (c - c^*)Q_0$

and the existing producers' profits are preserved.

On the other hand, when the invention is major, the procedure is not so immediate. Then, $P(Q^*) < P(Q_0)$, $Q^* > Q_0$, and the inventor must induce the existing producers to expand their output. (We assume that the structure of the industry is unchanged as a result of the innovation. The producers act individually to maximize their own profits, given the behavior of their rivals and the announced royalty and license fee.) To achieve the twin objectives of inducing the producers to expand their output and preserving their original profit, the inventor must employ both a royalty and a license fee. In our assumed Cournot oligopoly framework, a unit royalty $r = (n - 1)(a - c^*)/2n$ and a license fee $F = (a - c^*)^2/4bn^2 - (a - c)^2/b(n + 1)^2$ on each producer will do the trick. This can be verified by substituting $r + c^*$ for c in (1) and finding that this yields Q^* as the industry output. Subtracting nF from the gross aggregate profit $(a - c^*)^2/4bn$ of the existing producers when their unit costs are c^* and when they pay the unit royalty r, previously specified, discloses that they are left with their original profit $n(a - c)^2/b(n + 1)^2$. Thus for a major innovation, the inventor can realize a reward of

(4) $(a - c^*)^2/4b - n(a - c)^2/b(n + 1)^2$

It should be noted that the pre- and postinnovation levels of output do enter into the determination of the license fee by the inventor. The license fee, however, is a constant as far as the individual producer is concerned.

If the industry that uses a major innovation is a monopoly, the unit royalty is zero and the inventor collects his entire reward through the license fee. This has also been observed by Fixler (1979) using a different route. If, on the other hand, the innovation-using industry is perfectly competitive then there is no license fee and the inventor's reward is realized entirely through royalty payments.

This analysis gives rise to a number of observations related to the demand-pull hypothesis and market structure. The first four are based on the assumptions already employed and the remaining four on their relaxation. First, the inventor's total reward from the innovation increases with the competitiveness (n) of the industry to which he is licensing it. In the case of a minor innovation his total reward increases with the preinnovation level of output, as is evident from (3). It is largest when the industry is perfectly competitive and smallest when it is a monopoly. Likewise, his reward from a major innovation is greater when the industry is more competitive. The second term in (4) shrinks as the number of firms in the industry increases, approaching zero as n approaches infinity. Thus again his profit is greatest when the industry is perfectly competitive and smallest when it is a monopoly. In other words, because preinnovation profits vary inversely with the number of firms, he has to share less of the profit from the innovation with the existing firms as the industry becomes more competitive.

Second, the inventor's reward from a major innovation is not as large as the total benefit to society. That is, society gains his reward – the inventor is a member of the society and therefore his gain must be included – and also the addition to consumers' surplus from the drop in price from $P(Q_0) = P_0$ to $P(Q^*) = P^*$. The addition to consumers' surplus is $Q_0(P_0 - P^*) + (Q^* - Q_0)(P_0 - P^*)/2 = (P_0 - P^*)(Q_0 + Q^*)/2$. The latter benefit to society might tilt the balance in favor of undertaking a major innovation if the innovator could capture it. Thus a socially desirable innovation may not be undertaken if the inventor's rewards are inadequate. Even the largest possible reward to the inventor, as when the invention is to be used in a perfectly competitive industry, may be insufficient. In such a case even the sacrifice of static efficiency (a monopoly price prevails after the innovation) is not enough to call forth the innovation. The situation is worse still if static efficiency is to be maintained, because then the innovator would be obligated to set the postinnovation price at c^* and get no royalty at all. Assuming the perfectly competitive price c prevailed prior to the innovation, society's gain from the innovation would be $(c - c^*)(Q_0 + Q^*)/2$. However, it would not be realized because it leaves no reward to the inventor. Consequently, it is sometimes argued that innovation be carried out by the government. As indicated before, this alternative also has major drawbacks.

No gap between the social and private value of an innovation arises if it is minor, for then price and therefore consumers' surplus, remains unchanged. The innovator's total reward, according to (3), depends on the current level of output and the gap between pre- and postinnovation unit costs. This, Arrow suggests, may create a bias toward minor innovations because their entire rewards can be appropriated by the inventor. The difficulty with this argument is that the inventor is concerned only with the amount of the reward that he can realize. Thus a major invention with a higher reward to the inventor should be more attractive to him than a minor invention with a lower one. To the extent, however, that such a bias does exist, it provides an alternative explanation to Galbraith's for the presence of innovative competition and the absence of price competition. It will be recalled that Galbraith explained this in terms of a tacit agreement among firms in an industry not to compete on price.

The third observation from (3) and (4) is that the total reward increases with the size of the market. This is obvious in (3) – the larger the preinnovation level of output is, the larger is the total royalty. It is slightly less obvious for (4). A larger market means a northeast parallel shift in the demand curve – its vertical intercept a increases. Differentiating (4) with respect to a discloses that the total reward from a major invention increases with the size of the market. The intuitive reason is that new technology is not consumed or diminished as it is used to produce additional units of output. In other words, development costs are fixed costs, independent of the number of units of output produced with the new technology. But more revenue is collected if output is larger. This feature is sometimes referred to as the "indivisibility" property of an innovation. The incentive to develop a cost-reducing invention for a large market or for a larger share of a market is greater than for a small market or for a smaller market share, respectively. This supports Schmookler's emphasis on market size and growth as stimulants to innovation.

The positive effect of market size on the incentive to innovate led Demsetz (1969) to argue that comparisons of the incentives for different market structures, as in (3) and (4), were misleading without correction for differences in industry output. Thus according to Demsetz, it is incorrect to argue that a perfectly competitive market creates a greater incentive than a monopolistic one, because the competitive output is larger. By compensating for the scale effect, Demsetz showed that the incentive to innovate for a monopolistic industry was greater than for a perfectly competitive industry. But the appropriate way to remove the scale effect is not obvious. A competitively organized industry produces more than a monopolist does under the same circumstances. Similarly, were the monopolist always to produce the same amount as the perfectly competitive industry and thereby earn only normal profits, there would be no objection to monopoly. In any event Ng (1971) pointed out that in Demsetz's demonstration the scale effect is not eliminated but is merely shifted in favor of the monopolist.

The fourth observation is that the total reward for a major innovation increases with the elasticity of the industry's demand curve regardless of its market structure. This is demonstrated in Kamien and Schwartz (1970), wherein to isolate the effect of the elasticity of demand, the demand curves are adjusted so that preinnovation levels of output are identical in the industries being compared. The incentive to innovate for the industry with the more elastic demand curve is always greater than for the industry with the less elastic one. Intuitively, the innovation-induced price reduction results in a greater expansion in output in the industry with the more elastic demand curve. Also, as already noted, the total reward increases with the quantity of output to which the innovation applies. Because a major determinant of a product's elasticity of demand is the availability of substitutes, this suggests that the incentive to develop a cost-reducing innovation is greater for a product with close substitutes than for one with few substitutes. A price reduction for a product with close substitutes will draw customers away from those substitutes. A similar conclusion, using a different route, is reached in Kamien and Schwartz (1972b). Jackson (1972) concludes that market power and demand elasticity depress the incentive to innovate. His first conclusion is consistent with the analysis of (3) and (4). His second conclusion is couched in terms of percentages rather than in absolute amounts and therefore only appears to be in conflict with ours. Moreover, Jackson does not adjust for scale effects.

The fifth observation is that this analysis is partial equilibrium in nature. In evaluating the social benefit from an innovation in a general equilibrium framework, one takes account of cost changes in all industries, not just in the industry to which the innovation directly applies. For example, an innovation-induced cost reduction in a component may reduce the cost of the product of which it is a part, expand the product's market, and enable its manufacturers to employ a larger scale, more efficient method of production. On the other hand, expanded production in the industry using the innovation may increase the demand for some factor of production, raising its price, so that the final cost reduction is less than originally envisioned.

Arvidsson (1970) points out that if development is achieved by withdrawing resources from monopolistic production, there may be overinvestment in innovation, because the opportunity cost of resources withdrawn from monopolistic production is lower than their social cost (i.e., their value employed in a competitive industry). This phenomenon also underlies Hu's (1973) claim that a monopolist will have a greater incentive to innovate than a competitive firm does. The upshot of this digression is that an innovation has to be evaluated in terms of net rather than gross social benefit. The divergence between the two further complicates the inventor's ability to realize the full rewards of the invention. It also of course, makes it difficult for government to evaluate the benefits of an innovation.

Sixth, the hypothetical monopoly profit from the cost-reducing invention need not necessarily be shared between the inventor and industry's producers in the way described until now. The constraint that the firms retain their preinnovation profits was imposed merely to get at the relationship between the inventor's incentive to invent and the structure of the industry to which the invention applies, in the spirit of Arrow's original analysis. In reality, there is no reason to suppose that this is the way the profit from the invention will be split. Certainly, as Yamey (1970) observed, when the industry is completely monopolized, the inventor confronts a single buyer of his invention; this bilateral monopoly situation has an indeterminant outcome. Arrow finessed this problem by assuming that if the industry is monopolized, the monopolist himself is the inventor.

In bilateral monopoly a variety of threats and counterthreats are available to the two parties. The inventor can threaten to enter into production himself and deprive the monopolist of his profit. The inventor could not capture the monopolist's entire profit, for if he set a price above c, the current unit production cost, the monopolist could compete with him. On the other hand, the monopolist could threaten to develop a cost-reducing invention himself and deprive the inventor of any reward. Indeed, Salop (1979) has argued that a monopolist may engage in preemptive innovation to deter entry by an independent inventor. How much reward the inventor will capture depends on the credibility of the opposing threats. The situation becomes even more complicated when the inventor confronts an industry with several firms. Then, different coalitions among the industry members including the inventor are possible. Moreover, resale of the invention by its original buyers to others becomes a threat to suppress the inventor's reward. These possible bargaining situations and concomitant indeterminacies of how much the inventor will gain suggest that firms in concentrated industries may have an incentive to have their own research facilities and to purchase outsiders' inventions only on an exclusive basis. It also suggests a motive for vertical integration between, say, industrial equipment manufacturers and their customers, because by doing so, equipment suppliers can realize the rewards from equipment improvements directly.

The seventh observation is that in reality the inventor is neither likely to be alone in the development of an invention nor is development instantaneous or success certain – Others may be working on similar inventions; competition among inventors makes priority important; and the speed of imitation affects the rewards to the first inventor. The pace of invention therefore is determined by the degree of competition both among inventors and in the industry to which the invention applies. However, this brings us back to the supply side of innovation and the hypothesis regarding how it is affected by market structure. The modern theories of this relationship will be taken up in Chapters 4 and 5.

The eighth, and final, observation is that Arrow views innovation as the creation of a new piece of information. This conception gives an innovation the indivisibility property mentioned earlier. The indivisibility property makes an innovation similar to a Samuelsonian public good, Samuelson (1964). But technical advance need not be disembodied from the factors of production. An innovation may be merely a new recipe for combining the existing factors of production so as to realize a greater output, but in some cases the new technology is embodied in the factors of production, typically capital. In this instance a new technology cannot be utilized without purchasing some new equipment. Viewed this way, the demand for innovation question turns into the question of whether monopoly power inhibits or promotes the adoption of new technology. The issue is whether as an industry becomes more monopolistic, the pressure on the individual firms to adopt the newest technology declines. Does a monopolist prolong the use of his existing equipment beyond the time at which it would be replaced by new equipment in a competitive industry? This issue is sometimes posed in terms of the allegation that monopolists try to protect their investment in existing equipment by delaying introduction of new technology. In any event it is reasonable to suppose that a new method of production will be adopted more rapidly in a competitive industry than in a monopoly, for once it has been adopted by some firms, the others are compelled to follow or be at a competitive disadvantage. Fellner (1951) provides an analytical demonstration of this.

Remember, however, in making these comparisons that the advent of a new lower cost technology does not call for the immediate scrapping of all existing equipment by either a competitive industry or a social planner. Moreover, because future fixed costs are incurred in purchasing capital equipment, the size of the total market and the share of the market served by the firm influence the speed of adoption of new technology. Thus industry concentration may affect the adoption of new technology. Likewise, the firm's antic-ipation of its future market size can influence the speed with which it adopts new technology. It is shown in Kamien and Schwartz (1972c) that anticipation of a shrinking market retards the adoption of new cost-reducing technology. A firm that fears shrinkage of its market may decide that the new technology will not be economical because fixed costs will not be spread over enough units. This sug-gests that a firm with the monopoly power to preserve its market should be more receptive to the adoption of new technology than one without such power.

Summary

We have identified a number of hypotheses regarding the economics of technical advance due to, or inspired by, Schumpeter's paradigm of the modern industrial economy:

1. Innovation is greater in monopolistic industries than in com-petitive ones because
   (a) A firm with monopoly power can prevent imitation and thereby can capture more profit from an innovation.
   (b) A firm with monopoly profits is better able to finance re-search and development.
2. Large firms are more innovative than small firms because
   (a) A large firm can finance a larger research and development staff. There are other economies of scale in this activity also.
   (b) A large diversified firm is better able to exploit unforseen innovations.
   (c) Indivisibility in cost-reducing innovations makes them more profitable for large firms.
3. Innovation is spurred by technological opportunity.
4. Innovation is spurred by market opportunity (demand-pull).

The last two hypotheses are relevant to the first two in that they reflect possible influences on innovation that one must control for in a statistical test of the influence of market power or firm size on innovation. That is, in examining the relationship between market structure and innovation and firm size and innovation, across industries or through time, one has to factor out technological opportunity and market opportunity. A test of the first hypothesis is whether innovation increases more than proportionately with industry concentration, other things being equal. Likewise, a test of the second hypothesis is whether innovation increases more than proportionately with firm size, ceteris paribus.

Beyond the specifics of the hypotheses described in this chapter, the most important feature of the Schumpeterian view is the emphasis on competition through innovation. This of course is different from the emphasis on price competition that is prevalent in most economic theory, especially in general equilibrium theory. If the Schumpeterian view is more correct than one focusing on price competition, then economic theory will have to undergo significant changes. Moreover, governmental policies founded on the theory of price competition, such as the antitrust laws, should be modified accordingly.

Appendix

To derive the elasticity of "dead-weight" loss in the framework of a Cournot oligopoly model with a linear inverse demand function, as assumed in connection with equations (1) and (2), we define P_c, Q_c as the price–quantity combination under perfect competition. The "dead-weight" loss associated with any n-firm oligopoly is given by the area of the triangle with height $P - P_c$ and base $Q_c - Q$, where P and Q are given by (1) and (2), respectively. Using (1) and (2), we find that this area is $DWL = (a - c)^2 /2b(n + 1)^2$. We define the elasticity of "dead-weight" loss with respect to the number of firms as $(n/DWL)dDWL/dn$. (Alternatively, we could define an arc elasticity because the number of firms can change only by discrete amounts. The result is the same as in the continuous version except the calculations are more complicated). Carrying out the differentiation yields

$$(n/DWL)dDWL/dn = -2n/(n + 1)$$

This elasticity ranges between -1 when $n = 1$ (it does not make sense for n to be less than 1) and -2 as $n \to \infty$.

3

Empirical studies of the Schumpeterian hypotheses

Empirical testing of what we have called the Schumpeterian hypotheses is subject to a variety of difficulties. Perhaps the most fundamental is the identification of an innovation. In principle, an innovation can be regarded as either an upward shift of a production function or a new product, that is, a new dimension in a commodity space. In practice, it is extremely difficult to identify such changes. Production functions are generally not well specified and so observing changes in them directly is virtually impossible. Using a surrogate such as increased productivity is also imprecise because the improvement in productivity may be the result of economies of scale or improvements in the factors of production rather than an innovation.

Likewise, identification of a new product is not always simple. Certainly, dramatically new products are not difficult to identify, for example, commercial jet aircraft, digital computers, quartz watches or lasers. However, most new products are not so strikingly different from what exists and may constitute only small improvements. These improvements may be stylistic only and not involve an advance in technology. Indeed, the major task of the patent office is to determine whether a new product or process is a genuine improvement over the present one.

It might be thought, therefore, that patent statistics provide a means for identifying innovation, and in fact they are used for this purpose in many empirical studies. Their use, however, also has major drawbacks. First, patents are issued for minor innovations as well as for major ones. Giving all patents equal weight is inappropriate and impairs testing the Schumpeterian hypotheses for obvious reasons. Second, many patented products and processes are never commercialized. Third, many innovations are not patented.

The second major difficulty encountered in empirical testing of Schumpeterian hypotheses is defining the inputs into the innovation process. One measure of inputs is the number of workers specifically assigned to research and development. This is the number of scientists, or scientists and engineers, or both together with their support staffs. Refinements of this measure adjust the total figure by the experience distribution of the scientists and engineers and weight the professionals more than their support staff. More experienced scientists might be considered more productive than their junior colleagues, who in turn may be more productive than staff. In addition, account must be taken of the quality and quantity of equipment available to the research personnel in their efforts to innovate. However, even if these adjustments were made, measuring the inputs into the innovation process by the number of scientists and engineers would be inadequate because they are not the only source of innovation. Someone involved in the production process directly is sometimes responsible for the development of a new process or improvement of the existing one. Likewise, someone in marketing might initiate a new product. The distinction between research personnel and others is further blurred by the fact that research personnel may eventually end up in management; some managers have backgrounds in engineering or science.

An alternative measure of inputs into the innovation process is the total spending on research and development. This measure does not reflect the composition of the inputs – senior or junior personnel or equipment. Moreover, personnel not directly involved in research and development but who may contribute to the innovation process anyway are not taken into account. This measure depends on the accounting practices of the companies reporting research and development outlays. A particular shortcoming is that research and development spending is treated as a flow cost rather than as an investment. This method ignores the accumulation of knowledge and know-how through time that in fact constitutes an asset. Thus a potentially important input into the innovation process, accumulated knowledge, is left out when current expenditures alone measure innovative input.

A third difficulty is in the measurement of firm size. Sales, total number of employees, and total assets are three alternatives, but they are not perfectly correlated. At present, there is no theory about differences in the relationship between innovative activity (whether measured in terms of inputs or output) and each of the measures of firm size.

A fourth difficulty involves the measurement of monopoly power. Some indices of monopoly power focus on the performance of an industry as measured by the proximity of its equilibrium price to the price that would prevail under perfect competition. Others focus on market structure. The Lerner Index and the Dansby–Willig (1979) Index measure market performance, whereas the Herfindahl Index and the four-firm or eight-firm concentration ratio measure market structure. (A four-firm concentration ratio is the percent of industry assets, sales, or value added due to the four largest contributing firms in the industry.) The latter two, although focusing on the structure of an industry (the number of firms and their relative sizes), are supposed to be surrogates for measures of market performance through the notion that the more firms in an industry and the more alike they are in size, the closer the equilibrium price will be to the perfectly competitive price.

It can be shown, however, see, for example, Kamien and Schwartz (1980), that this link between market structure and performance is tenuous. The firms need not behave as Cournot oligopolists but may believe that their rivals will respond to changes in their output or price. A large number of equal size firms do not necessarily imply nearly competitive industry performance nor does industry composition of only a few large firms necessarily preclude it. Data availability has, however, constrained most studies to the use of four-firm or eight-firm concentration ratios as a measure of monopoly power. Moreover, industries are usually defined by the Standard Industrial Classification employed by the U.S. Department of Commerce. Although this classification is useful for some purposes, it has an important drawback in the study of competition through innovation. For, as already noted, innovation in one area may arise from an industry in an entirely different area, as defined by the Standard Industrial Classification.

A fifth difficulty in testing the Schumpeterian hypotheses arises from the indeterminancy of the direction of causality among the variables being studied. For example, market structure may be the consequence of innovation rather than a cause. An innovation, especially one that is relatively easy to imitate, may result in many new firms and the appearance of a relatively competitive industry. The number of firms in the industry may eventually decline as the market becomes saturated. This appears to be the pattern followed in the hand calculator market. On the other hand, an innovation that is difficult to imitate may lead to a decline in the number of firms serving a market, especially if the innovation results in substantial economies of scale in the production of an item. The decline in the number of independent automobile manufacturers in the early part of this century can be attributed at least in part to the introduction of the assembly line method of production by Henry Ford. This simultaneity between market structure and innovation suggests that tests of the Schumpeterian hypotheses be conducted in terms of simultaneous equations. This has been done in very few instances, however.

We have described some of the difficulties encountered in testing the Schumpeterian hypotheses as a warning to the reader in the interpretation of empirical studies that will be surveyed. They are of course not unique to testing the Schumpeterian hypotheses. The difficulties of identifying inputs and outputs also occur while estimating cost or production functions for transportation, health care services, and educational services, for instance. Even in estimating production functions of more tangible products, difficulty is encountered in connection with measurement of capital inputs of different vintages and in aggregating labor with differing skills. Also, as in most empirical studies in all branches of economics, the available data and the available statistical methodology tend to dictate the nature of the analysis. Economic theory tends to be more suggestive than definitive in specifying the functional forms that relate the variables being investigated. Thus we have chosen not to provide a methodological evaluation of each of the studies that will be presented. Certainly, they all do not merit equal weight in drawing conclusions about the Schumpeterian hypotheses; some are clearly better than others. This field of investigation, as already indicated, is at a relatively early stage of development with ample room for refinement. Overall conclusions about the Schumpeterian hypotheses at present have to be drawn from the reoccurrence of certain patterns in a variety of independent and dissimilar studies rather than from a few definitive investigations. What does emerge is that an industry with many moderate to large firms of relatively similar size and with a growing scientific base will tend to be the most technologically progressive. Neither the extremes of perfect competition nor perfect monopoly appear to be most conducive to technical advance.

In our survey of the empirical investigations, we shall not immediately discuss those dealing directly with the Schumpeterian hypotheses. We begin instead with studies seeking to establish a production function for invention or innovation. We shall then turn to investigations regarding the properties of this function, in particular, whether it exhibits increasing, constant, or decreasing returns to scale. Next we shall consider the role of other factors on the productivity of the inputs in the production of innovations. These factors include knowledge of opportunities for profitable innovation, internal organization, and the scientific base. We shall then survey the relatively brief literature on the effect of innovation on market structure. Finally, we shall take up the questions of how innovative activity is related to firm size and market structure. These questions will be addressed from two standpoints: When innovative activity is measured in terms of the level of inputs employed and when it is measured by the level of output. We have chosen this sequence of presentation because it builds up from the basic elements to the entire phenomenon of interest, thus paralleling the sequence of topics in microeconomics texts where discussion of production and cost functions precedes the analysis of markets.

It should be noted that most of the studies to be surveyed involve multivariate regressions. The investigator commonly tries to pack as many variables into his regression as the data allow. Rather than presenting the actual regression equations that were fitted, we give simple stylized regression equations that illustrate the hypothesis being tested.

Finally, we shall discuss some of the studies of the relationship between the rate of diffusion of an innovation and market structure. The rate of diffusion of innovations is critical in the overall rate of technical progress, because an innovation that is not used or whose use is limited contributes little to technical advance. From the standpoint of the innovator rapid diffusion of an innovation is desirable only if he is assured of collecting a royalty for its use. Such assurance may result from holding a patent that is not easily circumvented. If the innovator cannot assure himself of collecting the royalty, then he will prefer that the use of the innovation be limited to himself and that its imitation be slow. This of course is the major tension, previously mentioned, between the rewards to the innovator and the rewards to society from his efforts. The literature on diffusion is very broad, ranging from the classic studies by Griliches (1957) on hybrid corn to the work of Rogers and Shoemaker (1971) dealing with the sociology of the diffusion of innovations. We shall restrict ourselves to the much narrower literature on diffusion and market structure.

The inventive process

The first question is whether a positive relationship exists between the devotion of economic resources and the emergence of inventions. A regression equation of the form $Y = a + bX + u$ or of the form $Y = aX^b u$ may be fitted, where Y is a measure of inventive output, X is a measure of economic input, and u is a random variable. In the language of statistical hypothesis testing the null hypothesis is that there is no relationship between invention and the devotion of economic resources; that is, the parameter $b = 0$. Accepting the null hypothesis would mean that inventive output is unrelated to economic effort. Evidence to reject the null hypothesis is sought.

Note that if one takes logarithms of the second form, yielding $\ln Y = \ln a + b \ln X + \ln u$, the result is linear in the variables $\ln Y$ and $\ln X$ and can be estimated using ordinary linear regression techniques. The functional form is often called *log–linear* because it gives rise to an equation that is linear in the logarithms. The exponent b is the *elasticity* of Y with respect to X.

Passage from the abstract concept of inputs into the innovation process to its concrete empirical embodiment is difficult. Input measures include R&D spending, R&D employees, and scientists and engineers employed. Each of these, as well as other indices of innovational effort, has recognized deficiencies. For instance, as mentioned earlier, technical improvements arise in operating and other divisions as well as in the R&D department. Measures of scientific personnel accommodate this phenomenon but include employees with no R&D function or contribution. Modified indices of R&D employment include a distinction between total R&D personnel and professional R&D personnel. "Technical personnel" may be refined into all technical personnel or all scientists or scientists and engineers.

These measures are also susceptible to institutional distortions. For instance, David Novick (Blair, 1972, pp. 201–4) noted two significant jumps in reported R&D spending without commensurate increases in R&D activity. First, a 1954 change in the tax treatment of research expenditures provided an incentive for firms to classify additional activities as "research." Second, Sputnik and its aftermath made R&D more fashionable, particularly in military and space-related areas. The "fashion" aspect extends to other industries, where R&D may be viewed favorably by stockholders.

Innovational output has been measured alternatively by patents awarded, important patents awarded, important inventions or innovations, and sales of new products. Deficiencies of patents in this role include the facts that the patent recipient need not have been responsible for the invention, that patented inventions are of unequal importance, and that some important inventions go without patents. Nevertheless, systematic study of patenting behavior has led Schmookler, Scherer, and others to conclude that the number of patents granted a firm is a usable proxy for inventive outputs.

Schmookler (1966) found in his intensive study of patents and patenting that nonpatenting was not a serious problem before 1940, but post-1945 corporate patenting failed to keep pace with inventions. This was attributed both to the lengthening period to obtain patent approval and to a more hostile political and legal attitude toward patents, reducing the incentive to patent. Consequently, the post-1945 and pre-1940 patent statistics are not comparable. This shift in the patenting behavior was noted by Branch (1973) in his study of the relationship between patents awarded firms and their real sales growth; the regression coefficient of the patent variable was about one-fourth as large for 1928–39 as in 1950–64.

Some studies employed only "important" patents or inventions, as deemed by judges with competence in the field. Schmookler found that the time series of important inventions in a number of fields resemble those of all inventions in the field. A final measure of inventive output, employed by Comanor (1965), is the sales volume of new products in the two years immediately following introduction. Although the sales volume reflects the significance of the invention, it also depends on the size of the market and other factors.

Schmookler (1966) found similarity between changes over 1870–1950 in the numbers of scientists and engineers and of patents. He also found that patents and R&D expenditures were closely related in 1953 for eighteen major industry groups, with 85 percent of the interindustry variation in patents pending explained by the variation in expenditures on R&D. Using a sample from the 500 largest U.S. industrial firms in 1955, Scherer's (1965b) regression analysis indicated a very nearly linear relationship between the number of R&D personnel in 1955 and the number of patents issued a firm in 1959 (the four-year lag reflecting the average time for filing and processing applications).

In another study Comanor and Scherer (1969) compared three measures of innovative activity for fifty-seven pharmaceutical firms: sales volume of new products within two years after introduction, the number of R&D personnel, and the number of patents received. With firm size held fixed, the correlation between patents and the other measures of R&D input and output was positive and statistically significant. McLean and Round (1978), following the framework of the Comanor–Scherer study, investigated the correlations between three measures of inputs into the R&D process – the ratios of R&D spending to sales, R&D employees to total work force, and professional employees to total work force – and output as measured by new products or weighted new products (the weights reflecting their relative sales). Their sample consisted of 980 Australian manufacturing firms during 1971–2. For the entire sample, the correlation coefficients were positive and highly significant. The correlation between input and output was highest when input was measured by the ratio of R&D employees to total work force.

Mansfield (1968a) found, for a given firm size, a close relation in the long run between the rate of R&D spending and the total number of important inventions forthcoming. Comanor's (1965) study of the pharmaceutical industry reached a similar conclusion for his sample. Pavitt and Wald (1971) found across thirteen U.S. industries a high correlation between R&D intensity (R&D funds/sales) and rates of technical innovation, measured by the expected annual rate of new product introduction as a percent of sales. They also discovered, across ten OECD countries, a high correlation between national industrial R&D expenditures and national performance in technological innovation, after correcting for differences in population.

Without much doubt, on average, a direct relation between innovational effort and innovational output exists. However, it is also true that the transformation may depend on factors other than effort and may not be linear (but still monotone increasing). A further consequence of these results is that the use of either input or output as a measure of inventive activity is justified in the sense that there is a positive relationship between them. If the measures are not proportional, then the relationship between the R&D variable and some other variable will depend on the choice of the former.

For example, if $Y = aX^b$ and also R&D input X is related to firm size S by $X = cS^d$, then $Y = kS^{bd}$. If $b > 1$ so there are economies of scale in R&D and if $d < 1$ so R&D effort increases less than proportionately with firm size, then R&D output may, but need not, increase less than proportionately with firm size (i.e., $bd > 1$ or $bd < 1$ is possible).

There are circumstances, however, when it may be argued that one measure of inventive activity is superior to the other. If it is held that serendipity plays an important role in determining the outcome of R&D activity, then input is the appropriate measure. In this circumstance the inventor or the firm employing inventors can only control the level of effort devoted to invention and not the outcome. Thus for industries in which technical advance is largely the product of internal R&D activity, the level of resources devoted may be the appropriate measure of inventive activity. On the other hand, for industries in which technical advance is largely the product of R&D carried out elsewhere, inventive output (e.g., number of patents purchased) is the better measure, because in these industries the role of serendipity is irrelevant. They only purchase the final invention. Of course in any actual situation the investigator's choice of measures is influenced by the available data.

The roles of technological opportunity and economic opportunity

Rejecting the hypothesis that technical advance is entirely a random phenomenon still leaves open the possibility that chance is a very important element in the process. In particular, chance plays a role in the discovery of a new scientific law or principle. More generally, developments in basic scientific knowledge open up opportunities for invention. The importance of technological opportunity for invention, as previously noted, has been emphasized by Phillips (1966) and also by Rosenberg (1976). The competing hypothesis, identified with Schmookler, is that technological opportunity is not the dominant factor essential for invention. It is economic opportunity, according to the alternative hypothesis, that is dominant. An opportunity for economic gain leads to a quest for a solution that may draw on any branch of science or even go beyond the present state of scientific knowledge. As already mentioned, inventions have often preceded their underlying scientific base.

In a simple regression analysis the null hypothesis that technological opportunity is unimportant would mean that $a = 0$ in the equation $Y = a + bX + u$, where Y and X have the earlier interpretations. According to the technological opportunity hypothesis, $a > 0$ so that a certain amount of invention would take place even if no resources were devoted to this activity. In fact, the hypothesis is typically tested by accounting for interindustry differences in inventive activity. Those that cannot be accounted for by other factors are attributed to differences in technological opportunity. If interindustry differences were fully explained by these other factors, then obviously the technological opportunity hypothesis would not be supported.

To quantify and distinguish differences in technological opportunty, Scherer (1965b) ran cross-sectional linear regressions of patents granted against firms' sales in fourteen industries. Interindustry differences accounted for about as much of the total variance in corporate patenting as did interfirm differences in sales volume. The bulk of this interindustry variation, unrelated to sales, was attributed to differences in the underlying science base, or technological opportunity. Phlips's (1971) regression of research workers on total workers for twelve Belgian industry groups likewise revealed interindustry differences accounting for about as much of total variance as interfirm differences do. Moreover, the aggregation, based on regression coefficients, of the twelve industries into four groups led to no significant loss in explanatory power relative to the twelve groups. Although Scherer used innovational output (patents) and U.S. data, whereas Phlips used research input (R&D personnel) and Belgian data, the classification of industries was strikingly similar. Further evidence of the role of technological opportunity is provided by Kelly's (1970) investigation of 181 large multiproduct firms, divided into six industry groups. Measuring the 1950 inventive effort by the ratio of R&D employees to total employees, he found technological opportunity played a positive, significant role in the innovative activity of the chemical and petroleum industries relative to other industries studied.

Through association of technological opportunity with ease of achieving product differentiation, Comanor (1967) provided additional insight into its role in the inventive process. Based on McGraw-Hill surveys of the purposes of R&D and his own studies of the pharmaceutical industry (Comanor, 1964, 1965), he conjectured that a major goal of R&D is the development of new, differentiated products that afford a protected market position. Comanor then hypothesized that research effort would be greater in industries where prospects for successful product differentiation are better. From the results of the 1958 McGraw-Hill survey and of Bain (1956) regarding product differentiation as a barrier to entry in producer goods industries, he identified consumer durables and investment goods as industries with high potential for product differentiation and consumer nondurables and material inputs as those with low potential. Research effort was adjusted for firm size by using "predicted" research for the average firm size within each size class. The adjusted research levels were then grouped by the adjudged possibility of product differentiation. Comanor found, consistent with his hypothesis, that research levels tended to be far greater in industries producing consumer durables and investment goods than in those manufacturing consumer nondurables and material inputs. The distinction in research by product type was especially pronounced among large firms (over 25,000 employees) but was also evident among small firms (under 10,000 employees).

Schmookler (1966), on the contrary, found the role of technological opportunity of little significance. Chronologies of hundreds of economically or technologically important inventions in four fields revealed the stimulus typically to be a technical problem or opportunity conceived largely in economic terms. In contrast to the many accounts identifying economic problems as the immediate stimulus, in no instance was a scientific discovery specified as initiating the invention. A comparison of time series of important inventions and of patents within four fields lent no support to the possibility that inventions in a field beget further invention.

Having rejected the importance of technological opportunity, Schmookler argued that invention is largely an economic activity, pursued for gain; that expected gain varies with expected sales of goods embodying the invention; and that expectations of sales of improved capital goods are largely based on present capital goods sales. The number of capital goods inventions should therefore be expected to vary over time and among industries directly with and in response to sales of capital goods in that industry. He claimed support for his hypothesis from the similarity between the long-term time series behavior of capital goods inventions with investment in railroading, building, and petroleum refining. Regression analyses using cross-section data also supported the hypothesis and suggested that, on average, increasing the investment of an industry tends to increase – in about the same proportion – the number of capital goods inventions made for its use.

Schmookler also considered the relation between his findings and those of others on the role of technological opportunity and the rise of science- and engineering-based industries. In his study, inventions were attributed to the industry expected to use them; in contrast, other investigators classified inventions by the industry expected to supply the invented product or process. To see if this difference affected the conclusions, Schmookler regressed, in logarithmic form, the patents granted in 1959 on alternate measures of 1955 industry size using Scherer's data classified by industry supplying the invention. A similar regression was estimated using his own attribution of inventions by usage. The coefficient of size was significant and close to unity in each case. However, the latter regression (using Schmookler's classification) yielded a far higher correlation coefficient. The appreciably smaller portion of variance explained when inventions are classified by their industry source suggested to Schmookler that an economic objective can be achieved by a variety of technological means. The most efficient means available will usually be selected.

Schmookler inferred from these results that, on average, increasing the market served by an industry tends to increase in about the same proportion the number of goods invented for it to produce, just as increasing investment in an industry tends to increase proportionately the number of capital goods inventions for its use. The rise of the chemical and electrical industries may be a consequence of inventors' problems having been relatively efficiently solved by chemical and/or electrical means.

In attempting to discern factors underlying successful innovation, Freeman (1973) studied fifty-eight attempted, paired innovations (twenty-nine failures and twenty-nine successes) in chemicals and in scientific instruments. Failure and success, as well as similarity in pairs, were defined in economic terms of the market, not technical characteristics. Successful innovation generally involved greater attention to education of users, publicity, market forecasting, and selling. Most significantly, successful innovation was marked by an understanding of user needs. This understanding was needed by those in R&D performance as well as in marketing and general management.

Utterback (1974), reporting on his own findings and those of others, claimed that "sixty to eighty percent of important innovations in a large number of fields have been in response to market demands and needs." He suggests that this may also explain why freely available government patents and technical information do not get wide use. Likewise, Gerstenfeld (1976) found in a study of eleven successful innovations and an equal number of unsuccessful ones in West Germany, that the former (eight out of eleven) tended to stem from a perceived need, whereas the latter (nine out of eleven) were initiated by new technological developments.

In case studies of innovations in ten industries by Layton and others (1972) British companies were compared with companies in the United States and Continental Europe. Particular attention and emphasis was given the role of qualified scientists and engineers at every stage, from idea to successful innovation. Many instances were found in which skillful initial invention in the R&D department did not lead to successful innovation because of failure to carry through with skillful production planning and/or marketing. Good communication between the development and marketing departments was found particularly important in the capital goods industries. Langrish and others (1972) studied eighty-four innovations that won Queen's Awards in the United Kingdom for 1966 and 1967. Myers and Marquis (1969) studied 567 innovations in five U.S. industries. Both studies found that in initiating the innovation, the clear identification of a need that could be met was important more often than the realization of the potential usefulness of the discovery.

The emphasis on good management throughout the firm, with excellent working relationships and communications among the R&D, production, and marketing departments is a recurring theme in comparative studies of success and failure in innovations. Mansfield et al. (1971) insist these interrelationships cannot be over-emphasized. Besides the factors just mentioned, Carter and Williams (1957) also emphasized the role of communications between supplier firms and customer firms in stimulating and being receptive to technical advances.

In the discussion thus far technological opportunity has been implicitly viewed as unlimited though unequally available. The hypothesis that technical possibilities, and therefore inventions, become depleted was also tested by Schmookler. The time series of patents for railroad track was similar to that of patents for all other (nontrack) railroad patents. The similarity in patterns of invention, despite the dissimilarity in the underlying technology, suggested that technical progress slowed as it became less valuable, not because it approached exhaustion. A study of the course of invention in different aspects of shoe manufacturing (sole making, lasting, leather sewing, leather nailing and stapling, miscellaneous) yielded similar findings. Contrary results were reported by Baily (1972) investigating new drug introduction. He conjectured that the number of new drugs introduced in any year can be positively related to R&D spending in the pharmaceutical industry in preceding years (the development period) and negatively related to the depleted stock of research opportunities. As a measure of the depletion of research opportunities, he took a seven-year moving average of past total (all sources) new drug introductions. A regression indicated that the number of new drugs per dollar of R&D spending was indeed negatively related to this index. A subsequent reestimation of Baily's equation using data for 1954–74 showed a negative coefficient but it was not significant (Grabowski, et al., 1978).

All in all, the evidence suggests that technological opportunity does influence the pace and direction of technical advance in a broad sense and especially in the long run. Indeed, it would be rather surprising if it did not. Also, technological opportunity may have a strong impact on activities within an industry and on the growth of some industries and the decline of others. Yet when one gets down to the level of specific inventions, it becomes apparent that it is economic opportunity that is essential. In fact, of course technological opportunity and economic opportunity are complementary influences on the course of invention. A recent study by Stoneman (1979) supports the importance of economic opportunity but shows the complementary role of technical opportunity through its reduction in the cost of inventing. Economic opportunity accelerates the exploitation of technological opportunity and in the long run there is a feedback leading to new technological opportunities.

The innovation production function

Because economic inputs beget innovations, what is the nature of this relationship? What are the properties of this production function? Is there an optimal or most efficient scale research facility? In terms of a regression equation of inventive output against input of the form $Y = aX^b u$, the question is the value of b, the elasticity of output with respect to input. If $b = 1$, the production function exhibits constant returns to scale, whereas values of $b \gtrless 1$ indicate increasing and decreasing returns to scale, respectively. In empirical tests the null hypothesis is commonly taken to be $b = 1$. If the null hypothesis is correct, there is no single optimal size research facility; all sizes are equally efficient. On the other hand, rejection of the null hypothesis in favor of $b > 1$ would mean that a single very large research facility would be optimal, whereas the finding $b < 1$ would call for many research facilities, each of the smallest possible size.

This form of regression equation does not admit the possibility of an optimal intermediate scale research facility. To allow for that possibility, one can use a cubic equation. If the relationship is of the form $Y = aX + bX^2 + cX^3 + u$, with $a > 0$, $b > 0$, and $c < 0$, then the optimal scale research facility is given by $X = -b/2c$. An interval of increasing returns to scale is followed by an interval of decreasing returns; $X = -b/2c$ is the scale at which the average productivity of the input is the greatest.

Empirical investigations disclose an inverse, convex relationship between the total cost of project development and the time required to carry it out. That is, total R&D cost for a given project seems to increase at an increasing rate as the development period is shortened. Mansfield et al. (1971), in particular, found support for this relationship by estimating the time–cost trade-off functions for twenty-nine completed innovations by eleven firms in the chemical, machinery, and electronics industries, using data gathered in interviews with the innovation managers.

Mansfield's (1968a) regression study of firms in the chemical, petroleum, and steel industries indicated that when the size of firm is held constant, increases in R&D expenditures result in more than proportional increases in inventive output in the chemical industry. No such advantage of increasing R&D effort was evident in the other two industries, however.

Scherer (1965b), through regressions, found that patent intensity (patents per billion dollars of sales) varied inversely with firm size and increased with R&D intensity (R&D employment per sales dollar) but showed diminishing returns. The fitted quadratic function attained a maximum at an input intensity exceeded by only one firm in the sample. McLean and Round (1978) found a linear relationship between R&D inputs and output most prevalent when they disaggregated their sample into thirteen industries.

Comanor (1965) tested and found unsupported the hypothesis that a large support staff relative to the professional staff substantially increases the efficiency of the pharmaceutical research facility. He found at most highly tentative support for the hypothesis that rapid expansion of the R&D facility impairs its research efficiency.

Thus the scant evidence that exists indicates no economies of scale in the innovation process. Indeed, constant or even diminishing returns appear to be the more likely characteristic of the innovation production function. We turn next to the role of the size of the firm associated with the research facility.

As already observed, it is difficult to study the efficiency properties of a research laboratory in isolation. Most of them are associated with firms whose major line of business is not the sale of inventions as such. Thus it has become customary to study the externalities between the research facility and its parent firm, especially the impact of size of the latter on the performance of the former. In terms of a regression equation, this relationship can be expressed as $Y = aX^bS^du$, where S represents the size of the firm in which the research facility is embedded. The null hypothesis would be $d = 0$ and its rejection in favor of $d > 0$ (< 0) would indicate that firm size had a positive (negative) effect on the efficiency of the research facility.

Empirical studies over the last fifteen years have consistently shown that, although there may sometimes be certain advantages of size in exploiting the fruits of R&D, it is more efficiently done in small or medium size firms than in large ones.

Comanor (1965), in the preceding study, attempted to discern the relationship between research input, average (professional or total) R&D employment 1955–60, and new product output. R&D output, 1955–60, was measured by the proportion of sales attributed to either new chemical entities or products new to the firm. The regression included firm size and a diversification index as well. Comanor concluded that the marginal productivity of professional research personnel was inversely related to firm size. Estimated elasticities of research output with respect to research input exceed unity (1.4) for the smallest firms but fell well below unity for larger firms, suggesting economies of scale in R&D at low firm sizes but diseconomies as a firm becomes moderately large. Reestimation for 1965–70 by Vernon and Gusen (1974) resulted in a statistically worse fit, with firm sales being the only statistically significant variable. These authors then attempted to separate the effects of size on superior selling capability, on the one hand, and on economies of scale, on the other, by using the number of new chemical entities introduced by the firm as the dependent variable. Their regression suggested that in producing new chemical entities, there are diminishing returns to R&D employment for a given firm size. However, the marginal productivity of the research personnel was higher in larger firms.

Schmookler (1972) also concluded that beyond some not very large firm size, the efficiency of inventive activity tends to vary inversely with firm size. Firms in the largest size class (5,000 or more employees) spent more (on average, twice as much) on R&D per patent pending in 1953 than did firms in the smallest size class (under 1,000 employees). Further, in each industry except chemicals, large firms spent more per patent pending than did the intermediate size firms. The larger cost per patent is not attributable to a differential propensity to patent by firm size; Schmookler cited the independent findings of both B. S. Sanders and F. M. Scherer, which indicate small firms commercially employ a greater proportion of their patents than do large firms.

Mansfield (1968a), in the previous study, attempted to relate the number of significant inventions per dollar of R&D expenditure with firm size and the research budget. For a constant R&D outlay the effect of firm size on the average productivity of such spending was found to be negative. That is, inventive output per dollar of R&D spending was lower in the largest firms than in the small and medium size firms. Further corroborating evidence was subsequently secured by Mansfield et al. (1971). Twenty-three R&D executives and academicians were asked to rank the R&D programs of either ten major chemical firms or nine petroleum firms on the basis of their overall quality and their effectiveness per research dollar. A linear regression indicated that the average assessed effectiveness of R&D varied directly with the firm's total R&D budget and inversely with its size (sales). The regression coefficient signs were significant for the chemical but not for the petroleum industry.

Cooper (1964) interviewed about twenty-five development managers with experience in both large and small companies or in rapidly expanding development organizations. All were based in either the electronics or chemical industry. He also obtained actual cost figures for a particular parallel development effort by a large company and a small company. He found remarkably consistent estimates that a given product would cost three to ten times as much to develop by a large firm as by a small one.

A number of forces contribute to the superior efficiency of small firms in the R&D process. The larger firms seem to become enmeshed in bureaucracy and red tape, resulting in a less hospitable atmosphere for creative contributions by operating personnel. Superior technical personnel tend to be attracted to smaller companies where greater latitude may be afforded them. The larger the firm is, the more difficult it may be to understand the problems in need of solution. Finally, there is evidence of greater cost consciousness in smaller firms. Schmookler (1972) emphasized that inadequate attention has been given to the effect of firm size on individual incentives and opportunities to generate new ideas. Williamson (1975) describes at length the problems associated with innovation in the large firm.

Invention and development are not only more costly in large firms, but there is some evidence that big firms have actually suppressed inventions as well. Blair (1972) has presented evidence (law suits) that some large firms have endeavored to withhold inventions in the synthetic rubber, automatic glass, shoe machinery, cable, braking systems, matches, and golf clubs industries. The sluggishness of large firms in certain innovations has been explained by the desire to protect an investment in the then-current technology, satisfaction with the status quo, underestimation of the potential demand for a new item, neglect of the inventor, and misdirection of research, as well as by incompatibility of bureaucracy and creativity.

Our discussion so far has been in terms of quantity of inventive output, its cost, and its use. Another important dimension is the quality or importance of inventive output. Hamberg's (1966) review of his own and others' findings led him to conclude that large industrial laboratories tend to produce mainly minor inventions.

He claims that the fraction of total inventive output of these laboratories that can be classified as "important" is less than the comparable ratio for inventive output of other sources. Of twenty-seven major inventions in 1946–55 studied by Hamberg, only seven were products of large industrial laboratories. Of thirteen major innovations in the U.S. steel industry during 1940–55, seven were attributed to independent inventors. Hamberg also cited a study of W. M. Grosvenor published in 1929, according to which only twelve of seventy-two major inventions since 1889 orginated in corporate laboratories. In the Jewkes, Sawers, Stillerman (1969) study only twelve of sixty-one major inventions of the twentieth century were attributed to the laboratories of large corporations. They found that large research laboratories of industrial corporations have not been responsible for the greater part of significant inventions but have relied heavily upon other sources of original thinking.

W. F. Mueller's (1962) study of the origins of basic inventions underlying DuPont's major innovations during 1920–50 indicated that the DuPont laboratories were more successful in improving discoveries of others than in originating major inventions. Peck's (1962) study of the origin of inventions in the U.S. aluminum industry 1946–57 and Enos's (1962) study of the origins of major inventions in petroleum refining also support Hamberg's thesis.

Mansfield et al. (1971) found modified support for Hamberg's thesis. Up to some point, increases in firm size appeared to be associated with increases in the fraction of R&D expenditures devoted to basic research, increases in the technical progressiveness of projects, and increases in expected completion time. However, there was little if any difference in these areas between the behavior of the largest firms in the sample and of firms only half as large. Duetsch (1973) has dissented, at least regarding the ethical drug industry. He queried physicians to develop a list of important new drugs during 1940–67, as distinct from the comprehensive list of all new drugs. The contribution of ethical drug manufacturers in the discovery of new chemical entities (87 percent of U.S. total) was compared with their participation in discovery of important chemical entities (90 percent of U.S. total). Duetsch concluded that the ethical drug manufacturers have been as active in discovering important chemical entities as in finding new chemical entities. Layton et al. (1972), in their international study of innovation in ten industries, concluded that the best conditions for innovation are most often found in small companies where a common objective, with strategies to implement it, can be understood by all concerned.

Pavitt and Wald (1971) examined the empirical evidence developed during the 1960s and concluded that both large and small firms play essential, complementary, and interdependent roles in the process of innovation. Larger firms have tended to contribute most in innovation in areas requiring large-scale R&D, production, or marketing. Smaller firms tend to concentrate on specialized but sophisticated components and equipment. Small firms have often made very major innovations when large firms let the opportunity slip by.

The effects of technical advance on market structure

As noted earlier, the relationship between technical advance and market structure is not one directional. Although market structure may influence the pace of inventive activity, it is itself, at least in part, influenced by technical advances. Indeed, it may be difficult, in the study of technical advance in a particular market, to distinguish between cause and effect. Technical advances affect market structure in two primary ways. The first is through influencing the optimal scale of production in an industry. If the minimum efficient plant size (e.g., the level of output at which average cost is minimized) increases as a result of technical advance, then there will be a tendency for the industry to become more concentrated. Obviously, a decrease in the minimum efficient scale of operation will have the opposite effect on industry concentration.

The second way is through the erection of entry barriers. The first firm to introduce a successful major innovation may gain a significant advantage over its rivals. This advantage may derive from patents that cannot be easily circumvented, development of expertise that cannot be easily duplicated, realization of extraordinary profits that are available for additional research and development, and development of a favorable reputation and a loyal customer base. The last advantage is especially important for new durable goods, for they are not replaced often, by definition, and so the original supplier may capture a significant market share. Moreover, the original supplier may be able to maintain this advantage through time by making subsequent improvements in his product compatible with earlier versions or accepting the earlier versions as trade-ins. These advantages of being first constitute barriers to entry; to overcome them may require potential entrants to spend more money than the innovator needed to develop the product. Thus it is possible that a technical advance initiates a "success breeds success" spiral or what Merton (1973) calls the Matthew effect (in reference to the passage in the Gospel According to Saint Matthew describing how the rich will get richer and the poor poorer).

Although the bulk of empirical studies has focused on the influence of market structure on innovative activity, there have been a number of investigations of the opposite direction of influence. Blair (1972) very comprehensively reviewed the literature dealing with the impact of technological advance upon economies of scale. He concluded that from the late eighteenth century through the first third of the twentieth century, technical change exerted an impetus toward concentration, as advances in steam power, materials and methods of fabrication, and transportation (the railroad) permitted and encouraged scale expansion. Since then, newer technologies (electricity, materials and methods of fabrication, trucks) tended to have the opposite effect, reducing plant size and capital requirements for optimal efficiency. Hamberg (1967) reached similar conclusions. The most recent technical advances have tended to permit economic production with smaller plants and have also increased effective rivalry to older products through widening the range of substitutes. For instance, plastics, fiberglass, and high performance and prestressed concrete compete with steel.

The "success breeds success" hypothesis was first advanced by Phillips (1966). He sought, without much success, to support his theory with regression analysis, using data for eleven U. S. industry groups. He then undertook (1971) a detailed investigation of the commercial aircraft market in the United States during 1932–65. Advances in science and technology relating to aircraft manufacture often arose outside the industry but provided opportunities and incentives for manufacturers to develop new types of commercial aircraft. He concluded that the stream of innovations had the hypothesized effects. The number of manufacturers decreased, with large shifts in market shares. He also found that effective entry into this industry has been achieved only through some major technical change creating substantial cost and performance advantages for carriers. Relatively low operating costs seem to have been a necessary, but not sufficient, condition for an airplane to capture a sustained large market share. The effect of technical change as a barrier to entry in the commercial aircraft industry has been offset somewhat by an apparent proclivity of once successful manufacturers to remain too long with their original success. These firms have not always chosen to continue to be scientifically progressive and thereby retain their market position.

Other industry studies have reached similar conclusions. Comanor (1964) found that R&D is a major element of interfirm rivalry in the pharmaceutical industry, with profit largely dependent on a firm's continued innovative success. Effective entry usually requires some technical advance so the cost and risk of research, as well as high selling expenditures, constitute an entry barrier in this industry. Freeman (1965) found R&D to be an entry barrier in the oligopolistic international electronic capital goods industry. Rivalry occurs mainly in technical innovation and technical customer service. Because of the products' complexity, their manufacture relies on many existing patents that are obtained through cross-licensing, know-how agreements, and patent pools. The stronger a firm's own technical position is, the more readily it can obtain such technical agreements on favorable terms. At a minimum, a firm must have a strong development and engineering capability to assimilate, imitate, use, and improve upon the inventions of others. This minimum R&D capacity to maintain a defensive market position plus requisite marketing and technical service facilities constitutes a minimum size for entry. Stonebraker (1976) found the risk to industry entrants of losses or failure is positively related to the industry R&D spending/sales as well as to industry advertising/sales.

Mueller and Tilton (1969) have embedded the notion of R&D costs as a barrier to entry within a stages-of-development of the industry hypothesis. Their review of the available evidence plus two case studies (semiconductors, photocopying) of their own indicate that neither relative nor absolute size are requisite to invention, development, or technical imitation. However, the next stage, that of "technological competition," may be one in which R&D costs form a barrier to entry. They characterize this stage as one with many firms in the industry; the basic science, well understood; and the research, relatively sophisticated and specialized. The large industrial research laboratory is favored in such circumstances. The substantial costs of building and maintaining the large R&D capability constitute an entry barrier but need not spell demise for extant small firms with both a specialty and patent protection. The final stage in their scenario is one of standardization or maturity. Basic patents have expired and production techniques are standardized. Barriers to entry are not based on R&D requirements but rather on production and marketing scale. Price competition replaces technological competition.

Pavitt and Wald (1971) reached a similar conclusion. They found opportunities for small firms tend to be greatest in the earliest stages of the product cycle, when economies of scale are relatively unimportant, market shares volatile, and rates of entry and failure high. Successful entry is largely dependent on scientific and technological capability at this stage. They agree that as technologies mature, scale and efficiency in production become more important and the opportunities for small firms become fewer.

The hypothesis of "success breeds success" also finds support in Grabowski's (1968) study of R&D in the chemical, drug, and petroleum industries. One of three major determinants of firm research intensity was found to be an index of the firm's prior research productivity, measured by the number of patents received per scientist and engineer employed. In the sample, firms with higher patented output per scientific worker in the past were, ceteris paribus, more research intensive than their rivals. If Grabowski's findings are broadly indicative, past R&D success tends to lead to greater current R&D effort, which in turn could be expected to produce further innovational output and, in general, a widening gap between technologically successful firms and their rivals.

Finally, there is evidence of a positive empirical relationship between diversification and research activity. Diversification is the extent to which firms classified in one industry produce goods classified in another. It can proceed by internal development or by acquisition. Patterns of interindustry diversification seem to be the same whichever path is taken. Gort (1962), in his study covering 1929–54, found that industries entered most often by diversifying firms and industries in which diversifying firms were most often based were characterized by high technical personnel ratios. Wood (1971) examined diversification during 1959–62 and found that industries of frequent entry or origin were characterized by high proportions of R&D expenditures to sales after controlling for growth, profitability, and other variables. Wood suggests that high research intensity tends to encourage and facilitate diversification into similar industries.

It appears undeniable, at least in a broad sense, that the state of technology is a determinant of market structure through its definition of the minimum efficient scale of production. Beyond this, the necessity to carry on research and development activities in order to remain a viable competitor in certain industries imposes a barrier to entry. The success breeds success hypothesis has some direct support from several industry studies and indirect support from the finding that R&D-intensive firms find it easier to diversify into other industries. The last finding also suggests another procompetitive effect of technical advance, namely, the breeching of traditional industry boundaries. Firms in one industry must be on guard against competition from R&D-intensive firms in other industries, as well as from rivals in their own industry. Finally, there is also some evidence that "success begets failure." Either initial success leads to complacency or the successful firm is not as hungry as the newcomer or the behavior that led to the first success is maintained until it becomes obsolete in a changing environment.

We turn now to the two major strands of the Schumpeterian hypothesis: the relationship between firm size and inventive activity and between market structure and inventive activity.

Firm size and inventive activity

The hypothesis tested is that inventive activity increases faster or more than proportionately with firm size. Regression studies often relate a measure of R&D activity X to a measure of firm size S. If the functional form is assumed to be $X = aS^b u$, the hypothesis would be supported by a finding that $b > 1$, whereas for the equation $X = a + bS + cS^2 + u$, it would be supported by the finding that $c > 0$. Alternatively, a measure of innovational activity may be deflated by a measure of firm size to obtain an index of innovational intensity (i.e., innovational effort or innovative output relative to firm size), and the result regressed against firm size. The deflator is comparable with the numerator when possible. Thus R&D spending is often deflated by sales or assets, whereas R&D employees and scientific personnel are deflated by total employees. In regressions of the form $X/S = aS^b u$ or $X/S = a + bS + u$, the hypothesis that innovational intensity increases with firm size is supported if $b > 0$.

R&D activity might increase more than proportionately with firm size, it has been conjectured, if large firms can finance a larger R&D staff, if there are economies of scale in this activity (empirical studies, as we now know, suggest none), if they are better able to exploit unforeseen innovations, and if they can profit more from cost-reducing innovations because of their inherent indivisibility.

Studies of the relationship between inventive activity and firm size fall into two groups, those that measure inventive activity by inputs and those that measure it by output. To the extent that empirical evidence indicates constant returns to scale in R&D activity, these two measures should give the same results; in fact, the two groups of studies tend to agree. We begin with a review of the studies of the relationship between inventive inputs and firm size.

Innovative inputs and firm size

Firm size is alternately measured by sales volume, assets, or number of employees. These three variables are positively but not perfectly correlated and the results depend somewhat on the choice. Scherer (1965a) discussed their features and relative merits. He prefers sales, as it is neutral regarding factor proportions and because R&D budgets may be based on projected sales. But if measures of firm size are not proportional to each other, the results may be sensitive to the choice. If S_1 and S_2 are measures of firm size related by $S_2 = aS_1{}^b$, $0 < b < 1$, and if the R&D variable X is related to S_2 by $X = cS_2{}^d$, then the relation between X and S_1 is $X = kS_1{}^{bd}$. The elasticity of R&D with respect to firm size is then either b or bd, depending on the choice of firm size measure. Smyth, Boyes, and Peseau (1975) have examined the relation between alternate measures of firm size, using both U.S. and United Kingdom data. They find the measures not proportional. In particular, the elasticity of sales with respect to total assets or employment is significantly less than one in both countries. Therefore a finding that R&D activity increases less than proportionately with firm sales would indicate that R&D activity would increase still more slowly than an alternate measure of firm size.

Correlation studies by both Horowitz (1962) and Hamberg (1966) suggested at most a weak positive association between R&D input intensity and firm size. Using data for 1947 and 1951–2, Horowitz found industry ranking by value added per establishment to be positively but weakly correlated with both the breadth of participation in research by firms and the intensity of that effort, as measured by research expenditures per sales dollar. Likewise, Hamberg's investigation of 340 of *Fortune's* 500 largest firms in 1960 divided into seventeen industries disclosed the ratio of R&D employment to total employment to be only weakly correlated with total employment and total assets. Log–linear regression revealed the elasticity of R&D effort with respect to firm size to exceed unity in only three of the industries.

Worley (1961), using 198 very large firms, found this elasticity significantly greater than unity in just two of the eight industries. Both Worley and Hamberg concluded that although the results were mixed, the hypothesis was not strongly supported. Worley noted a tendency for firms near the middle of the distribution with respect to size to hire relatively more R&D personnel than the largest and smallest firms of the sample.

Scherer (1965a) criticized the data and the form of the regression employed in these studies. At best the results reveal the relationship between research intensity and firm size for firms with sizable research programs, because those without large research efforts were generally omitted from the sample. He also noted that the log–linear form of the regression equation cannot reveal inflection points or nonmonotonicity in the relationship between input intensity and firm size. To correct these weaknesses, Scherer, with a sample of 448 firms from the 500 largest in 1955, regressed R&D employment against the first three powers of sales and then repeated the regression with sales replaced by its logarithm. The use of the cubic function involves high collinearity of the independent variables but permits detection of inflection points and nonmonotonicity in the relationship. The relationship between R&D employment and firm size was found typically to have an inflection point, with R&D employment increasing faster than firm size among the smaller firms in the sample. R&D employment intensity tended to decrease among larger firms. The absolute level of R&D employment may even fall with firm size among the very largest firms in some industries. Finally, Scherer noted that the chemical industry and the giant leaders of the automobile and steel industries may be exceptional; their R&D intensity appeared to rise with sales.

Comanor (1967) also fit a log–linear regression form, with 1955 and 1960 data for 387 firms divided into twenty-one groups. For no industry was the estimated elasticity of research employment with respect to firm size (employment) significantly greater than unity; for seven of the twenty-one industries it was significantly less than one. Comanor suggested that his coefficients being smaller than Hamberg's might be attributable to the latter's broader industry classes; apparently larger elasticities may reflect aggregation of heterogeneous industries. Comanor next addressed the weakness of the regression form. Hypothesizing that the elasticity of research effort may vary with firm size, he estimated the equation separately for industries grouped according to average firm size. The results were interpreted as indication of increasing returns to scale in research effort up to a certain firm size, with constant returns to scale prevailing for larger firms. Shrieves (1976) used a broader range of firm sizes in his sample of over four hundred firms in twenty-three industry groups. Elasticity of R&D employment with respect to sales was significantly less than unity in eighteen of the twenty-three industries, and significantly greater than one in no case.

Mansfield (1968a) estimated a log–linear relation between R&D spending over 1954–9 and firm size for a sample of ten major firms in the chemical industry, nine in petroleum, eight in drugs, seven in steel, and four in glass. The coefficient of the firm size variable did not shift systematically over time. Except for the chemical industry, the largest firms in these industries spent no more on R&D relative to sales than did somewhat smaller firms. Smith (1974) likewise found that the largest firms in the electric power generation industry did not spend proportionately more on R&D relative to their size (measured by kilowatt hours) than smaller firms did. Indeed, inter-mediate size firms appeared to be most R&D intensive.

Using sixteen chemical firms and ten drug firms from the 1960 *Fortune* 500 listing, Grabowski (1968) regressed research expendi-ture, 1959–62, against sales and its square. Among the drug firms, research intensity initially increased but then decreased over most of the relevant range of firm size. In contrast, research intensity increased steadily with firm size for the chemical industry. Further examination of the data led Grabowski to suggest that the difference in the observed relation between research intensity and firm size in the two industries was largely attributable to other factors that are significant in explaining research intensity.

Smith and Creamer (1968) analyzed National Science Founda-tion data on industrial R&D during 1957–65 for companies per-forming R&D, classified by industry and firm size (a medium size firm has 1,000 to 4,999 employees). R&D input intensity, measured by company financed R&D as a percentage of net sales, averaged 1.4, 1.5, and 2.1 percent for the small, medium, and large firms, respectively. According to this index, small-firm R&D input intensity was not less than that of medium-size firms in six of twelve industries. Small-firm intensity exceeded that of large companies in three industries (other chemicals, communication equipment and electronic components, scientific and measuring instruments). Similar conclusions were reached when R&D input intensity was measured alternatively by R&D scientists and engineers per one thousand employees.

D. C. Mueller's (1967) four-equation econometric model of the firm, fit using a sample of sixty-seven firms over 1957–60, indicated that research intensity was negatively associated with firm size measured by sales. Kelly's (1970) multiple regression of the ratio of R&D employees to all employees against the logarithm of total assets and weighted market share failed to reveal any relationship between R&D intensity and either variable in his sample of 181 firms.

Loeb and Lin (1977), in analyzing 1961–72 time-series data relating sales to R&D expenditures for six major pharmaceutical manufacturers, found that a second-degree polynomial gave the best fit. Their results indicate that R&D expenditures increase with sales up to a point and decline thereafter. Likewise, Shrieves (1978) found from a sample of 411 firms in fifty-six three-digit industries that firms with relatively small sales employed proportionately more R&D personnel than firms with large sales. Using market share as a measure of firm size, J. B. Rosenberg (1976) found for a sample of one hundred firms among the *Fortune* 500 that the percent of R&D employees declined with firm size.

In a study of 883 companies with more than one thousand employees in 1964, which accounted for 91 percent of all the R&D performed in 1963, Griliches (in press) found only a proportionate relationship between firm size, as measured by the average of value added in 1957 and 1963, and the variety of measures of R&D spending. He did find, however, that capital-intensive firms also tended to be research intensive. Griliches's investigation of the relationship between the effectiveness of R&D expenditures and firm size disclosed no evidence either that the rate of growth of productivity is higher in larger companies or that the level of productivity is proportionately higher in the largest companies.

In a study of research effort and firm size among 301 Belgian firms doing research, Phlips (1971) found that the number of research employees grew somewhat faster than total employment for all but the ten or twelve largest firms; among the largest, research employment grew slower than total employment. Regressions of research personnel upon powers of total employment yielded a cubic as the statistically best fitting equation. It indicated that the number of research workers in Belgian firms grows faster than total employment up to about seven thousand employees and at a decreasing rate for larger firms. The research intensity (research employees per one thousand total employees) peaked at about ten thousand employees. This relationship for the aggregative economy was not replicated in the individual industries, because of great diversity in the industry patterns. In most industries, however, the elasticity of research employment was less than one.

In a subsequent study of 157 Belgian firms, Biname and Jacquemin (1973) found that in a regression of R&D expenditures against sales only the coefficient of the sales term to the first power was significantly different from zero both for the entire sample and for subsamples by industry. They conclude that for small and medium-size firms there is a threshold size beyond which R&D expenditures are proportional to size. Defay (1973), using the same data, found that the elasticity of research employees to total employment was significantly less than one.

Adams (1970) compared research activity in the United States and France to test the influence of firm size. He argued that because U.S. firms are larger than French ones, if absolute firm size were conducive to R&D effort, then R&D would be more highly concentrated among the very largest firms in France than in the United States. The share of the R&D performed by the largest three hundred firms in each country attributable to the four, eight, twenty, and so on largest firms in each group was cumulated and compared. Total R&D performance (private plus government funds) was less concentrated in France than in the United States, suggesting that absolute firm size is not conducive to R&D activity. Adams also reported that regression analysis revealed that R&D intensity in France is unrelated to firm size.

More recently, Howe and McFetridge (1976) studied the determinants of R&D spending by eighty-one Canadian firms in the chemical, electrical, and machinery industries during 1967–71. They found that R&D spending increased more than proportionately than sales in the chemical and electrical industries only for intermediate-size firms. Wilder and Stansell (1974) and Delaney and Honeycutt (1976) report that R&D intensity increases with firm size in the electric utility industry, but Link (1978) found that size is not especially conducive to R&D in that industry beyond some modest level.

Thus it seems that with the possible exception of the chemical industry, there is little support for the hypothesis that the intensity of innovational effort increases more than proportionately with firm size. In an early review of the literature Markham (1965) concluded that innovational effort tends to increase more than proportionately with firm size up to some point that varies from industry to industry. For still larger firms, innovational intensity appears to be constant or decreasing with size. Subsequent investigations are consistent with and tend to reinforce that generalization.

Three related caveats are worth noting. First, there are interindustry differences in the relation between firm size and innovational effort. Second, much of the evidence on the effect of firm size has not controlled for other factors that may be helpful in explaining innovational effort. Size may prove to be either more or less important as an explanatory variable once these other factors are discovered and taken into account. Third, the evidence on innovational intensity relates to firms that do have a sustained R&D effort and does not reflect research participation rates. The vast majority of large firms have, and the vast majority of small firms do not have, sustained R&D programs.

Innovative output and firm size

We turn now to studies of the relationship between innovative output and firm size. Mansfield (1968a) asked trade personnel to list and rank by importance the major innovations during 1919–38 and 1939–50 in each of three industries. The largest four firms in the coal and petroleum industries were found to be responsible for a larger share of their respective industry's innovations than of its productive capacity, but the four largest steel producers were responsible for fewer. In a later study (Mansfield, 1971), he found the market share of the four largest pharmaceutical firms exceeded their share of the industry's innovations. In this industry the large firms' performance was slightly better in terms of weighted than unweighted innovations, where medical weights were based on judgments of physicians and pharmacologists and economic weights were based on sales during the first five years following introduction.

Mansfield used these data to estimate the firm size at which innovational intensity is greatest. Noting the regressions fit the data only moderately well, he found maximum innovational output intensity occurred at about the size of the sixth largest firm in the petroleum and coal industries. In the steel industry, however, the maximum intensity obtained at the size of very small firms. For pharmaceutical advances over 1935–49 the maximum intensity appeared at the size of the tenth largest firm. The peak intensity of weighted pharmaceutical innovations over 1950–62 was found at about the size of the twelfth largest firm in that time period; for unweighted innovations, it occurred at the size of very small firms in the industry.

Scherer (1965b) used the number of patents issued a firm in 1959 as proxy for average inventive output four years earlier. A sample of 352 firms from the 1955 *Fortune* 500 disclosed sales volume to be consistently more concentrated among the largest firms than R&D employment, which in turn tended to be slightly more concentrated than patents. Smaller firms in the sample were responsible for a higher relative share of inventive activity than sales. A regression of patents on the first three powers of sales, fit for 448 firms, revealed a relationship increasing at a decreasing rate up to a point of inflection of $5.5 billion sales. Only three firms in the sample were larger than this. Thus patent output generally increased less than proportionately with sales among large corporations. The regression was repeated for fourteen industries and also for four consolidated industry groups. The essential findings were unchanged; the coefficients of the first and third powers of sales were positive, whereas the square term had a negative coefficient.

A similar study was conducted by Smyth, Samuels, and Tzoannos (1972) for eighty-six United Kingdom firms in chemicals, electrical engineering and electronics, and machine tools. Large firms were found more likely than small ones to participate in patenting. Patents granted during 1963–6 were regressed on the first two powers of firm size (1963 net assets), profits and cash flow. The number of patents awarded increased more than proportionately within the chemical industry and, for all but the largest firms, within the electrical engineering and electronics industry. In contrast, patenting decreased with firm size in the machine tool industry.

Freeman (1971) reported on a study of some twelve hundred post-1945 innovations in Britain. Small firms (under two hundred employees) accounted for about 10 percent of industrial innovations since 1945, compared with about 25 percent of employment and 21 percent of net output. The rank ordering of industries by the share of small firms in industry innovations corresponded fairly well with the ordering by their share in net output. Small firms contributed more than a proportionate share of innovations in scientific instruments, some types of machinery, electronics, and paper and board. These industries were characterized by low entry costs and low capital intensity and development costs for many products. Small firms contributed little, either absolutely or relatively, to innovations in industries of high capital intensity.

Johannisson and Lindstrom (1971) studied 181 Swedish firms with over five hundred employees, divided into twelve industrial sectors. Firm size and inventive output were measured by the number of employees in 1966 and the number of patent applications 1965–6, respectively. Excepting the four largest firms, large firms' share of total patent applications was consistently less than their share of employees. Patent applications increased faster than firm size in the chemical industry but less than proportionately in engineering and metal manufacturers.

Contrary findings are reported by Schwartzman (1976) for the drug industry. He claims that regardless of whether innovative activity is measured by the magnitude of inputs into the process or outputs, it increases more than proportionately with firm size, where size is measured by sales. Moreover, he claims that large firms enjoy substantial economies of scale in R&D.

Thus the conclusion about the effect of size on innovational effort tends to be supported and reflected in the evidence on size and innovational output. Beyond some magnitude, size does not appear especially conducive to either innovational effort or output in either this country or European countries. However, the patterns differ by industry. It seems noteworthy that the chemical industry is cited as an exception for both the United States and abroad. The reason for this exception appears to be in the technology of chemical process plants; Freeman (1968) found that the size of new plants increased by some four to five times over 1950–70. In case histories of thirty-one process innovations in the industry he discovered that two-thirds cost over a million dollars, whereas many cost over $5 million.

Market structure and innovation

Now we discuss what may be regarded as the heart of the Schumpeterian theory – namely, monopoly power is conducive to technical advance. The alleged reason is that innovation is both a means for realizing monopoly profits and a method of maintaining them afterward. Monopoly profits, however, can only be realized through innovation if imitation by rivals can be limited or prevented altogether. The power to exclude rivals is the key to the achievement and retention of monopoly profits. Thus firms possessing monopoly power should be more inclined to innovate, because they are better able to realize the rewards from innovation than firms that do not. Moreover, firms realizing monopoly profits should be better able to finance innovative activity. By investing a substantial amount of their own resources in a project, they can more easily attract outside investors. They are also more capable of financing the project entirely from internal resources. The last feature is especially important, for a failed R&D project leaves little in the way of tangible collateral that outside lenders can recoup. In addition, disclosure of the nature of the project in order to secure outside funding may undermine the competitive advantage the firm seeks. The other side of the picture, however, is that the firm already in possession of monopoly power feels less threatened by rivals and therefore less compelled to innovate. The tests of the Schumpeterian hypothesis to be reported in this section seek essentially to determine the relative strengths of these two offsetting forces.

Three types of studies will be reviewed in this section. The first group deals with the relationship between market structure and innovation. Market structure is measured in terms of the four-firm or eight-firm concentration ratio, that is, the share of the industry attributable to the largest four or eight firms. The implicit assumption is that firms in a more highly concentrated industry possess more monopoly power than ones in a less concentrated industry. This assumption, of course, is questionable on the grounds that the concentration ratio may reflect the underlying production technology in the industry rather than monopoly power. In addition, as already indicated, innovations in one area sometimes come from firms outside the traditionally defined industry boundaries. Despite these shortcomings, the concentration ratio is employed – largely because it is easy to compute. As in the studies of the relationship between firm size and inventive activity, both levels of input and levels of output are regressed against the concentration ratio. In terms of a regression equation of the form $X = a + bC + u$ or $X = aC^{b}u,$ where X is a measure of inventive activity and C is a measure of monopoly power, the null hypothesis is that $b = 0$. The hypothesis in this form is that inventive activity increases directly with monopoly power. Sometimes the second or third power of the measure of monopoly power is added to test for the existence of an "optimal" degree of monopoly for innovative activity or for an inflection point in the relationship, that is, a point at which inventive activity begins to increase at a decreasing rate with respect to monopoly power.

The second group of studies deals with the importance of the ability to self-finance for inventive activity. Some measure of inventive activity is regressed against profits or cash flow. The great difficulty in gauging this relationship arises from differences in accounting practices among firms. The third group of studies deals with whether firms with monopoly power attract the most talented innovators.

Maclaurin (1954) conducted an early study of the effect of market structure on innovation that does not fall directly into any of these groups. He compared a ranking of thirteen U.S. industries by their introduction of important innovations during 1925–50 with their ranking by the extent of monopolization in 1950. Each ranking was judgmental, corroborated in the first instance by the number of patents issued, the number of scientists with doctorates, and the presence or absence of a research department with responsibility for developing new products and processes. The ranking by monopolization considered the size of the price leaders in the industry and the ease of entry. The two rankings of industries were found not to coincide. He concluded that although some degree of monopoly power is necessary for technological progress, it is not sufficient. Ease of entry, entrepreneurial leadership, and a "competitive spirit" were considered essential. He also emphasized the role of the underlying engineering art or scientific base. Maclaurin's early conclusions have stood the test of time and subsequent investigation rather well. Some of the factors he emphasized have been quantified and their roles subjected to statistical analyses.

Concentration and research effort

The hypothesis that research input intensity is positively associated with concentration of industry sales was tested by Horowitz (1962). He found the four-firm concentration to be positively but weakly associated with research expenditure per industry sales dollar and negatively correlated with the percent of industry research laboratories in the largest 20 percent of the firms. Hamberg (1966) also found a weak positive correlation between company-financed R&D per sales dollar and industrial concentration. These findings weakly suggest that more highly concentrated industries tend to put forth a greater research effort. Further, participation in research seems to be more widespread in more concentrated industries, so the greater research intensity is not merely the reflection of the largest firms' efforts.

In Scherer's (1967a) reexamination of the hypothesis, research effort, the dependent variable, was measured by various indices of technical employment. Independent variables included a concentration index, 1960 industry employment, and such qualitative factors as the technological opportunity class and the type of good (producer or consumer, durable or nondurable). His first test involved logarithmic regressions. The coefficients of the concentration variable were positive and highly significant when qualitative factors were omitted. When these factors were introduced through dummy variables, the coefficients of the concentration index remained positive and significant but the incremental explanatory power of "concentration" was far smaller.

In the second test, research effort intensity, measured by technical employment as a fraction of total employment, was regressed on the concentration index and qualitative dummy variables. The concentration coefficient was barely significant at the 10 percent level for two of the measures of technical employment and not significantly different from zero in the third case. In a third test, with regressions of technical employment intensity against concentration for the two technology classes with the most observations, the concentration coefficients were positive and significant at 10 percent or better. Scherer (1967a) concluded that the hypothesis of positive association between concentration and the intensity of research effort was supported. The fact that the incremental explanatory power of concentration fell sharply on introduction of dummy variables was attributed to the positive correlation between concentration and technology class. Scherer suggested this last correlation might support Phillips's hypothesis that technological innovation arising from opportunity has led to increased concentration.

Scherer (1967a) also tested the hypothesis that increases in concentration are conducive to technical vigor only in relatively atomistic industries, becoming unimportant once a certain threshold is crossed. The square of the concentration index was added in the third set of regressions previously indicated. The relation between technical employment intensity and seller concentration was found to be concave, but the coefficient of the squared term was significant at the 5 percent level in only one case. In all four cases technological employment per one thousand employees reached a predicted maximum at concentration levels between 50 and 55 percent. The threshold level appeared to be above 10 to 14 percent.

In Comanor's (1967) study estimated elasticities of research effort were regressed against average firm size and an eight-firm concentration ratio. The coefficient of average firm size was reported positive and significant, but no effect of concentration was apparent. Comanor conjectured that because product differentiability may be an important component of the research decision, the effect of concentration upon research might depend on whether differentiability is high. To test this, he grouped industries by whether the eight-firm concentration ratio exceeded 70 percent. Research levels adjusted for firm size, as described earlier, were grouped by both concentration and differentiability classes. Comanor concluded that high concentration tended to be associated with high research in cases where it is not a major element of market behavior, that is, where prospects for product differentiation are relatively weak.

Kelly's (1970) study of 181 multiproduct firms disclosed that maximum research intensity appears to occur at a 50 to 60 percent concentration ratio, in close agreement with Scherer's results. Also, the four-firm concentration ratio and its square have significant coefficients at the 10 percent level when dummy variables reflecting technological opportunity are omitted but are not significant otherwise.

Adams (1970) tested the hypothesis of positive association between seller concentration and research activity by comparing the R&D-spending intensity and the four-firm concentration index by industry in France and the United States. He found that for each of the high technology industries except instruments, the country with the larger concentration index had the smaller R&D-spending intensity. Among the lower technology industries, the results of the comparison were mixed. The hypothesis was rejected. Applying regression analysis to the French data, he also concluded that differences in research intensity among French firms were unrelated to differences in seller concentration.

Phlips (1971) tested the hypothesis by using Belgian data. The number of research personnel was regressed against total personnel and the concentration index. Provision was made for each technological opportunity group to have its own coefficient for the concentration variable. The slope coefficients were positive for both the chemical and electrical equipment industries but not significantly different from zero for the moderate and nonprogressive groups. As a corroborating test, Phlips regressed research intensity (research personnel as a fraction of total employees) of the four largest firms on the concentration ratio, permitting each technological group to have its own slope coefficient. Concentration had a significant influence only in the chemical and possibly in the electrical equipment industries. Phlips concluded that for Belgian industry, concentration and research effort tend to be positively associated in those industries with greatest technological opportunity, that is, in those industries where research is most intensive.

Even this modest support for a positive relationship between innovative activity and concentration is challenged by Finet (1975). In a study of 301 Belgian firms grouped into a chemical sector, an electronics sector, a moderately progressive sector, and the rest, he found that the ratio of research personnel to a firm's total employment is only very weakly related to the four-firm concentration ratio. He attributed the difference between his findings and Phlip's to the latter not allowing the regression for each industry group to have its own intercept.

Globerman (1973) tested the roles of concentration and technological opportunity in research effort in Canadian manufacturing industries during 1965-9. The fifteen industries were divided into nine with greater and six with lesser technological opportunity, based largely on Scherer's classification. R&D personnel per one thousand employees, among firms engaged in R&D, was regressed against a four-firm concentration index, the fraction of industry assets held by non-Canadian corporations and a measure of governmental subsidy. Globerman found that for industries with greater technological opportunity, research intensity varied inversely with concentration (and directly with both foreign ownership and government financing). All coefficients were highly significant. In contrast, for industries with lesser technological opportunity, all signs were reversed but no significant relationship was present.

J. B. Rosenberg (1976) found that the percent of R&D employees in a firm increased with industry concentration. However, his study also indicated that concentrated industries with firms of equal size (market share) would be most R&D intensive. Further, he found that entry barriers, as measured by capital requirements, necessary advertising levels, and economies of scale, tended to have a positive effect on R&D intensity. The presence of entry barriers, however, appears to reduce the importance of technological opportunity.

Somewhat similar results are reported by Shrieves (1978). He also finds that firms in concentrated industries tend to be more R&D intensive, as measured by R&D associated personnel, than firms in less concentrated ones. Within concentrated industries, however, he found that the largest firms do proportionately less R&D than smaller firms. Shrieves points out that the relationship between concentration and R&D intensity depends on the type of industry product and market served. In industries where product imitation is relatively easy and the short-run cross-elasticity of demand is relatively high, such as in consumer nondurables, concentration tends to be conducive to innovative activity. On the other hand, for products difficult to imitate and with relatively low short-run cross-elasticity of demand, such as consumer durables, the first firm to introduce a new product may gain a significant advantage over rivals and industry concentration does not appear to have a positive influence on innovative activity. In the durable goods industries, demand after the initial purchase is largely for replacement. In order to accelerate this replacement demand a newcomer must introduce a product with a very significant advantage over the existing one. This provides existing suppliers a certain degree of security and a possible dampening of their incentive to innovate.

In reviewing the diverse findings on research efforts and concentration, we find little concensus. In most instances it has been difficult to discern a statistical relationship among these variables. There is agreement that the relation may vary with the "technological opportunity class" of the industry.

Concentration and innovation output

Studies relating concentration to productivity increases have found high concentration alternatively harmful, neutral, and helpful. Stigler (1956) compared the rate of technical progress, measured by the decline in unit labor requirement, 1899–1937, in fourteen industries of high concentration with that in seven industries with declining concentration and in eight in which it was low. The largest reduction in labor requirements occurred in industries with rapidly declining concentration during the period and the smallest, in industries of continued high concentration. These statistical results were interpreted by Stigler to suggest that competition of new rivals in an industry spurs rapid technical advance. Allen (1969), updating Stigler's study using data for nineteen industries over various periods during 1939–64, found no significant differences in productivity growth rates by industry concentration class.

Using changes in productivity of labor and horsepower per employee as indices of technical change, Phillips (1956) found that in twenty-eight U.S. industries between 1899–1939, those with high concentration or large factories showed greater technical change. Carter and Williams (1957) followed the pattern of Phillips's study for twelve United Kingdom industries for 1907–48; there was some positive correlation between the degree of concentration and the increase of output per employee hour. Weiss (1963) found productivity growth in the United States positively related to output growth in both 1937–48 and 1948–53, but no significant association was found between the average four-firm concentration ratio and productivity increase in either period. Bock and Farkas (1969) did find a positive association between productivity and concentration in the United States for 1963.

Scherer (1965b) tested the hypothesis that technological output tends to increase with industrial concentration. The number of industry-related patents issued in 1954 to the leading four firms in the industry was regressed against their sales and the four-firm concentration ratio as well as dummy variables for technological class. No support for the hypothesis was found.

Mansfield's (1968a) study of important innovations indicated that although the largest four bituminous coal and petroleum refining firms carried out a larger share of innovations than their share of the market, the largest four steel producers carried out fewer. To explain these findings, Mansfield developed a model that predicts the largest four firms in an industry tend to account for a relatively large share of the innovating when (1) the investment required to innovate is large relative to the size of the potential users, (2) the minimum firm size to use the innovation profitably is relatively large, and (3) the average size of the largest four firms is much greater than the average size of all potential users of the innovations. This model could explain Mansfield's data in the three industries mentioned and in the railroad industry as well.

Williamson (1965) employed the data developed by Mansfield for the three basic industries for the periods 1919–38 and 1939–58 to see if a simple hypothesis was also consistent with them. He regressed the largest four firms' share of innovations, relative to their market share, against the concentration index. Both linear and log–linear forms of the equation were estimated. The influence of concentration on the relative innovational performance of the largest four firms was found to be negative. That is, the relative share of innovations contributed by the largest firms appeared to be decreasing with their monopoly power. For a concentration ratio above 30 to 50 percent the largest firms supply less than their proportionate share of innovations.

The inconclusiveness of studies on concentration and innovational effort is reinforced by the studies discussed in this section. Mansfield's work suggests that even "technological opportunity class" may not be enough to sort out the underlying relationship sought; a deeper study of components of industrial structure may be required.

Other elements of market structure

The ease of entry into an industry is an element of market structure that might influence research intensity. Comanor (1967) has argued that a principal goal of research activity is creation of entry barriers through product differentiation. Therefore he thought research outlays would tend to be low where there are high entry barriers of other forms. To test this hypothesis, Comanor ran a regression of average research personnel, adjusted for firm size, against dummy explanatory variables, reflecting classification of an industry by its concentration, by its opportunities for product differentiation, and as having a high, moderate, or low technical entry barrier due to scale economy. To construct the last classification, he took average plant size among plants accounting for the top 50 percent of industry output to be the minimum efficient plant scale. The entry barrier created by scale economies was defined to be the ratio of this minimum scale to industry shipments.

Comanor found the effect of high entry barrier and of low entry barrier not significantly different from zero. However, the impact of moderate technical entry barriers appeared positive and significant, after other factors were taken into account. Comanor rejected his original hypothesis and revised his views. He concluded that when technical entry barriers are either quite low or very high, the incentive for research appears to be substantially less than that existing at some intermediate level. Thus industrial research effort is strongest in industries with some technical entry barrier, so rapid imitation is impeded, but also where entry has not been effectively foreclosed.

Stekler (1967) assessed technical progressiveness in the U.S. aerospace industry in the postwar period. He found evidence that the industry became increasingly technologically progressive as the federal government, its major customer, became less protective of the industry members. Johannisson and Lindstrom (1971) found for Swedish industry no effect of firm's market share on its patent applications, when firm size is taken into account. In Freeman's (1973) paired comparison study of success and failure in industrial innovation, the "competitive environment" of the would-be innovator did not seem to influence whether the attempt to innovate would be successful. Freeman emphasized that the presence of competitive pressures may nevertheless be important in stimulating attempts to innovate.

The stimulating effect of rivalry on R&D activity was investigated by Grabowski and Baxter (1973). Using a sample of eight chemical firms during 1947–66, they tested the hypothesis that firm R&D expenditures respond positively to a rival's R&D outlays. A multiple regression was estimated of the current change in the firm's R&D expenditure on lagged changes in its own and a rival's R&D outlays, changes in the firm's cash flow and its market value, and a dummy variable to reflect sales or earnings decline. The relevant rival was selected by best statistical fit as either the firm with the largest R&D outlay or the immediate successor in magnitude of R&D budget. Cash flow appeared to be the single most important explanatory variable. Change in rival's expenditure on R&D was significant in four cases and the firm's own lagged spending change in three. Neither firm valuation nor the dummy variable offered considerable explanatory power. Thus this phase of the study provided some evidence of responsiveness among firms to each others' inventive activity, especially between the two leading firms. Grabowski and Baxter (1973), seeking further confirmation, then tested the hypothesis that rivalry in R&D will be stronger, the more oligopolistic the industry is. They argued that as the concentration ratio increases, the firms' R&D intensities will become more similar, leading to a decreasing coefficient of variation in firm research intensity. Using a sample of twenty-nine three-digit industries and an eight-firm concentration ratio, they found a significant negative relationship in the rank correlation between concentration and the coefficient of variation of research intensity. Thus concentration does appear to induce conformity in R&D expenditure among firms. It should be noted, however, that this does not imply that high concentration leads to high levels of research activity.

More recently, Grabowski and Mueller (1978) did a cross section study of eighty-six firms in nine industry groups, ranging from technologically progressive to nonprogressive. Although their main objective was to determine how much of the variance in unadjusted profit rates was due to counting advertising and R&D spending as current expenses rather than to capitalizing them as investments in intangible capital stocks, they also looked into the relationship between concentration and R&D rivalry. Using R&D spending during 1951 to 1966 as a measure of the intensity of this activity, they found that higher market concentration in research-intensive industries increases intraindustry rivalry in R&D.

Our review of the impact of market structure on innovation has netted little more than reaffirmation of the early observation that both competitive pressures and market opportunities are important. Further work is required. There are two suggestions in the literature. First, evidence on both size and the market structure elements indicates the sought after relationships are quite likely to be nonlinear. Intermediate values of the market structure elements may be most conducive to research effort and its success, with extreme values providing less incentive for such efforts. Second, "technological opportunity," broadly interpreted, seems to condition the relationship. It is not clear whether the influence is through relative scale, as Mansfield's work hints, or through the effects of research's role in interfirm rivalry.

Liquidity and profitability

It has been argued that because R&D is largely internally financed, only firms generating a substantial cash flow can support a sizable R&D effort. The firms with high liquidity are generally large, monopolistic firms. A closely related hypothesis suggests that high current profits are necessary for a sizable R&D effort because they are a source of liquidity. Alternatively, current profits may be viewed as an indicator of future profits; a firm enjoying past success may be more inclined to take the risks of R&D in expectation of future success. Both aspects support the notion that large monopolistic firms are the most likely source of technical advance because they are in the best position to reap sizable profits. It has also been suggested that profits may tend to influence the development effort inversely. A firm experiencing declining profits may feel under more pressure to innovate. To test these theoretical arguments, several investigators have included measures of liquidity and/or profits in their regression analyses.

For a sample of 405 firms in twenty-one U.S. industries for 1960 Hamberg (1966) regressed the ratio of R&D personnel to total employees against profits and depreciation (a source of liquidity), along with sales, federal R&D contracts, gross investment, and the past scale of R&D – all deflated by gross fixed assets. The fit was rather poor. The direction of effect of profits (as well as of sales and gross investment) varied among industries. The liquidity variable, depreciation, had little apparent influence on R&D intensity. The clearest conclusion was that the past scale of R&D positively influences current R&D.

Grabowski's (1968) study of selected firms in the chemical, drug, and petroleum industries included internally generated funds as an important determinant of R&D expenditure intensity. Internal funds were measured by the sum of after-tax profits, depreciation and depletion in the previous period – all deflated by sales. This variable was included along with a measure of diversification and an index of prior research productivity as explanatory variables in a regression with R&D expenditures per sales dollar as dependent variable. The regression coefficient of the "internal funds" variable was positive and significant at the 1 percent level for each of the industries. All the regression coefficients and the correlation increased with the research orientation of the industry involved, being lowest in the petroleum industry and highest for the drug industry in each case. Grabowski inferred that the more important research is as a competitive strategy in the industry, the greater is the effect of the independent variables, including internally generated funds, on research intensity. Further support for this contention is provided in the Grabowski and Baxter (1973) study previously described.

Mueller (1967) constructed and estimated, using observations of sixty-seven firms over 1957–60, a four-equation econometric model of the firm to explain R&D, capital investment, advertising, and dividend payment. In the fitted equation for R&D intensity the coefficient of depreciation was positive for all years, but significant only for 1958. Its greater impact on R&D in the recession year, coupled with its low coefficient for that year in the investment equation, indicated a shift of resources from capital investment to R&D when returns to the former may be low. The industry R&D intensity best explained firm R&D intensity.

Elliott (1971) investigated the determinants of R&D spending for fifty-three firms in sixteen industries over 1953–66. He was especially interested in whether profits' role in research-spending decisions is primarily "expectational," as indicative of future profitability, or is as a source of liquidity or funds. For each year 1957 through 1966 he regressed R&D spending per sales dollar against current and lagged R&D-spending intensity, industry growth rates, firm share of market and of R&D expenditure, and relative firm size and growth. By including or excluding each variable in the regression for each year of the study on the basis of its statistical performance, Elliott accounted for most of the variation in R&D-spending intensity. Lagged R&D was the only explanatory variable to appear consistently in the equations: Both the sign and magnitude of its coefficients fluctuated from year to year. However, the sum of coefficients of R&D lagged one through four years was reasonably stable over the ten-year period.

Next, Elliott introduced three measures of profits (gross profits, profits after taxes and dividends, sales margin over cost of goods sold) and two measures of liquidity (cash flow, discretionary income). Each was tentatively added to the regression already fit and was retained in the equation if its inclusion lowered the residual variation. The best lag specification was also selected statistically. He concluded that effects of internal profit expectations proxies tended to be more significant in general than effects of internal funds-flow variables, given the best fitting specification of other (external) variables. "Gross profits" was deemed the most significant internal variable. Finally, the funds-flow variables were judged to have a greater influence on R&D intensity when GNP was growing slowly than when GNP grew more rapidly.

Scherer (1965b) was unable to find any significant relationship between either 1955–60 profits or 1955 liquid assets, on the one hand, and 1959 patenting or 1955 R&D effort, on the other. The Smyth, Samuels, and Tzoannos (1972) study of determinants of patented output in three United Kingdom industries found firm profitability, measured by average profits net of tax and interest payments for 1948–63, deflated by net assets, to have no significant effect in any industry. Cash flow, measured by average undistributed profits plus depreciation, had a positive coefficient in each case, but it was significant for only the chemical and machine tools industries. The Johannisson–Lindstrom (1971) study of patent applications in Swedish industry found neither liquid assets (current assets less short-term liabilities) nor cash flow (net profits prior to depreciation, taxes and allocations to financial funds) especially conducive to inventive output. They acknowledge possible statistical difficulties due to the very high correlation between these financial variables and firm size.

In sum, the empirical evidence that either liquidity or profitability are conducive to innovative effort or output appears slim. Grabowski has made perhaps the strongest empirical case. Yet the failure to support the hypothesis may not indicate the lack of importance of this variable. Liquidity or profitability may be "threshold factors," necessary in some degree for R&D activity, but with no direct functional (linear) relation with innovative activity. No direct test of this "threshold" version of the role of these financial variables appears to have been conducted.

Diversification and entrepreneurial talent

Another argument supporting the role of the large monopolistic firm in innovation rests on its supposed diversification into many product areas. Diversification is logically distinct from both size and market power but may be a frequent accompaniment. A firm's degree of diversification will positively influence its expected profit from R&D effort, it is argued, because a more variegated firm will be better able to utilize its research outputs. The output of R&D may be difficult to predict. Search for a product with certain properties may yield what is sought, or it may reveal something else of potential value. A firm doing business in a narrowly prescribed area may be unable or unwilling to produce and market a new product provided by the R&D laboratory but unrelated to the firm's main business. On the other hand, a widely diversified firm might utilize profitably serendipitous findings. Because the expected profit of R&D effort increases with the firm's diversification, it is argued, R&D intensity may increase as well.

To test the hypothesis just outlined, Grabowski (1968) included an index of diversification in his regressions to explain R&D-spending intensity. That index was the number of separate five-digit SIC product classifications in which the firm produces. The regression coefficient was positive in all three industries but significant only in the chemical and drug industries.

Comanor's (1965) study of R&D output, the proportion of sales attributed to new products, in the pharmaceutical industry included an index of diversification reflecting the firm's participation in forty therapeutic markets defined on the basis of apparent medical usage. The regression included other dependent variables reflecting the R&D input intensity and firm size. Comanor found that the diversification index was negatively associated with his index of R&D output, suggesting R&D effort may be more productive if it is concentrated toward a few product areas. Vernon and Gusen, in their sequel to Comanor, found their diversification index to be insignificant.

Scherer's (1965b) investigation of patents introduced a diversification index, the number of consolidated industries in which the company operated, into regressions of patents on sales for the aggregate sample and each of the fourteen industry groups and into a regression of R&D employment on sales. The findings were mixed. The index seemed to capture the effect on companies based in industries with relatively low rates of patenting of also operating in high patenting industries. Scherer concluded that diversification as such does not appear necessarily favorable to patented invention.

Johannisson and Lindstrom (1971), employing a diversification measure in their regression to explain patent application in Sweden, reported findings very similar to those of Scherer; diversification did not seem helpful in explaining variations in inventive output, except as it reflected diversification from a low patenting industry into an industry that is more technically progressive.

Kelly (1970) employed the percent of shipments outside the firm's primary three-digit SIC category in his sample of 181 multiproduct firms as a measure of diversification. He found "diversified firms more likely to invest in a higher proportion of research but the advantages of diversification for research occur for technically related products in the same two-digit SIC industry group."

Another supposed advantage of the large firm in innovation is that it attracts and retains the best entrepreneurial talents by offering the greatest challenges and opportunities. Because the best entrepreneurs are the most progressive, it is argued, the larger firms will tend to be the technological leaders. To test this hypothesis, Adams (1970) reasoned as follows: Americans, as a group, are widely acknowledged to be better entrepreneurs than Frenchmen. Therefore the hypothesis suggests that even moderate size firms in the United States would tend to be reasonably progressive, whereas the limited entrepreneurial talent of France would tend to be concentrated among the very largest firms. Hence the hypothesis that "entrepreneurship" and R&D intensity are positively related implies a greater concentration of R&D effort among the larger firms in France than in the United States. Adams tested the hypothesis by checking this implication. He found that U.S. R&D spending tends to be more concentrated in large firms than is production; in France, on the other hand, large firms' share of R&D is less than their share of industry output. In sum, contrary to the prediction, small firms' role in R&D appears greater in France than in the United States.

Market structure and diffusion of innovations

The rate of imitation of an innovation is a determinant of its profitability to the innovator. If it can be easily and quickly imitated, then it will yield a smaller profit to its developer than an innovation with the opposite properties. Thus resources for innovative activity tend to be directed toward those innovations that are the most difficult to imitate and are therefore most profitable, ceteris paribus. The empirical studies of Comanor (1967) and Shrieves (1978) reviewed earlier tend to support this expected bias. They found, for example, that innovative input intensity is higher, ceteris paribus, in industries producing goods that are difficult to imitate, such as consumer durables, than in those producing easily imitated goods, such as consumer nondurables. The ease of imitation of a good may also be affected by the existing monopoly power of its developer. An established firm with some monopoly power may be able to retard imitation of a new product by imposing entry barriers (say, through advertising) on a potential imitator. The Comanor and Shrieves studies do indicate that market concentration, a proxy for monopoly power, is more important in explaining the intensity of innovative activity in those industries producing an easily imitated product than in those producing one difficult to imitate.

Another view of the rate of imitation is the rate of diffusion. The more rapidly an innovation is imitated, the sooner it comes into widespread use. The most widely tested theory of the diffusion of industrial innovations was advanced by Mansfield (1968a). The gist of his theory is that the diffusion of an innovation throughout an industry follows a logistic or learning curve. Further diffusion is more rapid when the innovation is more profitable and less costly relative to the firms' assets. The rationale for the S-shaped diffusion pattern through time is that adoption of an innovation accelerates initially as it becomes more widely known and competitive pressure compels its adoption. Eventually, the pace of adoption slows as the number of firms not employing the innovation declines. The prospect of high profits from adoption of an innovation tends to offset the risks associated with the use of a new process or manufacture of a new product and thus hastens its diffusion. Likewise, low cost of adoption relative to firm resources speeds it up.

Mansfield tested his model on a sample of twelve process innovations in four industries – bituminous coal, iron and steel, brewing, and railroads. He found that his model explained the actual diffusion patterns very well, as measured by the usual standards of statistical hypothesis testing. He then explored interindustry differences in the rate of diffusion and found some support for the contention that the rate of diffusion is more rapid in more competitive industries. In a subsequent study of diffusion of numerical control of machines in the tool-and-die industry during 1960-8 Mansfield et al. (1971) also found that concentration had an adverse effect on the rate of adoption. Finally, Romeo (1977) studied the diffusion of numerical control of machines among 152 firms in ten industries over different periods of time – aircraft engines (1950-7), airframes (1950-69), printing presses (1954-69), coal mining machinery (1956-69), digital computers (1956-69), large steam turbines (1956-8), machine tools (1956-65), farm machinery (1957-68), tool-and-die (1961-9), and industrial instruments (1964-9). He found that diffusion of this process innovation followed an S-shaped pattern in all the industries, consistent with Mansfield's model. There were, however, interindustry differences in the rate of diffusion. Romeo sought to explain these differences by a number of factors, including the number of firms in the industry and the variance in their size. His findings, using regression analysis, indicate that diffusion was more rapid in industries with many firms of equal size (employees) than in industries with few firms of unequal size.

There are few studies of the relationship between market structure and rate of diffusion of innovations, as this survey indicates; however, they all appear to indicate that the rate of process innovation diffusion is positively related to the competitiveness of the industry into which it is introduced.

Summary

Studies of the economics of technical advance suffer the shortcomings common to many empirical investigations – the choice of measures of inputs and outputs of innovation is guided largely by data availability rather than by a conceptual framework. However, ingenuity is often displayed in wringing out interesting observations from a meager data base. No serious attempt to cope with simultaneity elements, through modern econometric techniques, appears to have been made. This would seem to be a high payoff direction for further empirical work.

A picture of the relationship between resource allocation and technical advance, though fuzzy, does emerge from these studies. The quest for profit and the devotion of resources do influence the rate and direction of inventive activity despite the large role of serendipity and other goals motivating discovery. Moreover, the relationship appears to be bidirectional, with the state of knowledge shaping and being shaped by profit opportunities and availability of resources. Examination of the nature of the innovative process seems to reveal an almost neoclassical production structure with increasing returns up to a threshold level of resource commitment and nonincreasing returns beyond. The threshold for efficient operation does appear to constitute an entry barrier in certain industries although perhaps not always a formidable one.

Availability of data has allowed more extensive investigation of the relationship between firm size and inventive activity than between market structure and inventive activity. A commonly tested hypothesis is that R&D activity increases more than proportionately with firm size. Measures of firm size employed include total assets, total employment, and total sales. R&D activity is measured either by input intensity variables such as the ratio of technical and scientific personnel to all employees or fraction of annual budget devoted or by output intensity measures based on patents or innovations. Use of either R&D input or R&D output measures would give similar results if there were a linear relationship between the two; there is some evidence of this, subject to eventual decreasing returns. The bulk of the empirical findings indicate that inventive activity does not typically increase faster than firm size, except in the chemical industry. R&D activity, measured by either input or output intensity, appears to increase with firm size up to a point and then level off or decline, as is consistent with the evidence on the nature of the R&D process.

Studies of market structure and R&D activity commonly employ a concentration ratio as a measure of monopoly power. Evidence suggests that rivalry in R&D may be related to the industry concentration ratio. The standard hypothesis tested is that the R&D activity increases with monopoly power. Little support for this hypothesis has been found. Instead, a new hypothesis has emerged that a market structure intermediate between monopoly and perfect competition would promote the highest rate of inventive activity. Some theoretical support for the hypothesis has been advanced. A defect of the empirical investigations of the relationship between either monopoly power or firm size and R&D activity is the failure to deal with the inherent simultaneities.

The hypothesized positive association between diversification and R&D activity has been weakly supported in some studies. The direction of causality is unclear. Investigation of the supposition that large firms have the best innovative talent have disclosed almost the exact opposite. The largest firms appear to be far less efficient innovators than smaller rivals.

4

Modern theories of market structure and innovation: the decision theoretic approach

The economics of technical advance appears to have followed a traditional pattern: from hypothesis formulation to explain casual observation to more rigorous testing of these hypotheses and then to the synthesis of new more general hypotheses. The hypotheses proposed by Taussig, Schumpeter, and Galbraith were based on casual observation. Others conducted empirical tests with results as surveyed in Chapter 3. These empirical studies have inspired new theories. Also, other events, such as the recent energy crisis, have increased interest in the relationship between market structure and innovation. For example, when the prospect of exhausting the earth's fossil fuels began to be seriously contemplated, attention turned to technical advance as a panacea.

In the modern theories of market structure and innovation competition among potential innovators is thought of as a race to be first. The amount of resources an innovator devotes to the development of a new product or process affects its completion date. This relationship may be exact or probabilistic. There is a monetary reward for being first, which may, but need not, exceed the value of being second. There may, in fact, be no reward for being second. A follower may diminish the reward to the innovator. The main questions addressed in the modern theories are how profits, costs, and the "intensity of rivalry" determine the speed of development of an innovation. The "intensity of rivalry" is related to market structure and to the number of rivals but is identical to neither. That is, a potential innovator may feel threatened, as Schumpeter claimed, even if he appears to be alone in developing an innovation, because, as discussed ealier, there are often a variety of routes to the same result. Thus the innovator may take the possible existence of unidentified rivals into account in deciding how rapidly to develop his innovation. In focusing on the role of competition among potential innovators, the modern theories are closer in spirit to Schumpeter's emphasis than to Arrow's (1962) analysis, with its focus on the market structure of the industry that was to use the innovation.

An important question is the extent of accuracy of Schumpeter's (1975) assertion that long-run growth warrants sacrifice of short-run allocative efficiency. A related question is whether the implied trade-off is required. The consensus on the second question appears to be yes. No serious economist has suggested that we can have both. Much of the reasoning behind the conclusion that short-run allocative efficiency and technical advance are incompatible has been informal. Short-run allocative efficiency is incompatible with technical advance because the former is identified with perfect competition, and perfect competition in innovation means there are enough potential innovators that the return to this activity equals the return to any other activity. It further suggests immediate imitation after introduction of the innovation, assuring that the innovator will not have a monopoly and thereby preventing misallocation of resources after the innovation. This also discourages the quest to innovate. Ruff (1969) demonstrated this result rigorously in the context of a stylized two-sector growth model. The first and primary question remains open.

Even without attempting to address the main question, modeling the economics of technical advance poses great difficulties. Technical advance involves many of the features, such as externalities, uncertainty, nonconvexity, and dynamics, that are difficult to incorporate into even the most refined general equilibrium models. Thus the modern theories of market structure and innovation have been somewhat confined to addressing those questions that can be analyzed with current economic and mathematical tools.

The questions addressed by the modern theories can be divided into two broad categories. The first deals with the influence of various factors on the innovating firm's choice of the speed of development. In particular, it is asked, how is the expected profit-maximizing speed of development influenced by (1) the reward of being first, (2) the reward to imitation, (3) properties of the development cost function such as economies or diseconomies of scale, (4) uncertainty in the cost of development, (5) uncertainty regarding the identity of rivals and their development plans, (6) whether development costs are incurred at the outset with no opportunity for revision or whether they can be revised or terminated upon rival preemption, (7) the realization of monopoly profits on a current product that will be superseded by the firm's own innovation or a rival's innovation, (8) the necessity to finance development of the innovation out of the firm's current and past profits, (9) the possibility of costless imitation if preempted by a rival or of complete nullification of the firm's development efforts to date, and (10) the perceived intensity of rivalry?

The second category of questions deals with the relationship between market structure and innovation. The questions include: (1) What is the optimal number of parallel research efforts for a given total level of expenditure? (2) Under alternative assumptions about the development cost function, will a competitive or a monopolistic market structure lead to the optimal number of parallel research efforts if development costs are contractual (i.e., not subject to revision)? (3) Reconsider the second question if development costs are noncontractual (i.e., subject to revision). (4) Will a competitive or a monopolistic market or neither allocate the socially optimal level of resources to innovative activity? (5) Is there a market structure intermediate between perfect competition and monopoly that leads to the most rapid development of an innovation?

The first category of questions – those dealing with firm behavior – are analyzed in a decision theoretic framework. That is, certain elements of the firm's environment are taken as fixed or exogenous, including the rewards for innovation and imitation, the development cost function, and the intensity of rivalry. Of particular importance in the decision theoretic framework is the assumption that the firm believes its choice of the level of R&D spending does not influence the R&D-spending levels of its rivals. Indeed, it does not identify specific rivals. This assumption, as we noted earlier, may be justified when there are perhaps many ways of achieving the same innovation, so that the firm's rivals may not be in its present line of business.

In the second category of questions – those dealing with market behavior – interdependence among rivals' R&D-spending decisions is recognized. The intensity of rivalry is an endogenous variable in this analysis. The assumption of interdependence of R&D spending among rivals is, as mentioned earlier, appropriate when the innovation can be achieved in only a relatively few ways and so rivals are few and identifiable. A game theoretic framework is employed for the analysis.

The analysis of individual firm behavior presented in this chapter is largely based on seven of our papers (Kamien and Schwartz 1972a, 1974a, 1974b, 1976b, 1978a, 1978b, 1980b). This work was stimulated by Barzel's paper (1968) containing the claim that intense rivalry among potential innovators could result in overinvestment in innovative activity as compared to the "social optimum." Barzel did not, however, specify how each firm took into account the presence of rivals. Thus we set out to rectify this and to embed his model into a more general and explicit framework.

The game theoretic analysis of aggregate market behavior will be presented in the next chapter. Its antecedent is the paper by Scherer (1967b) in which rivalry among potential innovators was modeled in a Cournot oligopoly framework. Horowitz (1963) had conducted a similar analysis. The current analyses by Loury (1979), Lee and Wilde (1980), Kami (1979), Kelley (1979), Dasgupta and Stiglitz (1980b), and Reinganum (1979) differ from Scherer's in the assumption that the development cost function is stochastic rather than deterministic. Olivera (1973) anticipated much of this work but did not carry forth his efforts to addressing the questions posed here.

Returning to the analysis of individual firm behavior, our first objective was to determine the circumstances under which innovation might be premature relative to the social optimum and when it might be belated. The determination of the social optimum poses some conceptual difficulties that plague both the decision theoretic and game theoretic models of innovation, as will become evident later. In our earliest investigations we supposed that development cost was contractual, which means that once the firm decided to engage in the development race, it made an irrevocable commitment of resources. The firm could not cease its development effort upon preemption by a rival and thereby halt spending. All development costs are regarded as fixed costs in this formulation. The validity of this assumption varies with the cases. There are circumstances when the development of a new product or process is done on a contractual basis – as when another firm or independent laboratory is engaged to develop a specific product or to achieve a desired performance level in production for a fixed fee. More realistically, the contractual development cost assumption should be viewed as an approximation, better for development projects with relatively high fixed costs.

Later we modified the assumption that development cost is contractual. The firm may revise its development plan (and spending) upon rival preemption by accelerating, decelerating, or ceasing development altogether. This new assumption is closer to reality; however, it adds technical difficulties. Rather than specifying the development cost as a function of the development period, one must specify the development technology so that the optimal rate of spending throughout the development period can be determined. Furthermore, when development costs are contractual they are also certain, whereas noncontractual costs are also uncertain. The actual development costs to be incurred cannot be known at the outset when they are noncontractual because they depend on how the plan is revised upon rival preemption and, especially, upon the uncertain date of that preemption. We also identified two sources of uncertainty – technical uncertainty and market uncertainty. Technical uncertainty refers to uncertainty regarding the development cost function. It may not be known exactly how much money it will take to complete an innovation. Market uncertainty refers to the firm not knowing exactly how much money rivals are spending on the development of a substitute innovation, or, more exactly, if or when a rival innovation will appear. Thus even in the absence of technical uncertainty, development costs may be uncertain because of market uncertainty regarding the plans of rivals. This formulation gives rise to the interesting question of what circumstances will lead the firm optimally to accelerate, decelerate, or cease development altogether upon rival precedence. It turns out, as might be expected, that the firm is most likely to cease development if it is preceded by a rival at an early stage of its effort and continues on otherwise.

The innovating firm may or may not be currently producing a product or employing a process that earns it a monopoly profit and for which the innovation is a substitute. We investigate the relative importance of the opportunity for new extraordinary profits, the "carrot," versus the defense of existing profits, the "stick," as motivators of inventive activity. The decision to accelerate or decelerate development upon rival precedence rests importantly on which of these motives is dominant.

There is a third source of uncertainty regarding the profitability of the innovation. The profitability of an innovation depends on many factors, including the prices of substitutes, competing innovations, and complementary innovations, all of which may not be known exactly by the innovator at the outset. These sources of uncertainty have not been treated fully in either the analysis of this chapter or the next.

We have investigated the roles of the assumptions that development of an invention is financed through borrowing in the capital markets and that development involves no technical uncertainty. The first of these assumptions was replaced by the supposition that the firm must finance development entirely out of retained earnings. As already noted, because of both the intangibility of the outcome of an R&D project and the desire to maintain secrecy so as not to lose a competitive edge, R&D financing is thought to be done largely internally. The main question in this context is how the necessity to self-finance constrains the R&D activity of the firm.

Put another way, how much advantage accrues to the firm with high current profits available for investment in R&D? Relaxing the assumption of no technical uncertainty enables us to ask how much difference its presence makes for the optimal development plan of the firm. Technical uncertainty is a source of market uncertainty, for it is impossible to know precisely when a rival will introduce his invention if the development process is stochastic.

We also consider the possibility of costless imitation to see if it then becomes optimal for each rival to wait for one of the others to develop the invention. It need not be. We also study the consequences of assuming that imitation is totally impossible and of different durations of patent protection from imitation.

These generalizations of the first model followed a typical sequence, starting with the simplest, analytically most tractable formulation and progressing to more realistic, analytically more difficult ones. The conclusions reached from the analysis of these models are plausible, although many of them might not have been guessed at the outset. One of the most interesting results is the demonstration that an intermediate intensity of rivalry, one in which the innovator is neither entirely unthreatened by rivals nor severely threatened, may yield the fastest pace of innovation. That is, this decision theoretic model is consistent with the empirical finding that an intermediate market structure is often the one in which innovative activity is the greatest. The closest link between the results of the empirical testing of the Schumpeterian hypotheses and modern theorizing occurs here. This result also has stimulated the modern game theoretic modeling of innovation and market structure, because, it has been argued, the optimal behavior of a single innovating firm may differ from the aggregative behavior of all the innovators.

The presentation in this chapter goes well beyond what has been previously published in terms of the generality of the models. Results that we published earlier have been quite robust with respect to increasing realism and complexity of the assumptions. We present an integrated treatment, reflecting our current knowledge.

We turn now to the description and analysis of the models.

Formal analysis and proofs appear in the appendix to this chapter; appendix sections are ordered and titled according to the text sections they support.

The rewards and probabilities of collecting them

At the beginning of our story our firm is selling a product yielding a net profit flow of r_0 (set $r_0 = 0$ if the firm is a newcomer). These receipts will evolve over time, perhaps growing for a while, and then declining after the appearance of a superseding product in the market. In turn, the superseding product becomes the current product, eventually to be replaced by yet another improvement, and so on. To highlight the decision about a single potential innovation, we make some simplifying assumptions. We consider just one round – one new good – even though it too will subsequently be replaced. Although each product may have its own life cycle, we suppose that the underlying market may be growing (or declining) at a constant proportionate rate g.

Because the market is growing or declining at a constant proportionate rate g, profit on the initial good will be $e^{gt}r_0$ at time t. Others may sell similar products; we assume a stable division of the market has been reached. The market and the profit stream may be growing, so $g > 0$; it may be stationary ($g = 0$); or it may be declining, reflecting exogenous technological obsolescence (so $g < 0$ is the rate of decline). The firm contemplates a new superseding product. Because new ideas often occur to several people simultaneously, other (unidentified) entrepreneurs may have similar plans. Some may be current rivals of the firm, but others may not. In the next few pages the profits the firm can earn under various circumstances are stated. We let r's reflect receipts on the current good and p's reflect receipts on a new good. Capital P's reflect the capitalized value of a stream of receipts on a new good.

If our firm is the first to introduce a new product into the market, it receives a profit flow of $e^{gt}p_0$ for all t after innovation so long as it is the monopoly seller of the new good. If the firm's innovation is imitated, then the profit stream changes. Let $e^{gv}P_1(v - T)$ be the value at the moment v of imitation of the innovator's entire earnings stream after imitation. It may depend on the lag $v - T$ between innovation and imitation. The later a follower appears, the greater the foothold we shall have established in the marketplace, so the derivative $P_1' \geq 0$, typically (but not necessarily). Only its capital value P_1 matters; the time profile of receipts may be monotone or rising at first and then falling, in accord with a product life cycle. If receipts grow steadily, equal to $e^{gt}p_1$ at t, then $P_1 = \int_0^\infty p_1 e^{-(i-g)s}ds$. Although imitation usually reduces the profit available to the innovator, it is also possible that the presence of other sellers may broaden the market and so increase his profit.

If some other firm introduces a new competing product before our firm's own new product development is completed, our firm's net profit from its current product falls to $e^{gt}r_1$ at t, which it receives until it brings out its own new product. Suppose a rival innovates at time v; then by imitating with its own new product at time $T > v$, the firm can earn a stream of profits worth $e^{gT}P_2(T - v)$ at T. The greater our lag in following is, the smaller is the remaining market, so the derivative $P_2' \leq 0$ typically. Letting T and v be the times our firm and a rival respectively introduce their new products, we can summarize these receipts by the schematic

if our firm innovates, or

if it imitates, where the term e^{gt} has been omitted for brevity.

All these profits are assumed to be nonnegative with $r_0 \geq r_1$ (rival innovation does not increase the profit from the old good). There are many possible relationships among these parameters. For instance, in case our firm would be a new entrant with no current good to be replaced, $r_0 = r_1 = 0$. This equation also holds in case the firm is currently selling in other markets and its new good replaces none of its existing products. In case a rival's new good would eliminate the profits from the firm's current good, $r_1 = 0$.

The firm's profits from the innovation may be diminished or enhanced by the presence of followers. It may get more or less as follower than it would lose to others if its innovation were imitated. If the winner takes all, the first firm to bring out the new good gets the entire reward from that moment forward and followers get nothing.

The reward to the firm as monopolist includes all returns from the innovation, whether the firm uses or markets the innovation itself or licenses it to others. In each case the rewards available to our firm are the best that the firm believes it can obtain, given the predicted behavior of consumers and rivals. This "best" may be reached using tacit collusion, leader–follower relations, or other means and is taken as data.

The firm does not identify a single source of innovative rivalry but, rather, is aware that a competing product may appear from a myriad of sources: from current rivals, firms in other markets, or entirely new entrants. It recognizes the potential innovators by a single subjective probability distribution over the introduction date of any rival product. Let $F(t)$ be the firm's assessment at time $t = 0$ of the probability that the composite rival will have introduced its improved product or process by time t. Then, the probability density that the composite rival will introduce its innovation in the next moment, given that it has not done so prior to time t, is

$$(1) \qquad H(t) \equiv F'(t) / (1 - F(t))$$

where prime indicates derivative. This function, equation (1), is called the hazard rate. Because

$$-d \ln (1 - F(t)) / dt = H(t)$$

it follows on integrating that

$$(2) \qquad 1 - F(t) = \exp\left(-\int_0^t H(s)\, ds\right)$$

Because we are especially interested in the effects of an increase in rivalry, realized as an increase in the hazard rate (conditional probability density of rival entry at any moment), we write the hazard rate as a hazard function $u(t)$, multiplied by a hazard parameter h:

(3) $H(t) = hu(t)$

An increase in the hazard parameter h results in a constant proportionate increase in the hazard rate. We assume $u(t)$ is a nondecreasing function so the hazard rate is nondecreasing through time. The exponential distribution (which has been used exclusively in the previous literature) corresponds to $u(t) = 1$; the Weibull distribution is $u(t) = wt^{w-1}$; and the extreme value distribution is $u(t) = we^{wt}$. The exponential distribution is a special case of the Weibull with $w = 1$; it has a constant hazard rate. The extreme value distribution and the Weibull distribution with $w > 1$ (as we assume) both have hazard rates that increase through time, reflecting a conditional probability density of rival entry that increases through time.

Using (3), we can write (2) equivalently as

(4) $1 - F(t) = e^{-hv(t)}$

where, by definition,

(5) $v(t) \equiv \int_0^t u(s)\, ds$

We note that $v(t) = t$ for the exponential distribution, $v(t) = t^w$ for the Weibull distribution, and $v(t) = e^{wt} - 1$ for the extreme value distribution. Then, also, the probability density of rival entry at t is

(6) $F'(t) = hu(t)e^{-hv(t)}$

The expected time of rival entry can be written as

(7) $E(t) = \int_0^\infty e^{-hv(s)}\, ds$

Clearly, an increase in the hazard parameter will hasten the expected time of rival entry. (See Sivazlian and Stanfel, 1975, Chap. 3.)

Discounting future profits at rate i, the firm's expected profit stream if it introduces its new product at time T is

$$(8) \quad W(t) = \int_0^T e^{-(i-g)t}(r_0(1 - F(t)) + r_1 F(t)) \, dt$$

$$+ \int_T^\infty e^{-(i-g)t}[p_0(1-F(t)) + P_1(t-T)F'(t)] \, dt$$

$$+ \int_0^T e^{-(i-g)T} P_2(T-t)F'(t) \, dt$$

To understand (8), note that so long as the firm has not introduced a new product $(t < T)$, the firm gets $e^{gT}r_0$ if no rival has brought out a new good by t (probability $1 - F(t)$) and gets $e^{gt}r_1$ if a rival has done so by t (probability $F(t)$). If the firm innovates and still holds a monopoly (probability $1 - F(t)$, $T \le t$), it gets $e^{gt}p_0$. It gets a stream worth $e^{gt}P_1(t - T)$ if it was first but an imitator appears at t (probability density $F'(t)$, $t > T$). Finally, the firm gets a stream worth $e^{gT}P_2(T - t)$ at T as follower if another firm preceded it at t (probability density $F'(t)$, $t < T$).

The cost

The new good will be introduced as soon as its development is complete. Development takes both time and money. Delaying introduction of the new good saves costs in two ways. First, the later money is spent, the lower is its present value. This time value of money or opportunity cost is reflected in i. Second is the inverse time–cost trade-off introduced by Scherer (1967b) and studied by him and Mansfield (1971). Both classical diminishing returns tendencies and also the heuristic and uncertain features of the research and development process lead to diminishing returns to time compression of research. More rapid spending may involve overtime and premiums for more intensive use of factors of production and may involve greater use of parallel rather than sequential lines of inquiry.

We suppose there is no important uncertainty about the feasibility of completing development by any desired date T by expenditure of a known requisite sum of money $C(T)$. That is, $C(T)$ is the value at time zero of the cost stream needed to develop the product by time T. The details of precisely how this will be accomplished need not be known, however. We assume that this cost is positive and that it decreases at an increasing rate as the completion time T is extended; that is,

(9) $C(T) > 0, \quad C'(T) < 0, \quad C''(T) > 0 \qquad$ for all $T > 0$

We also assume $C(0)$ is so large that immediate entry is not worthwhile.

Speed of development

Let the difference between the expected rewards from introduction at T and the cost of doing so be

(10) $V(T) = W(T) - C(T)$

Development is assumed undertaken under contract so the development schedule will not be modified should a rival appear before T. There is no opportunity to recoup committed funds. (Alternative assumptions are made later.) The firm seeks the introduction time T^* that maximizes (10). Substituting from (8) into (10) and setting the derivative of (10) with respect to T equal to zero gives an implicit expression for the optimal introduction time, if one exists (see appendix). It is possible that it is best not to introduce the product at all.

The marginal condition for choice of introduction time involves balancing the marginal gain from a moment's delay against the marginal cost from doing so (see appendix). The marginal gain from momentary delay is the reduction $C'(T)$ in development cost. The marginal loss depends on whether a rival has already appeared by T. If a rival has not appeared, then one gives up the innovational reward in favor of the return on the existing good for the moment of delay. In addition, the delay reduces the expected lag between our innovation and rival imitation, which may reduce our rewards after imitation if they depend on the length of the lag.

If a rival has appeared first, then during a slight delay in our introduction, we surrender the imitational reward in favor of the reduced receipts on the existing good for that moment. Also, the lag between rival innovation and our imitation is increased, so the total reward stream from imitation may be reduced. Finally, if a rival would enter during the moment of delay, the firm becomes a follower rather than an innovator; we lose the reward stream to the innovator with followers and get instead the stream to the follower.

If the project is worthwhile, how does the optimal introduction date T^* vary with the pre- and postinnovational returns? Implicit differentiation of the first-order condition for T^*, assuming that the second-order condition holds with strong inequality, shows (see appendix) that the "carrot" of innovational profits p_0 and P_1 stimulates innovation, for offensive reasons. The larger these rewards are, the earlier is the new product introduction. On the other hand, the larger are the profits r_0 and r_1 from the current good to be replaced, the later will be new product introduction. Current profits are lost upon innovation, thereby reducing the net gain from innovation. Thus, other things equal, a new good that does not supplant an existing one marketed by the firm will appear more rapidly than one that replaces a current product. Likewise, the incentive to bring out a new good is greater for a firm that is new to the industry than for an incumbent, again, other things equal. (In this case, other things may not be equal; the incumbent may have other advantages not possessed by the new entrant.)

The greater the loss $r_0 - r_1$ from rival precedence is, the greater is the stimulus to development and the sooner development will be completed. The threat of loss from rival innovation acts as a "stick," encouraging more rapid development for defensive reasons. As shown later, an effect of the "stick" may be the development of a good less profitable than the current one.

The impact of an increase in rivalry (i.e., in the hazard parameter) upon the planned introduction time can be determined if having followers is preferable to being a follower ($P_1 > P_2$) and these rewards are independent of the lag between innovation and imitation ($P_1' = P_2' = 0$). It is shown in the appendix that there are just two cases. First, the development period may increase with the intensity of rivalry h; then no rivalry at all ($h = 0$) yields the fastest development and thereby the maximum inventive activity. In the second case the development period decreases with increasing rivalry up to a point h^* and then further increases in innovational rivalry lead to a lengthening of the development period. Maximum inventive activity, or minimum development time, occurs at a degree of rivalry intermediate between competition (h approaches infinity) and monopoly ($h = 0$). (These results also depend on the supposition that $u(T)/v(T)$ is a decreasing function, as is the case for the exponential, Weibull, and extreme value distributions.)

Thus far we have supposed that the probability distribution over the time of rival entry was unaffected by our firm's innovation. This reflects an assumption of symmetry among the firms, whereby each of the rivals' R&D is contractual and unalterable in response to actions of others. We now relax this assumption. If the firm innovates, rivals may change their development pace, accelerating or decelerating their own efforts as a consequence. (They may change their pace because the innovation reveals how to do it easier or blocks current efforts, or because the available rewards are changed. These issues are discussed at length later in the chapter.)

Let $F_1(t)$ be the firm's assessment of the probability of rival innovation by time t, and let $F_2(t - T)$ be the firm's assessment of the probability of rival imitation by time $t > T$, given that no rival had innovated by T when the firm introduced its own new product. Then

$$(11) \qquad 1 - F(t) = \begin{cases} 1 - F_1(t) & 0 \le t < T \\ (1 - F_2(t - T))(1 - F_1(T)) & T \le t \end{cases}$$

is the continuous probability distribution function over the time of rival entry. Note that $F(t)$ now depends on T for $t > T$. We shall write F_1 in the form of (4) so h is the innovational hazard parameter.

Substituting (11) into (8) and collecting terms gives

$$(12) \qquad W(T) = \int_0^T e^{-(i-g)t}(r_0(1 - F_1(t)) + r_1 F_1(t)) \, dt$$

$$+e^{-(i-g)T}\left[(1-F_1(T))\bar{P}+\int_0^T P_2(T-t)F_1'(t)\,dt\right]$$

where

(13) $\qquad \bar{P}\equiv\int_0^\infty e^{-(i-g)s}[p_0(1-F_2(s))+P_1(s)F_2'(s)]\,ds$

(see appendix). $e^{gT}\bar{P}$ is the value of the stream of expected receipts from innovation, discounted to the moment of innovation. It includes receipts after innovation while the monopoly is maintained and the capital value of the receipt stream that is awarded when the innovation is imitated.

The total expected receipts (12) consist of expected receipts during the development period (first integral term) plus expected receipts upon completion. The latter consists of the expected reward to the innovator, just discussed, if no rival has preceded him and of the expected reward as follower if a rival has preceded. The formulation reflects the assumption that the postimitation rewards may depend on the duration of the monopoly.

Note that the innovational rewards p_0 and $P_1(t)$ and the expected duration of the monopoly enter $W(T)$ only through the expected reward for innovation $\bar{P}$. Only this expected reward matters and not its composition. Thus high monopoly profits for a short period followed by none once imitators appear can be equivalent to a moderate return over a longer period. Whether the appearance of followers enhances or diminishes the reward flow to the innovator does not matter as such, nor does the time profile of receipts matter. The aggregative amount $\bar{P}$ summarizes all that is relevant about innovational rewards.

The expected profit to be maximized by choice of introduction time T is $V(T)=W(T)-C(T)$. Substituting from (8) and differentiating gives necessary conditions obeyed by the optimal introduction time T^* (see appendix). The interpretation of the marginal condition is similar to that given earlier under the supposition of no change in the function $F(t)$. A marginal delay in introduction results in a savings of development costs $C'(T)$. This equals the marginal change in expected receipts: We get the reward on the old good instead of on the new good during the moment of delay (for which the exact expressions depend on whether a rival has entered). In addition, if a rival has appeared, the lag between innovation and imitation will increase, which may reduce the total stream available to us as imitator. Finally, if the rival should enter during the moment of delay, then we give up the innovator's stream and get that for the imitator.

The sensitivity of the optimal introduction time to the various rewards is the same as that found for the earlier model with no change in anticipated rival behavior. An increase in the expected reward for innovation $\bar{P}$ (carrot) accelerates development, as will a decrease in the reward for the current good or an increase in the loss $r_0 - r_1$ (stick) due to rival innovation. (See appendix.)

The effect of changed innovational rivalry upon the speed of development is as already found. The degree of rivalry that renders the development period shortest may be said to maximize the rate of innovation. The same two cases may occur. For projects offering moderately good improvement in rewards, an increase in innovational rivalry h (see (4), with F replaced by F_1) will lengthen the development period. In this case no rivalry at all ($h = 0$) yields the shortest development period and thereby, maximum inventive activity. On the other hand, for very good projects offering a large increase in expected receipts, an increase in innovational rivalry will hasten development, up to a point h^*; still further increases in h will cause a slackening in effort. The minimum development time would occur for a degree of rivalry h^* of intermediate intensity. Further, the more attractive the project is, the larger will be the innovation maximizing (development period minimizing) degree of rivalry and the shorter will be that minimum development period (at least when $r_0 - r_1$ is small). (We assumed that our reward for imitation is independent of the lag between innovation and imitation ($P_2' = 0$) and that $u(T)/v(T)$ for F_1 is a decreasing function but did not restrict either the probability of imitation distribution $F_2(t)$ or the functions describing rewards for innovation.) See appendix for demonstrations.

A patent of life L can be modeled as a special case. Suppose imitation is impossible during the life of the patent and is immediate and eliminates supranormal profits upon expiration. This is reflected by letting $F_2 \equiv 0$ and replacing p_0 by $p(1 - e^{-(i-g)L})$, where receipts are pe^{gt} for t within the life L of the patent. We find that the longer the patent life L is, the greater is the reward from innovation, and hence the sooner the new product will appear. Innovation is most rapid if an infinite lived patent is available. A project can always be discouraged by a short patent life but even an indefinitely long patent will not bring forth development effort unless the benefit is sufficiently large.

New product pricing

If the firm introduces a new product, the probability or speed of imitation may depend on its price or profitability. The higher the price is, the more attractive entry may appear to potential rivals and the shorter may be the innovator's monopoly. Thus the innovating firm may wish to set the product's price to balance the effects of a marginal price change on the profit level during the monopoly period against the effect on its duration. This additional consideration is easily incorporated into our model in case the imitation probability function F_2 is exponential with hazard rate k and if the innovator's reward after followers appear does not depend on the duration of the monopoly ($P_1' = 0$). (See appendix.)

The profit flow from innovation exclusive of development cost will be $e^{gt}p_0(c(t))$ at time t if product price is $c(t)$ at t and no imitator has yet appeared. We assume p_0 is a concave function of price. Suppose that the maximum monopoly return is greater than the equivalent return available once there are followers: $(i - g)P_1 < \max_c p_0(c)$. The constant hazard rate k is replaced by an increasing convex function of price $k(c)$. The modified problem is to choose an entry time T and price policy $c(t)$ during the monopoly period to maximize expected profits, given the modifications in p_0 and k. We find (see appendix) that all the earlier results regarding the introduction time T hold when the problem is generalized as indicated. In addition, the optimal price for the new product is constant over time. It is generally less than the monopoly price that would be charged if there were no threat of rival entry. The optimal price balances the marginal loss of current profits during the monopoly against the marginal increase in its expected duration.

The nonrivalrous solution

The special case of no rivalry for new product introduction, no imitation, and no profits from existing goods to be endangered by new product introduction provides a benchmark for comparison with the rivalrous situation discussed earlier. The nonrivalrous solution and corresponding optimal introduction date T^s have the desirable properties that there is no uncertainty about the rewards to be received (no rivals to encroach on the benefits stream), no duplication of developmental costs, and no retardation to protect current profits. Although the time T^s may not coincide with the socially optimal timing when consumer surplus associated with a new product is taken into account, it serves as a reference against which to compare the results of innovation in a setting of rivalrous competition.

We find that the firm's introduction date T^* may be premature or belated compared with the nonrivalrous solution T^s (see appendix). After our earlier findings that an increase in rivalry may either hasten or retard development, this result may not be surprising.

Intense rivalry

Barzel (1968) argues that rivalry will accelerate development so much that the net present value of the supramarginal innovation is driven to zero. He implicitly assumes that the winner takes all, no good is being supplanted, and no diminishing returns to compression of the development period exists. Yet it can readily be shown that the firm's optimal introduction time under these restrictions is always strictly later than the zero profit introduction time that Barzel expects to observe. (See appendix.) Rivalry cannot force a profit-maximizing firm to introduce so early that there are no profits. Indeed, under Barzel's assumptions, the optimal introduction time for the firm T^* may not even be earlier than the nonrivalrous date T^s. If rivalry becomes sufficiently intense, the firm will not pursue the project at all. (See appendix.)

Finally, we drop Barzel's special assumptions and examine the consequences of perfect competition on the speed of innovation. We interpret perfect competition as a situation in which no supranormal profits are earned on the current good, no innovational rivalry is anticipated, imitation will be immediate, and the firm gets little reward for its innovation once followers have appeared. Under these circumstances, the firm will not undertake development at all. (See appendix.)

A particular cost function

It will be useful to develop a particular cost function satisfying (9). Let $y(t)$ be the rate of dollar spending for the research project at time t, and let $z(t)$ be the cumulative effective effort devoted to the project by t. The total effective effort required to complete the development is a known amount A. The rate of spending and the growth of cumulative effective effort are related by

$$(14) \qquad z'(t) = y^a(t), \quad z(0) = 0, \quad z(T) = A$$

where $0 < a < 1$. This specification reflects the assumption of decreasing returns to spending money faster. It may be viewed as a production relation whose inputs are monetary expenditures and whose output is the completion date T. The greater is the extent of diminishing returns to time compression of the development, the smaller is the parameter a. The total discounted expenditure is

$$(15) \qquad \int_0^T e^{-it} y(t) \, dt$$

to be minimized subject to (14). Solving gives the optimal spending program (see appendix). It is characterized by expenditures that rise at a constant proportionate rate

$$(16) \qquad y'(t)/y(t) = i/(1 - a)$$

throughout the development period. This exceeds the discount rate i. For an intermediate case of $a = \frac{1}{2}$ spending grows at twice the discount rate. The more sharply diminishing the returns to spending money faster are, the lower is the proportionate rate of change of development spending. Although the absolute rate of spending $y(t)$ depends on the amount of effort A required for the project and on the due date T, the proportionate spending growth rate is independent of both A and T.

Define

(17) $n \equiv a/(1 - a)$

Then, the least cost of development by a given completion date T is (see appendix)

(18) $C(T) = A^{1/a}(in/(e^{inT} - 1))^{1/n}$

This cost function has the properties posited in (9).

Is development worthwhile?

The optimal introduction time has been characterized in cases that it is profitable (in an expected value sense) to undertake development. But under what circumstances is this so? This question is answered here by specializing our model somewhat. Let the cost function $C(T)$ be given in (18) and suppose that F_1 is exponential ($u(t) = 1$). Assume that rival precedence forecloses any opportunity for additional profit from imitation, so the firm would earn the same with its current good as it would by imitating the rival's new good: $r_1 = (i - g)P_2$. After specializing appendix equation (A10), using (18), we find that $W'(T) = C'(T)$ implies

(19) $e^{(g-h)T}(1 - e^{-inT})^{1/a} = (Ai)^{1/a}n^{1/n}/B_0$

provided that

(20) $i/(1 - a) + (g - h)(e^{inT} - 1) > 0$

(so the second-order condition will be satisfied. This means that the left side of (19) must be increasing with respect to T at the optimum), where

(21) $B_0 \equiv (i - g + h)\bar{P} - r_0 - hP_2 > 0$

The right side of (19) is roughly a cost/benefit ratio. Relations (19) to (20) implicitly specify the optimal development period T^*. If there is no introduction time satisfying (19) and (20), then development is not undertaken.

Clearly, B_0 must be positive for R&D to be worthwhile. This reflects the expected net reward from innovation. Naturally, it increases with the direct rewards from innovation. On the other hand, the more profitable the good to be displaced is, ceteris paribus, the smaller is the net benefit of innovation.

The extent of innovational rivalry anticipated matters also. Without potential rivalry, a new product would be developed only if it yielded greater profits than the current one. However, a project that would be rejected if there were no fear of rival entry may nevertheless be worth developing and introducing if rivals may bring out a new good that reduces or destroys the profitability of the current one. (Specifically, suppose for simplicity the winner takes all, with profits on the new product less than current profits: $(i - g)\bar{P} = p_0 < r_0$. Further suppose rival innovation leaves the firm no profits, so $P_2 = 0$. Then if $(i - g + h)\bar{P} > r_0 > (i - g)\bar{P}$, B_0 is positive so development may be worthwhile even though the new good will be less profitable than the old one.)

The possibility of rival preemption reduces the expected value of the current product because receipts would fall upon rival entry. This enhances the relative value of the new product. Thus innovation may be attractive for either offensive reasons (profits are expected to rise) or for defensive reasons (rivals' actions may reduce the firm's profits), in support of the current line of business.

Returning to the question of whether development will be undertaken at all, we find that there are two cases, depending on whether g exceeds h. If the market growth rate g exceeds the hazard rate h of rival entry, and if $B_0 > 0$, then there is always a unique positive optimal introduction time T^*. (The left side of (19) is increasing with respect to T when $g > h$ so (20) is satisfied, and it assumes all positive values so there is a solution T^* to (19).) In this case development is undertaken regardless of the amount A of effort required. (The required effort A will, of course, affect the optimal speed of development.)

On the other hand, if the hazard rate of rival entry is at least as large as the market growth rate, B_0 must be sufficiently large relative to the effort A required to complete develoment. Specifically, in case $g = h$, development is worthwhile in just those cases where the required effort is small relative to the benefits to be received:

(22) $(Ai)^{1/a}n^{1/n} < B_0$

(because the left side of (19) is an increasing function of T, with least upper bound of one, when g = h). If $g < h$, the condition for undertaking development is similar to (22) but more stringent. The right side of (22) must then be a certain multiple of the left side, with the required multiple increasing with $h - g$. (Condition (19) can be satisfied only if the right side of (19) is not larger than the maximum of the left side. The maximum of the left side with respect to T is less than one when $g < h$ and is smaller as $h - g$ is larger.) The larger is the hazard rate relative to the growth or decay rate, the better the project must be, measured by B_0, in order that it be worth undertaking. If (19) has a solution T when $g < h$, the optimal introduction time T^* is the smaller of the two roots of the equation (so that (20) is satisfied). Otherwise T^* tends to infinity and development is not undertaken.

In sum, if the expected net advantage B_0 of the project is positive and if the market growth rate exceeds the hazard rate of rival entry, innovation will be worthwhile in an expected value sense. This is true even if the project would be rejected in the absence of potential rivalry. Also, it is true regardless of the amount of effective effort A required to complete development. But if the market growth rate is no larger than the hazard rate, a project will be undertaken only if the expected benefit is sufficiently large relative to the effort required.

Noncontractual development

Until now, development was assumed to be contractual in the sense that once the planned introduction date T was chosen, cost $C(T)$ was incurred regardless of rival behavior. Henceforth the firm may stop spending on development if and when a new rival good is introduced. However, the firm may also continue development, perhaps at an altered pace, if it chooses. In addition, it has been assumed implicitly that development could be financed entirely through borrowing. We shall also analyze the requirement that R&D be financed internally from the firm's current profits and accumulated funds.

Conventional wisdom on research and development holds that R&D generally must be self-financed. (Therefore a firm must have some monopoly power, and associated monopoly profits, to do R&D.) As noted, two reasons are frequently offered for a self-financing requirement. First, it may be difficult to borrow money without substantial tangible collateral to be claimed by the lender if the project fails. But an R&D project that fails generally leaves behind few tangible assets. Second, the firm may be reluctant to reveal detailed information about the project that would make it attractive to outside lenders, fearing its disclosure to potential rivals. These observations are supported by anecdotal evidence and case studies documenting the difficulties of obtaining adequate external financing for R&D and innovation. Nevertheless, as we have seen, regression tests generally lend scant support to the hypothesis that corporate financial liquidity is important for innovation.

Let the various receipt streams, discount rate, market growth rate, and probability distribution over rival entry time be as before, with one exception. We now admit the possibility that rival precedence may inflict losses on the firm's current product; that is, r_1 may have any sign. Let $y(t)$ be the rate of development spending at time t, and let $x(t)$ be the cash balance at t. If a rival introduces a new product at some time t prior to our firm's completion, then our firm will either cease development and exit (collecting zero), cease development and continue marketing its old good (collecting $e^{gt}r_1$ for all t thereafter), or modify its development schedule optimally (spending at an optimal rate – to be determined – until completion and then collecting a stream worth $e^{gt}P_2$). Discussion of the circumstances under which the firm's optimal response will be each of these options is postponed. Let $G(t, x(t), z(t))$ denote the value at time t of the maximum net return the firm can earn from t forward if a rival good precedes its own at time t. This may in general depend on the date of rival appearance, the firm's cash balance $x(t)$ at that moment, and the amount of development already completed $z(t)$.

The present value of the expected receipts to our firm if it plans to complete its new product development at T is

$$(23) \quad W(T) = \int_0^T e^{-it}[e^{gt}r_0(1 - F_1(t))$$
$$+ G(t, x(t), z(t))F_1'(t)]\,dt$$
$$+ e^{-(i-g)T}(1 - F_1(T))\bar{P}$$

where $\bar{P}$ is the expected innovational reward given in (13). The firm gets $e^{gt}r_0$ before innovation, G upon a rival's innovation, and $e^{gT}\bar{P}$ upon its own innovation. The expected net profit to be maximized is

$$(24) \quad \max W(T) - \int_0^T e^{-it}y(t)(1 - F_1(t))\,dt$$

The maximization is subject to the cash balance constraint

$$(25) \quad x'(t) = ix(t) + e^{gt}r_0 - y(t), \qquad x(0) = x_0,$$
$$x(t) \geq 0, \quad 0 \leq t \leq T$$

The cash balance $x(t)$ grows by the interest it earns (at rate i) and the profit on the current good and is diminished by spending on development. An initial cash balance x_0 is given. The balance must be nonnegative throughout the development period. (It turns out in this problem that a terminal nonnegativity condition assures nonnegativity throughout.)

In addition, accumulated effective effort $z(t)$ grows with spending according to the relationship given earlier, namely,

$$(14) \quad z'(t) = y^a(t), \quad z(0) = 0, \quad z(T) = A$$

where $0 < a < 1$, initial accumulated effort is zero, and effort A must be accumulated by the time T of planned new product introduction. (It is not possible to indicate a general cost function, because total spending is stochastic.)

The problem is to choose T and $y(t)$, $0 \le t \le T$ to maximize (24) subject to (25) and (14). The optimal planned spending path will be followed until our firm innovates at T, provided no rival entrant appears. But if a rival enters at some time before T, then the development plan is discarded and a revised plan is followed thereafter. The value at t of the revised plan is $G(t, x(t), z(t))$.

The firm may cease development upon rival precedence, only slow the pace of development, or accelerate development. We begin our analysis under the supposition that the first option obtains and then we turn to the other options.

Development ceases upon rival entry

Suppose the appearance of a rival before development is complete leads the firm to stop its own development efforts. This is optimal if either completion will not raise receipts after rival innovation or if the gain in receipts is small relative to the required effort and the rival enters early in the development period. Suppose also that the cash constraint does not limit the development pace so that (25) may be ignored.

Under the circumstances just outlined, the optimal spending rate grows according to (see appendix)

$$y'(t)/y(t) = (i + hu(t))/(1 - a)$$

The proportionate spending growth rate is larger as the discount rate i or the hazard parameter h (extent of innovational rivalry) is larger; it is smaller when the extent of diminishing returns to compression of the research period is greater. (Contractual spending is a special case in which $h = 0$; that is, $h = 0$ as far as spending is concerned.)

Under these suppositions, the optimal development period can be shown (see appendix) to depend on the parameters qualitatively the same as in the case of contractual R&D. Development is hastened by an increase in the rewards to innovation or by a reduction in the effective effort required. Profits on the current good to be displaced act as a drag on the rate of development, because they reduce the net reward to be realized. An increase in the market growth rate usually makes the innovation more attractive and hence hastens its development. A firm without innovational rivals will develop a modest project more rapidly than a firm facing such rivalry. But a highly profitable project will be most rapidly introduced if there is a degree of rivalry intermediate between monopoly and competition. The more attractive the innovation is to the developer, the larger is the innovation-maximizing (i.e., development period minimizing) degree of rivalry.

It turns out (see appendix) that there is a significant difference in the criteria for undertaking development when R&D is contractual and when it may be terminated upon rival precedence. We examine the special case that F_1 is exponential. When development is done under contract, a project with a positive net benefit is undertaken regardless of the development effort required only if the market growth rate exceeds the constant hazard rate h. In contrast, if expenditure can be halted upon rival entry, then the project with a positive net benefit will be undertaken regardless of effective effort required, provided only that the market growth rate is *positive*. It is therefore typically much easier to meet the criterion for undertaking a project if spending can be terminated upon preemption than if spending is contractual. Of course, without innovational rivalry, the two cases coincide.

A range of innovations

Although we are primarily concerned with projects of given magnitude, we briefly suppose that the firm can choose the magnitude of innovation. A larger innovation, with larger benefits, can be attained with greater effort. We suppose the benefit is an increasing concave function of the effective effort A. Assuming that the market growth rate is zero, but otherwise retaining our previous assumptions with an exponential probability of rival entry, we find (see appendix) that firms facing greater innovational rivalry will select smaller projects than firms with lesser rivalry. We also find that an increase in patent life, or other change that raises the potential reward for the whole range of potential innovations, will enlarge the innovation attempted.

DeBondt (1977), using a formulation similar to the one described here and in the previous section on entry retarding pricing, studied how the firm can optimally employ the magnitude of innovation as a deterrent to entry. He found that the optimal magnitude of the innovation will be the largest when the exogenous threat of entry is intermediate between no chance of rival entry and virtually certain rival entry. This is consistent with our finding that an intermediate market structure may lead to the most rapid pace of inventive activity.

Self-financing

Under what circumstances will the self-financing requirement affect the place of development? That is, when will the constraint be tight? And if it does matter, how does it alter the development plan? How does the optimal development program of a firm with considerable liquidity differ from the plan of a firm without it? These questions are explored using the model (24), (25), and (14), assuming that rival precedence will cause the firm to cease development.

Development can be optimally financed from *current* receipts alone for a remarkably broad range of projects. If

$$(26) \qquad (i - g + hu(T))\bar{P} \le r_0/a + hu(T)r_1/(i - g)$$

development spending never exceeds current receipts and the self-financing constraint will not retard development (see appendix). This is true regardless of the effective effort A required. Of course if g is no bigger than h and the difficulty A is too large, then the project is rejected.

Several remarks can be made about the applicability of the self-financing condition. First, (26) is more apt to hold so that self-financing is readily accomplished, the larger the returns on the current product are, the smaller are expected returns on the contemplated product, the smaller the innovational rivalry is, and the greater are diminishing returns to time compression of research. Thus if the expected reward from the new product modestly exceeds that of the current one or if there are sharply diminishing returns to hastening development, the optimal development schedule is so leisurely that it can be fully financed from current receipts.

Second, because in many instances expected rewards from the new product will not greatly exceed expected profit from the current product, the solution with the cash constraint inactive has extensive applicability. Moreover, (26) is only a sufficient condition that cash availability will not be an impedence; development can be financed from current and accumulated past receipts for a far broader range of parameter configurations. The cash constraint can always be rendered inactive by a sufficiently large initial cash balance.

Third, a firm earning high profits from its current product or facing little innovational rivalry is better able to finance product development from current profits than one earning low profits or facing intense rivalry. However, a newcomer (for whom $r_0 = 0$) nevertheless may develop a superior product more rapidly than the incumbent will. A newcomer facing the same parameters will develop more rapidly because his potential net innovational reward exceeds the incumbent's (because the incumbent gives up current rewards, whereas the newcomer has none to relinquish). However, a newcomer needs a substantial initial cash balance so that development will not be impeded by a cash constraint. An entrant with ample cash will develop faster than an otherwise identical firm that is already in the market. But if the would-be entrant is limited by cash availability, his speed of development may or may not exceed the incumbent's. The cash required increases with the innovational reward because a larger reward encourages faster, costlier development. It increases with required effort A for A small, as increased development effort requires more cash. However, for large A this effect is more than offset by the impact of lessened profitability in reducing the development pace; cash required then decreases with A. (See appendix.)

Although the substantial initial cash balance required of a newcomer may pose a barrier to the individual innovator, it need not hamper entry of a firm currently in another line of business. This helps explain why the innovator of a superior product in a particular line of business is often a firm already in another line. It also underscores the point made earlier that firms currently in a market may not be the only potential innovators.

Now suppose that the self-financing requirement is active. That is, the development program implicit in the preceding discussion is not feasible because the firm does not have enough cash to finance it. Several observations are pertinent about the best development schedule that can be financed for a worthwhile project. First, development spending increases throughout the development period. Second, the proportionate rate of growth of spending y'/y is intermediate between the one that holds when spending is contractual, $i/(1 - a)$, and the one that obtains when spending is not limited by cash availability and may be stopped upon rival precedence, $(i + hu(T))/(1 - a)$. (See appendix.)

Third, if there is no innovational rivalry $(h = 0)$, these two bounds coincide and spending rises at the constant proportionate rate $i/(1 - a)$ in each case. The sole effect of the cash constraint in case $h = 0$ is to reduce the absolute spending rate to maintain feasibility, thereby extending the development period. The proportionate rate of growth in spending is $i/(1 - a)$ in case $h = 0$, whether or not the cash constraint is active.

Fourth, if innovational rivals cannot be ignored, $h > 0$, then the proportionate growth rate of spending as well as its absolute value is affected by the financing requirement. The proportionate spending growth rate decreases with increasing severity of the constraint (measured by its implicit multiplier in the optimization problem). An active cash constraint reduces the level and (if $h > 0$) the proportionate growth rate of spending at comparable times and must lengthen the development period, relative to the optimal plan with adequate liquidity.

Fifth, the cash balance will never be zero before project completion. In particular, a solution in which R&D spending just equals profits cannot be optimal for any interval of time. If the cash constraint is binding, the cash balance will be single peaked with respect to time, either decreasing throughout or building up early in the development period while expenditures are low, and eventually peaking and decreasing to zero.

If there is little or no innovational rivalry and the cash constraint is binding, optimal development is more rapid when the initial cash balance is larger, the current receipts r_0 is greater, and the required developmental effort A is smaller. (See appendix.) The impact of the initial cash balance and required effort are as expected. The dominant role of r_0 is its effect on cash availability, as initial cash. This is the opposite of r_0's impact when cash was not scarce; then the dominant effect of increased r_0 is a reduction in the net reward for innovation, reducing the development pace.

An increase in the expected benefit from innovation generally hastens development, although there is one interesting exception. If there is no innovational rivalry, the reward does not affect the speed of development; it affects only the decision to undertake the project. Good and excellent projects proceed equally rapidly, just governed by cash availability and required effort. Further, in the absence of innovational rivalry, a deficiency of financing may retard development, but the condition governing whether the project is sufficiently attractive to be undertaken is independent of financial resources. In other words, without innovational rivalry, product improvements will not be bypassed solely because of limited cash. (See appendix.)

Rival precedence need not halt R&D

Suppose a rival appears at time v when effective development effort is $z(v) < A$. The firm may exit and collect zero profits thereafter, or it may stop development but continue selling its old product. These cases were previously discussed. The third option is to complete development, possibly at an altered pace. To explore this third option, as well as to determine the circumstances under which each option is best, we make some simplifying specializations. Specifically, we assume the market is stationary $g = 0$, assume rival entry time is thought to follow an exponential distribution, let the development function parameter $a = \frac{1}{2}$, and assume there is adequate financing so the cash constraint is not tight.

If a rival new product appears, the expenditure-effort relationship may be modified thereafter. Accumulation of effective effort may become easier if the firm can learn something from the rival's innovation. It may, alternatively, become more difficult if the innovator has patented a product or process similar to the firm's own approach, so that a new one must be developed. To capture these notions, we write the expenditure effort relationship after rival innovation at v as

(27) $z' = my^{1/2}, \quad v \le t \le T_1, \quad z(v) \text{ given}, \quad z(T_1) = A$

where T_1 is the revised completion date. The parameter m reflects the possible advantage $(m > 1)$ through imitation, or disadvantage $(m < 1)$ through foreclosure of some options of being the follower. If the technical difficulty is unchanged, then $m = 1$. Completion may also be impossible after rival innovation $(m = 0)$ or it may be immediate through costless copying $(m = \infty)$.

The firm's optimization problem involves two steps: (1) to determine what to do if preceded by a rival and to find the maximum profit thereby available and (2) to find the optimal development plan to employ from $t = 0$ until completion or rival appearance, whichever occurs first. The second problem cannot be solved without the answer to the first.

If the firm were to continue development after rival precedence, it would select a revised completion date T_1 and expenditure plan $y(t)$, $v \le t \le T_1$ to

(28)   maximize $\int_v^{T_1} e^{-it}(r_1 - y(t)) \, dt + e^{-iT}P_2$ subject to (27)

The integral contains the reduced profits from the existing product, marketed until the new one is ready, less development expenditures. The second term is the profit from the new product for the firm as follower. If the net benefits of completion are sufficiently large relative to the required effective effort remaining and the difficulty of accumulating it

(29) $(iP_2 - r_1)^{1/2} > i(A - z(v))/m$

then completion has value (see appendix)

(30) $e^{-iv}(P_2 - 2(iP_2 - r_1)^{1/2}(A - z(v))/m + i(A - z(v))^2/m^2)$

(This is the maximum in (28).) Otherwise further development is not worthwhile.

To find the best option, we must compare the maximum return (30) from completing development, together with the condition (29) under which it is available, with the return from the other options. The firm's optimal behavior upon rival entry depends on the extent of profit erosion due to the rival product, rewards available to the firm if it completes development, the remaining effective effort required for completion, and the difficulty of accumulating that effort. If $r_1 > 0$, then the old product is still profitable. The maximum reward available is (30) if (29) is satisfied and is $e^{-iv}r_1/i$ otherwise. If $r_1 \leq 0$, the current product is unprofitable after rival entry so leaving the market is the relevant alternative; the maximum reward available is then (30) if that expression is positive and is zero otherwise.

Substituting the appropriate maximum value in (23) and (24) with our specializations enables us to complete the solution by finding the optimal planned introduction date T_0 and corresponding spending schedule to follow until T_0 or rival precedence.

Case 1: Development ceases upon rival precedence

The firm surely would discontinue an incomplete project upon rival precedence if the reward as follower is no more than the (reduced) profit from the old product, that is, if $p_2 \equiv iP_2 \leq r_1$. This case has already been discussed.

Case 2: Development begun is completed

There are two situations in which development, once undertaken, will be completed regardless of when a rival product appears. The first is that the benefit of being second with a new product exceeds the reward from the old product after rival entry by an amount that is large relative to the effective effort required and the difficulty of achieving it after rival entry:

(31) $p_2 > r_1 \geq 0$ and $(p_2 - r_1)^{1/2} > iA/m$

The second involves temporary losses while a rival has a monopoly in the new product, but the reward to the firm as follower is large relative to the total development effort and its difficulty of accumulation after rival precedence:

$$(32) \qquad r_1 \leq 0 \quad \text{and} \quad (p_2 - r_1)^{1/2} - (-r_1)^{1/2} \geq iA/m$$

If completion after rival entry would be profitable, should development begin prior to that entry? The answer is yes if completion would be expected to raise the profit stream from its current level, that is, if

$$(33) \qquad B_3 \equiv \bar{P} - P_2 + (p_2 - r_0)/(i + h) > 0$$

Note in particular that a firm may optimally try to innovate even if imitation were still more profitable; that is, $B_3 > 0$ and $p_2 > p_0$ are consistent.

Might all development effort be postponed until rival introduction and then be undertaken? For this to happen, completion must be worthwhile so either (31) or (32) must hold. In addition, it must not be worthwhile for development to begin at $t = 0$ so $B_3 \leq 0$ is needed. The expected benefit as follower is large enough to justify the costs of being one. But the expected benefit stream seen at $t = 0$ does not exceed current profits on the firm's existing product. The combined conditions are stringent but might occur.

Analysis of the optimal planned introduction date T_0 in the present case shows (see appendix) that greater rewards for innovation or greater loss due to rival innovation spurs completion. Completion is retarded by a larger profit from the current product and by greater total required effort. Thus both the carrot of rewards for innovation and the stick of loss from failing encourage speedy development. Conversely, high monopoly profits from the current product or a large required development effort postpone the planned introduction date. These findings are the same as those of Case 1 when rival precedence would halt the firm's development efforts.

The firm follows the development schedule from problem (24) until completion or precedence. The spending rate is of a different functional form than in the other cases examined thus far. Rather than being a simple exponential function of time, spending is a function of two different exponential terms. The revised development plan if a rival appears at $v < T_0$ is obtained by putting $z(v)$ from (24),(14) into (28),(27). Development may be either hastened or prolonged by rival entry. If the difficulty of development is unaltered by rival entry ($m = 1$), then development slows upon rival entry if the gain from completion as revised upon rival entry is less than calculated initially. This condition is equivalent to $B_0 > 0$ (with $g = 0$).

As mentioned, either larger rewards for innovation or a larger penalty from rival innovation spurs development. Upon rival introduction, however, only the loss is relevant because the potential reward of being first is no longer available. If it was the anticipation of large profits, the carrot, that spurred development, then its sacrifice upon rival entry retards it to reduce development costs. On the other hand, if it was fear of a large loss in the event of rival entry, the stick, that originally spurred development, then rival precedence hastens it to reduce the duration of losses from the rival's new product monopoly.

Case 3: Early precedence causes the firm to stop development

Whether the firm stops development upon rival precedence may depend on the time at which that precedence occurs. In the present case if it occurs early when relatively little has been achieved (before a critical time v_0), the firm stops development and just continues selling its old good. But if rival entry occurs when the firm has already completed much of its own development work (after the time v_0), the firm revises its development schedule and completes development. This case arises if profits can still be earned on the old product after rival entry ($r_1 \geq 0$) and if the gain from imitation is relatively small so development of the new product would not be initiated without the possibility of innovational rewards ($iA/m > (p_2 - r_1)^{1/2}$). Development begins in this case only if the prospect of innovational rewards B_3 is substantial relative to the effort required for completion.

Rival innovation before the critical time v_0 stops the firm's development. Rival entry after v_0 tends to delay the firm's new product introduction under a wide range of circumstances. Greater innovational rewards mean the firm is more apt to begin development; complete it, given any particular rival entry date; and complete it sooner. Intuitively, higher innovational rewards lead the firm to complete more development by any date. With more development already done, completion is more attractive.

Case 4: Early precedence forces the firm from market

The remaining case is that rival innovation inflicts absolute losses on the firm if it continues selling its old product ($r_1 < 0$). Further, the rewards as follower are insufficient to make development worthwhile on that basis alone (the second part of (32) fails). If the firm stops selling its old product, it must either market a new one or exit. (The possibility of temporarily withdrawing from the market while completing the development falls in Case 3 because then effectively $r_1 = 0$.) The firm will halt development and exit if a rival enters "early" but will continue development and sales (accepting temporary losses) if the rival appears "late."

Impossible imitation and costless imitation

Two extreme cases highlight the role of changed difficulty of product development after rival precedence. First, rival introduction makes completion impossible, $m = 0$. Second, imitation of a rival can be immediate and costless, $m \to \infty$.

If completion is impossible and no profits are available on the old good ($m = 0$ and $r_1 \leq 0$), the firm ceases both development and business upon rival preemption. This fits Case 1. Innovational development will be undertaken only if the excess of expected rewards for innovation over current profits are large relative to the development effort required.

If $m \to \infty$, rival introduction allows instantaneous costless completion. However, if the rewards from being a follower are no more than the rewards on the old good, $p_2 \leq r_1$, then development ceases upon rival entry. Although it would be costless to finish, it would not be worthwhile: The old product yields a higher reward than the new one. Case 1 applies. Note that we get to this same position if it is either impossible to be a follower, as in the preceding paragraph, or merely unprofitable to follow, as in this paragraph.

If it is worthwhile to be a follower when $m \to \infty$, then Case 2 applies. With large rewards for innovation, development will be undertaken immediately even though costless imitation may be possible later. The prospect of being a free rider need not result in indefinite postponement. The firm is more likely to choose innovation instead of costless imitation if the rewards from innovation are high, the rewards from imitation are low (as they may be because all could share them), the status quo profits low, and the required innovational effort is low. Monopoly profits on the current product impose a drag on innovation.

Solutions in all variants of these polar cases have the same structure, whether it is impossible, costless but unprofitable, or both costless and profitable to be a follower. (See appendix equations (A46) to (A48) for the general structure.) The sole difference is the expected net benefit of product development, which accounts for differences in the criteria for undertaking development and in the planned development period.

Summary

Our analysis discloses that the presence of extraordinary profits on the existing product or process retards a firm's development of a new superseding product or process, because the firm sees only the difference between its current profits and profits from the innovation as the reward. The net reward to the firm from innovation, therefore, is smaller when the profit on its current product or process is larger. Thus a firm currently earning zero or just normal profits will develop an innovation more rapidly than a firm earning monopoly profits on its current product or process. This of course all pertains to the case where the innovation is a substitute for the current product or process. Therefore, a newcomer, in the sense of a firm whose products or processes will not be superseded by the innovation, may develop it more rapidly, regardless of the profits it is realizing, than an established firm. In other words, a firm may have a greater incentive to develop innovations for use in other industries or sectors of the economy than in its own. This reinforces the selection of the decision theoretic modeling of innovative activity by indicating why potential innovational rivals may be unidentifiable.

Both the prospect of large rewards from innovation, the carrot, and the fear of large losses from failure to innovate, the stick, speed up development. The latter motive may even cause a firm to develop and introduce a product or process that is less profitable than its present one. A project that might not be undertaken in the absence of rivalry may be undertaken in its presence. On the other hand, rivalry might be so intense that a project will not be undertaken by anyone even if the innovator were to receive patent protection forever.

The firm's optimal introduction date may be premature or belated relative to the social optimum. The date at which development costs just balance expected benefits, the break-even introduction date, is never an optimal choice for the innovating firm, at least in our formulation. It is not optimal in the game theoretic formulation of the next chapter either. Under perfect competition, in which immediate imitation completely erodes the extraordinary profits from innovation, innovation is never optimal for the firm. As the intensity of competition perceived by the firm declines, innovations that promise a modest return will be introduced more rapidly. On the other hand, the speed of introduction of innovations with a large payoff will increase with an increase in the intensity of competition up to a point but then slows down as it continues to increase. The intuitive explanation for this is as follows. Initially, the fear of losing the race spurs additional expenditure on development but as the intensity of competition continues to grow, the firm begins to fear that it will not get the reward from being the first and will also lose the development costs. It then reduces investment in development and thereby postpones the planned introduction date.

The firm is more likely to undertake development of an innovation when development costs are noncontractual than when they are contractual. When costs are noncontractual, the firm risks a smaller loss in case it is not the first to innovate than if costs are contractual. Likewise, the presence of rivalry causes the firm to invest in more modest innovations, from the standpoint of effort required for success, than in its absence. That is, again, the firm seeks to reduce the possible loss if it is not the first to innovate.

The firm will speed up development upon rival precedence if it initially undertook to innovate to defend its current profits, whereas it will slow down if it was motivated by the prospect of large extraordinary profits. In the former case, where the stick is the main motivator, rival precedence makes the fear of losses a reality that can be minimized by rapid completion of the innovation. On the other hand, the rewards from being first are lost by rival precedence and thus once this carrot is gone, the firm slows its development so its costs will be consistent with the more modest reward from imitation.

The necessity to finance development of the innovation from internal sources does not impede the firm's development as long as the expected rewards are not much larger than the profits being earned on the current product. When they are much larger, the firm might want to hasten development to beat rivals and find itself limited by the self-financing requirement. More intense rivalry, and therefore a greater need to develop quickly, may also cause the self-financing condition to become an impediment. Obviously, when the self-financing condition is binding, development takes longer than when it's not binding. The result that the self-financing constraint is not a limiting factor except for innovations whose expected profits are many times larger than current profits may help to explain why the empirical studies reviewed in the last chapter generally find that ability to self-finance does not have a significant impact on the intensity of R&D activity.

Finally, we should comment upon the consequence of allowing for technical uncertainty even though there has been no formal analysis of this situation in the chapter. Technical uncertainty has been omitted because its inclusion would considerably increase the mathematical details without adding much to the substance. The details of the analysis of the firm's behavior in the presence of both market uncertainty and technical uncertainty can be found in Kamien and Schwartz (1974a). It is shown there that the firm's behavior under technical uncertainty is qualitatively similar to behavior with technical certainty, previously discussed. There is, however, one observation from that paper that deserves mention here, which ties in with the analysis of the next chapter.

We can introduce technical uncertainty into the analysis by supposing that the required effective effort for successful completion of the innovation is no longer a known amount A. Instead, we assume that the probability of successful completion at any time is an increasing function of cumulative effective effort at that time $z(t)$. Specifically, define $F(z(t))$ as the probability that the innovation will be successfully completed with effective cumulative effort less than or equal to $z(t)$. Thus $1 - F(z(t))$ is the probability of no success with effort $z(t)$. We can endow this function with the properties $F(0) = 0$, $F'(0) = 0$, $F'(z(t)) \geq 0$, and $\lim_{z(t) \to \infty} F(z) = 1$; the probability of success without any effort is zero, it increases with effort, and success is feasible in the sense that it will occur with a large enough accumulation of effort. [See Kamien and Schwartz (1971) for a discussion of R&D under technical uncertainty.] If there are n firms, each of which is independently seeking to develop the innovation and facing the same probability distribution governing success, then the probability that $n - 1$ will not succeed when each has accumulated $z(t)$, assuming each accumulates at exactly the same rate, is

(34) $1 - \hat{P}(t) = [1 - F(z(t))]^{n-1}$

The probability of one of these $n - 1$ having succeeded by time t is, therefore,

(35) $\hat{P}(t) = 1 - [1 - F(z(t))]^{n-1}$

Differentiating (35) with respect to t yields

$$\hat{P}'(t) = (n - 1)[1 - F(z(t))]^{n-2}F'(z(t))z'(t)$$

Recollection of (34) and some algebra yields

(36) $\hat{P}'(t)/(1 - \hat{P}(t)) = (n - 1)z'(t)F'(z(t))/[1 - F(z(t))]$

Now $h(z(t)) = F'(z(t))/[1 - F(z(t))]$ is the conditional probability density that a firm will succeed in innovating with the next increment to cumulative effort $z'(t)$, given that it has not succeeded with effort $z(t)$. The right side of (36) is the conditional probability density that one of the $n - 1$ firms will succeed in innovating in the next moment, given that none have succeeded to date. We define, therefore,

(37) $\hat{h}(t) = (n - 1)z'(t)h(z(t))$

as the hazard rate faced by the nth firm, where $z(t)$ is the optimal effort function. Of course each of the n firms faces (37). This expression demonstrates how technical uncertainty generates market uncertainty even if rivals are identified and their level of cumulative effort is known. In viewing (37) as the hazard rate faced by each of the n firms, we tacitly assume that the firms are identical and all begin their development efforts at the same time. Equation (37) is an equilibrium condition for solution of the n-firm industry problem, much as appears in Cournot-type analysis.

Apart from linking technical and market uncertainty, (37) provides the basis for game theoretic models, further developed by others, which will be described in the next chapter. The fundamental idea in these models is that each firm takes (37) as given and chooses its optimal increment to its own cumulative effort. The aggregate of these individual decisions determines the expected introduction date of the innovation. In this formulation an increase in the number of rivals heightens the intensity of rivalry.

We are now ready to proceed to the game theoretic formulation of the race to innovate.

Appendix

Speed of development
Combining text equations (8) and (10) gives

(A1) $V(T) = \displaystyle\int_0^T e^{-(i-g)t}[r_0(1 - F(t)) + r_1F(t)]\,dt$

$$+ \int_T^{\infty} e^{-(i-g)t}[p_0(1 - F(t)) + P_1(t - T)F'(t)]\,dt$$

$$+ e^{-(i-g)T} \int_0^T P_2(T - t)F'(t)\,dt - C(T)$$

as the expected net profit to be maximized by choice of development period T^*. If T^* is finite and if $F(t)$ is differentiable, then T^* satisfies

(A2) $\quad V'(T) = e^{-(i-g)T} \times [(r_0 - p_0)(1 - F(T))$

$$+ (P_2(0) - P_1(0))F'(T)$$

$$+ \int_0^T (r_1 - (i - g)P_2(T - t)$$

$$+ P_2'(T - t))F'(t)\,dt]$$

$$- \int_T^{\infty} e^{-(i-g)t}P_1'(t - T)\,F'(t)\,dt - C'(T) = 0$$

(A3) $\quad V''(T) \le 0$

Alternatively, the optimal solution may not be finite; it may be best to forego the project, that is, $T^* \to \infty$. Equation (A2) has been interpreted in the text.

To see how T^* varies with the rewards, we perform a comparative statics analysis of (A2), assuming (A3) holds with strict inequality. Let $M \equiv V'(T^*)$. Then $\partial T^*/\partial b = -(\partial M/\partial b)/(\partial M/\partial T^*)$. Since $\partial M/\partial T < 0$ by (A3), we have sign $\partial T^*/\partial b = $ sign $\partial M/\partial b$ for any parameter b. Bearing in mind this equation, the first, second, and fourth columns of the table readily follow:

b	r_0	r_1	$r_0 - r_1$	p_0	P_1	P_2
$\partial T^*/\partial b$	+	+	−	−	−	?

To see the effect of loss from rival precedence, rewrite the terms in r_0 and r_1 in (A2) as $e^{-(i-g)T}(r_0 - (r_0 - r_1)F_1(T))$. This expression is decreasing in $r_0 - r_1$ (given the initial value r_0), so the third column of the table follows.

To examine the effect of a uniform proportionate shift in the functions P_1 and P_2, replace these functions by m_1P_1 and m_2P_2, respectively, where m_1 and m_2 are parameters. The marginal impact of changing m_i from its initial value of unity is determined in the usual way and recorded in the preceding table in the column for the corresponding P_i.

We examine the effect of increased rivalry upon the speed of development in case the rewards after the follower's appearance are independent of the length of the lag between innovation and imitation and it is better to be followed than to follow: $P_1' = P_2' = 0$ and $P_1 > P_2$. Rewrite (A2) using text equations (4) and (6) as

$$(A4) \quad V'(T) = e^{-(i-g)T}[(r_0 - p_0)e^{-hv(T)}$$

$$+ (r_1 - (i-g)P_2)(1 - e^{-hv(T)})$$

$$+ (P_2 - P_1)hu(T)e^{-hv(T)}] - C'(T) = 0$$

This equation implicitly defines the optimal introduction time T^*. Still calling the left side M, we compute

$$(A5) \quad \partial M/\partial h = \exp(-(i-g)T - hv(T))v(T)[(p_0 - r_0 + r_1$$

$$- (i-g)P_2) + (P_2 - P_1)u(T)(1/v(T) - h)]$$

To sign this expression, we use an indirect argument. Fix all parameters but h and define the function $T^0(h)$ implicitly by

$$(A6) \quad u(T)(1/v(T) - h) = (p_0 - r_0 + r_1 - (i-g)P_2)/(P_1 - P_2)$$

The left side is decreasing in h. It is also decreasing in T so long as $u(T)/v(T)$ is a decreasing function, as it is for the exponential, Weibull, and extreme value distributions. (Recall we assumed that $u(T)$ is nondecreasing.) Let us suppose that $u(T)/v(T)$ is a decreasing function. Then $T^0(h)$ is a decreasing function. For given h, with $T^*(h)$ implicitly defined by (A4), we have $\partial T^*/\partial h \gtrless 0$ as $T^* \gtrless T^0$ in view of (A5), recalling that $\partial M/\partial h$ and $\partial T^*/\partial h$ have the same sign. This means that viewed as functions of h, $T^*(h)$ is falling, stationary, or rising when it lies, respectively, below, on, or above $T^0(h)$. Therefore a stationary point h^* of $T^*(h)$ is a minimum. Hence at most three behavior patterns are possible for $T^*(h)$:

(i) $T^*(h) > T^0(h), \quad h > 0$

(ii) $T^*(h)$ has a stationary point $h^* > 0$ so $T^*(h) \lessgtr T^0(h)$
as $h \lessgtr h^*$

(iii) $T^*(h) < T^0(h), \quad h \geq 0$

In case (i) T^* is an increasing function. In case (ii) T^* is decreasing for small h, attains a minimum at h^*, and is increasing for $h > h^*$. We now show that case (iii) is impossible.

Since $V(T; h)$ is continuous with $V(0; h) < 0$ by assumption, there is a fixed number $T_1 > 0$ such that $V(T; h) < 0$ for $0 \leq T \leq T_1$. The optimal introduction time $T^*(h)$ renders V positive, so $T^*(h) > T_1 > 0$. Hence since $P_1 > P_2$,

$$p_0 - r_0 + r_1 - (i - g)P_2 + (P_2 - P_1)u(T(h))(1/v(T(h)) - h)$$

$$> p_0 - r_0 + r_1 - (i - g)P_2$$

$$+ (P_2 - P_1)u(T_1)(1/v(T_1) - h)$$

Because the right side becomes arbitrarily large as h does, the left side must also become large. Hence the left side becomes positive for sufficiently large h, and so $\partial M/\partial h$ and therefore $\partial T^*(h)/\partial h > 0$ for all sufficiently large h. This eliminates case (iii).

Two cases remain. In case (i) the development period is increasing with the intensity of rivalry, and no rivalry at all ($h = 0$) yields the shortest development period and thereby maximum inventive activity. In case (ii), however, the development period is decreasing with increasing rivalry up to h^*, and then is increasing as rivalry becomes still more intense with values of h greater than h^*. Maximum inventive activity, or minimum development time, occurs at an intermediate degree of rivalry.

In case rivals are thought to alter their development pace after our innovation, in accord with text equation (11), expression for the expected receipts is text equation (12) where

$$(A7) \quad \bar{P} \equiv \int_T^\infty \exp(-(i-g)(t-T))(p_0(1 - F_2(t-T))$$

$$+ P_1(t-T)F_2'(t-T)) \, dt$$

Changing the variable of integration from t to $s = t - T$ produces the equivalent expression of text equation (13).

The marginal revenues foregone by delaying introduction slightly are found on differentiating text equation (12),

$$(A8) \quad W'(T) = e^{-(i-g)T}[(r_0 - (i-g)\bar{P})(1 - F_1(T))$$
$$+ \int_0^T (r_1 - (i-g)P_2(T-t) + P_2'(T-t))F_1'(t)\,dt$$
$$+ (P_2(0) - \bar{P})F_1'(T)]$$

We get the return on the old good rather than the expected receipts on the new one during the delay; the expression depends on whether a rival has entered. If our reward as follower depends on the lag between innovation and imitation, then that reward will be changed (because the lag is lengthened by the delay). Finally, if a rival enters during the delay, the entire innovational reward is replaced by the follower's reward.

The optimal introduction time, if finite, satisfies

$$(A9) \quad W'(T) - C'(T) = 0$$

The response of the introduction time to a change in the rewards is readily found by comparative statics as before, and with the same results:

b	r_0	r_1	$r_0 - r_1$	$\bar{P}$	P_2
$\partial T^*/\partial b$	+	+	−	−	?

To see the effect of an increase in the hazard parameter h, suppose that P_2 is constant. (We need make no special assumptions about $\bar{P}$ or its components.) Substitute from text equations (4) and (6) for $F_1(T)$ and $F_1'(T)$ into (A8) with $P_2' = 0$:

$$(A10) \quad W'(T) = e^{-(i-g)T}[(r_0 - (i-g)\bar{P})e^{-hv(T)}$$
$$+ (r_1 - (i-g)P_2)(1 - e^{-hv(T)})$$
$$+ (P_2 - \bar{P})hu(T)e^{-hv(T)}]$$

Then

$$(A11) \quad \partial W'(T)/\partial h = \exp(-(i-g)T - hv(T))v(T)[(i-g)B_1$$
$$- (r_0 - r_1) + u(T)B_1(h - 1/v(T))]$$

where

(A12) $B_1 \equiv \bar{P} - P_2$

Expression (A11) has the sign of the square-bracketed term. Define the function $T^0(h)$ implicitly by

(A13) $u(T)(1/v(T) - h) = i - g - (r_0 - r_1)/B_1$

We can now complete the argument along the lines used earlier. The left side of (A13) is decreasing in h and in T (so long as $u(T)/v(T)$ is a decreasing function) so that $T^0(h)$ is a decreasing function. For given h, with $T^*(h)$ implicitly defined by (A9), we have $\partial T^*/\partial h \gtreqless 0$ as $T^* \gtreqless T^0$ so that $T^*(h)$ is falling, stationary, or rising when it lies respectively below, on, or above $T^0(h)$. The same three potential behavior patterns are determined and the third is eliminated by an argument analogous to that used earlier. There are just two patterns – either the development period increases with innovational rivalry or it is reduced for modest amounts of rivalry to a minimum and then increases with further rivalry.

To determine the circumstances under which each of these two patterns may prevail, we recall that $T^*(h)$ is a U-shaped function; the minimum occurs for a negative value of h^* in the first case and a positive value of h^* in the second case. Thus we examine the sensitivity of h^* to the rewards. The development period T^* and the value h^* are the simultaneous solution to (A9) and (A13). Assume $W'' - C'' < 0$ and suppose $r_0 = r_1 = r$. Then the total differentials of these two equations have the following sign pattern:

(A9) $(-)dT + (0)dh = (+)d\bar{P} + (-)dr$

(A13) $(-)dT + (-)dh = (0)d\bar{P} + (0)dr$

Applying Cramer's rule, we find that

(A14) $\partial T^*/\partial \bar{P} < 0 \qquad \partial h^*/\partial \bar{P} > 0$

$\partial T^*/\partial r > 0 \qquad \partial h^*/\partial r < 0$

By continuity, (A14) holds for $r_0 - r_1$ small as well as for zero. Thus the larger the expected innovational reward $\bar{P}$ is and the smaller are the receipts r on the old good, the larger h^* will be and the more apt it is to be positive. Thus case (i) with the development period increasing as h increases is most apt to occur for moderately good projects, in terms of the improvement in rewards, whereas case (ii), with an intermediate degree of rivalry providing the most rapid innovation, will hold for projects offering a big increase in rewards. The minimum development period is shortened as innovational rewards are increased.

New product pricing

Because we are considering a new product whose price affects the speed of imitation, we set the returns on the current good to zero: $r_0 = r_1 = 0$. Let the monopoly receipts $p_0(c)$ be a concave function of price c. Assume $P_1' = 0$. The probability distribution of rival imitation F_2 is exponential with parameter k. In fact, let the hazard rate $k(c)$ be a nondecreasing convex function of price c. With these specializations, the firm's problem is to choose a planned introduction time T and a price policy $c(t)$, $t \geq T$ to

(A15) $\quad \max e^{-(i-g)T}[(1 - F_1(T))\bar{P} + \int_0^T P_2(T-t)F_1'(t)\,dt] - C(T)$

We solve the problem stepwise. First, hold the planned introduction time T fixed and find the corresponding optimal price policy. Second, find the optimal introduction time.

The optimal price policy is employed only after innovation. Examining (A15), we see that the optimal price policy $c(t)$ will

(A16) $\quad \max (\bar{P} = \int_0^\infty e^{-(i-g)t}(p_0(c(t))(1 - F_2(t)) + P_1F_2')\,dt)$

$\quad\quad\quad$ subject to $\quad F_2' = k(c(t))(1 - F_2(t))$

(Recall text equations (12), (13), and (1).) Substituting from the constraint into the objective function for F_2' yields an optimal control problem in a single control variable $c(t)$ and a single state variable $F_2(t)$. Let $m(t)$ be the current value multiplier associated with the state variable. Then the current value Hamiltonian at t is

$$H = [p_0(c) + P_1 k(c) + mk(c)](1 - F_2)$$

Necessary conditions for solution, in addition to the constraint, are

(A17) $\quad H_c = [p_0'(c) + (P_1 + m)k'(\text{c})](1 - F_2) = 0$

(A18) $\quad m' = (i - g + k(c))m + p_0(c) + P_1 k(c)$

From (A17) the price that maximizes H satisfies

(A19) $\quad p_0'(c) + (P_1 + m)k'(c) = 0$

Replacing c in H by its maximizing value $c(m)$ determined in (A19) gives the current value Hamiltonian. Because the maximized current value Hamiltonian is linear and hence concave in the state variable F_2, a solution $(c(t), F_2(t), m(t))$ to the necessary conditions is also a solution to the optimization problem. These conditions are satisfied by the constant price c^* and constant multiplier m^* implicitly defined by

(A20) $\quad -m = (p_0(c) + P_1 k(c)) / (i - g + k(c))$

(A21) $\quad p_0'(c) / (p_0(c) - (i - g)P_1) = k'(c) / (i - g + k(c))$

The right side of (A21) is nonnegative by hypothesis and is typically positive. Because the denominator of the left side is to be positive, the numerator is likewise positive, which means that the optimal price is generally such that the current return at t, $p_0(c)$, would increase with a price hike. Therefore the optimal price is less than the monopoly price if rival entry is sensitive to price. The extent of sacrifice of current returns depends on the anticipated responsiveness of potential rivals to the price.

The second part of the problem is to find the optimal introduction time T. But because the optimal price is constant, the optimal value of p_0 and k will also be constant, indicating the timing problem is identical to one already solved and the properties of the solution are unchanged.

The nonrivalrous solution

Setting $r_0 = r_1 = F_1 = F_2 = 0$ in (7) to (9) gives the first-order condition satisfied by the nonrivalrous introduction date T^s:

(A22) $p_0 \exp(-(i-g)T^s) = -C'(T^s)$

The firm's introduction date T^* satisfies $V'(T) = W'(T) - C'(T) = 0$; it may be premature or belated compared with T^s. To see this, evaluate $V'(T)$ at T^s, using (A22) for $C'(T^s)$ and recalling (A8):

$$V'(T^s) = \exp(-(i-g)T^s)\,[(r_0 - (i-g)\bar{P})\,(1 - F_1(T^s))$$
$$+ \int_0^{T^s} (r_1 - (i-g)P_2(T^s - t)$$
$$+ P_2'(T^s - t))F_1'(t)\,dt$$
$$+ (P_2(0) - \bar{P})F_1'(T^s) + p_0]$$

If $V''(T^s) < 0$, then we expect $T^* \gtreqless T^s$, when $V'(T^s) \gtreqless 0$. Since $V'(T^s)$ may have any sign, our demonstration is complete. The firm's introduction may either precede or follow the nonrivalrous date.

Intense rivalry

Barzel's implicit assumptions of winner take all ($F_2 = 0$), no current good ($r_0 = r_1 = 0$), and no diminishing returns to compression of the development period ($C(T) = e^{-iT}C_0$, C_0 constant), lead to the optimal introduction time

$$T^* = (g - h)^{-1}\ln(iC_0(i-g)/(i-g+h)p_0)$$

provided that the hazard rate is less than the growth rate ($h < g$). Otherwise development is not worthwhile.

The zero profit introduction time T^b that Barzel expects to observe (defined by $V(T^b) = 0$) is

(A23) $T^b = g^{-1}\ln((i-g)C_0/p_0)$

Comparing T^* and T^b, with $h < g$, shows that the firm's optimal introduction time under rivalry T^* is always strictly later than the zero profit introduction time T^b. Thus rivalry cannot force a profit-maximizing firm to introduce so early that there are no profits.

Under Barzel's assumptions, the firm's optimal T^* may not even precede the nonrivalrous date T^s. Under his assumptions, (A22) specializes to

$$T^s = g^{-1} \ln(iC_0/p_0)$$

so

$$T^* > T^s \quad \text{if and only if}$$

$$(h/g) \ln(iC_0/p_0) > \ln((i - g + h)/(i - g))$$

Even under these restrictive assumptions, the optimizing introduction time may or may not precede the nonrivalrous introduction time.

Suppose that rivalry becomes very intense. Then the hazard rate exceeds the market growth rate and there is no positive finite optimal introduction time. Introduction is either immediate or postponed forever. If Barzel's introduction time T^b is to be nonnegative, then the argument of the ln function in (A23) must be at least unity: $(i - g)C_0 \geq p_0$. Then, under current assumptions, the expected profit from immediate introduction $V(0) = p_0/(i - g) - C_0$ is not positive; immediate introduction is not profitable. The best choice must then be $T^* \to \infty$; development is postponed forever. Hence if the firm believes that a rival introduction is imminent, or even that the conditional probability h of rival introduction at any time exceeds the rate of growth of the benefits stream, then the firm will not pursue the project at all. Any firm facing this situation that embarks on development (seeking an expected profit maximum) believes that the market growth rate g exceeds the hazard rate h and will choose its development time T^* later than the time T^b suggested by Barzel.

The consequence of perfect competition on the firm's optimal introduction date can also be indicated, dropping the restrictions imposed when considering Barzel's hypothesis. We translate the requirements for perfect competition in our model as: the firm earns no supranormal profits on its current good ($r_0 = r_1 = 0$), it perceives no innovational rivals ($F_1 \equiv 0$), imitation will be immediate ($F_2 \equiv 1$), and the firm reaps a minuscule portion of the benefits of innovation once followers appear ($P_1 \to 0$). Under these circumstances, the first-order condition determining T can be satisfied only if T tends to infinity and innovation is postponed indefinitely.

This is the classic result that under perfect competition, innovation is not worthwhile for the firm.

A particular cost function

The cost function is the minimum value of the discounted expenditure stream

(A24) $\quad \int_0^T e^{-it} y(t) \, dt$

subject to accumulation of the required total effective effort

(A25) $\quad \int_0^T y^a(t) \, dt = A$

Append the constraint to the objective with a constant multiplier λ:

$$\int_0^T (e^{-it} y(t) - \lambda y^a(t)) \, dt$$

Set the derivative under the integral with respect to y equal to zero and solve for

$$y(t) = (a\lambda e^{it})^{1/(1-a)}, \qquad 0 \le t \le T$$

Therefore

(A26) $\quad y(t) = y(T) \exp(i(t - T)/(1-a)), \qquad 0 \le t \le T$

Put (A26) into the constraint, integrate, and rearrange to

(A27) $\quad y(T) = (inA/(1 - e^{-niT}))^{1/a}$

where

(A28) $\quad n \equiv a/(1 - a)$

Combining (A26) and (A27) gives the optimal spending rate

(A29) $\quad y(t) = (inA/(e^{inT} - 1))^{1/a} e^{it/(1-a)}, \qquad 0 \le t \le T$

for any given completion date T. Putting (A29) into (A24) and integrating gives the associated minimum cost of development by date T

(A30) $C(T) = A^{1/a}(in/(e^{inT} - 1))^{1/n}$

Development ceases upon rival entry

Suppose the appearance of a rival before development is complete leads the firm to stop its own development efforts. (The conditions under which this is optimal are described later.) If it continues to sell its old good, the firm will get a stream worth $e^{gt}r_1/(i - g)$ at the moment of rival entry. If $r_1 < 0$, then it is best to leave the market and collect nothing thereafter. Replacing r_1 by zero gives the correct expression in this case. Suppose also that the cash constraint is not tight, so it can be ignored. Then the firm's problem is to select a spending plan $y(t)$ and planned introduction date T to

(A31) $\max \int_0^T e^{-(i-g)t}[r_0(1 - F_1(t)) + (r_1/(i - g))F_1'(t)]\, dt$

$\qquad + e^{-(i-g)T}(1 - F_1(T))\bar{P} - \int_0^T e^{-it}y(t)(1 - F_1(t))\, dt$

$\qquad$ subject to $z'(t) = y^a(t), \qquad z(0) = 0, \qquad z(T) = A$

Because the receipts depend only on T, we solve this problem stepwise, by finding the minimum expected expenditure for completion by any given date T and then finding the optimal date T.

Let the minimum expected expenditure of planned completion at T be $C_N(T)$ (the cost function in the noncontractual case):

(A32) $C_N(T) = \min \int_0^T e^{-it}y(t)(1 - F_1(t))\, dt$

$\qquad$ subject to $z' = y^a, \qquad z(0) = 0, \qquad z(T) = A$

To solve, rewrite F_1 according to text equation (4) $(1 - F_1(t) = e^{-hv(t)})$ and proceed as in the contractual case. Append the constraint to the objective with a constant multiplier

$$\int_0^T (e^{-it-hv(t)}y - \lambda y^a)\, dt$$

Set the derivative with respect to y under the integral equal to zero and solve for

(A33) $\quad y(t) = [a\lambda\exp(it + hv(t))]^{1/(1-a)}, \qquad 0 \le t \le T$

Substitute (A33) into the constraint and solve for the multiplier:

(A34) $\quad (a\lambda)^n = A / \int_0^T \exp(nit + nhv(t))\, dt$

where $n = a/(1 - a)$ as before. One can substitute (A34) for λ into $y(t)$ and then into $C_N(T)$ to find that

(A35) $\quad y(t) = \left[\exp(nit + nhv(t))A / \int_0^T \exp(nit + nhv(t))\, dt\right]^{1/a}$

(A36) $\quad C_N(T) = A^{1/a} / \left[\int_0^T \exp(nit + nhv(t))\, dt\right]^{1/n}$

Note that

(A37) $\quad y'(t)/y(t) = (i + hu(t))/(1 - a)$

An increase in the hazard parameter h raises the growth rate of spending and reduces the expected cost of planned completion by any date T. Of course the larger h is, the earlier is the expected rival entry date, and so the firm is less apt actually to complete the development.

It follows from (A36) that $C_N'(T) < 0$, as desired. However, $C_N''(T) > 0$ only if

(A38) $\quad e^{niT+nhu(T)} / \int_0^T e^{nit+nhv(t)}\, dt > an(i + hu(T))$

This inequality is always satisfied for the exponential case ($u = 1$, $v = t$). We have been unable to determine what distributions, if any, fail to satisfy this condition.

It remains to find the optimal planned completion date T^*. Rewriting F_1 in terms of the hazard function and combining (A31), (A32), and (A36), we find that T^* maximizes

(A39) $\quad V(T) = \int_0^T \exp(-(i-g)t - hv(t))(r_0 + r_1 hu(t)/(i-g))\, dt$
$$+ \exp(-(i-g)T - hv(T))\bar{P}$$

$$- A^{1/a} / \left[\int_0^T \exp(nit + nhv(t)) \, dt \right]^{1/n}$$

Compute

(A40) $\quad V'(T) = \exp(-(i-g)T - hv(T)) \left[(r_0 + r_1 hu(T)/(i-g)) \right.$

$$- (i-g+hu(T))\bar{P} \right] + A^{1/a} \exp(niT + nhv(T))$$

$$/n \left[\int_0^T \exp(nit + nhv(t)) \, dt \right]^{1/a} = 0$$

which implicitly gives T^* (if there is a finite optimal introduction date). This may be rearranged to

$$[(i - g + hu(T))\bar{P} - r_0 - hu(T)r_1/(i-g)]n/A^{1/a}$$

$$= e^{-gT} \left[\exp(niT + nhv(T)) / \int_0^T \exp(nit + nhv(t)) \, dt \right]^{1/a}$$

in which the left side is a benefit/cost ratio. In addition, T^* must satisfy

(A41) $\quad V''(T) \leq 0$

If (A41) holds with strict inequality, it readily follows from comparative statics applied to (A40) that

b	r_0	r_1	$\bar{P}$	A
$\partial T^*/\partial b$	+	+	−	+

Thus as in the case of contractual R&D, larger innovational rewards accelerate development, whereas larger returns on the current product retard development. In addition, the greater the required development effort A is, the longer development will take.

To examine the circumstances under which development will be worthwhile and to see the effects of rivalry upon speed of development, we specialize the model by assuming that F_1 is exponential, that is, $u(t) = 1$, $v(t) = t$. Then (A39) is equivalent to (i.e., differs from (A42) by an additive constant)

(A42) $\quad \max_T \exp(-(i - g + h)T)B_2$

$$- A^{1/a}((i + h)n/(\exp((i + h)nT) - 1))^{1/n}$$

where

(A43) $B_2 \equiv \bar{P} - (r_0 - r_1)/(i - g + h) - r_1(i - g)$

Expression (A43) reflects the net advantage of innovation. The first derivative (A40) specializes to

(A44) $e^{gT}(1 - \exp(-(i + h)nT))^{1/a}$

$$= (A(i + h))^{1/a}n^{1/n}/(i - g + h)B_2$$

The second-order condition (A41) requires

(A45) $(i + h)/(1 - a) + g(\exp(n(i + h)T) - 1) \geq 0$

It is worth noting that if an expected reward of B (whatever the composition of B) can be collected upon completion of R&D and if development is worthwhile, then the optimal development period is given implicitly by (A44) on replacing B_2 by B. In particular, if $g = 0$, we can solve explicitly: T satisfies

(A46) $\exp(-(i + h)nT) = 1 - A((i + h)n)^{1-a}/B^a$

provided that

(A47) $n(i + h)A^{1/(1-a)} < B^n$

If (A47) fails, then development should not be undertaken. (When $g = 0$, (A45) is satisfied.) If (A47) holds, then the maximum value in (A42) with $g = 0$ is positive and equal to

(A48) $B^a - A(n(i + h)^{1-a})^{1/a}$

Returning to our main argument, conditions (A44) to (A45) invite comparison with text conditions (19) to (20) that hold in case the development is contractual and $r_1 = (i - g)P_2$ so that the firm is indifferent about whether it follows a rival's innovation or continues selling its old good. Note that if the firm would get the same profit after rival precedence whether or not it replaces its old product with a new one ($r_1 = (i - g)P_2$), then B_2 is proportional to B_0.

We show how the firm's choice of development period depends on the degree of innovative rivalry in the present case. It simplifies matters and suffices to take the special case of a stationary market environment $g = 0$. Further, suppose that rival entry does not alter the return from the current good: $r_0 = r_1 = r$. Then specializing (A44), the firm's planned introduction date T satisfies

(A49) $1 - \exp(-(i + h)nT) = w$

where

(A50) $w = A(i + h)^{1-a}n^{1-a}/[\bar{P} - r/i]^a$

Differentiating (A49) gives

(A51) $(i + h)^2n\exp(-(i + h)nT)\partial T/\partial h = (1 - a)w$

$$+ (1 - w)\ln(1 - w) \equiv f(w)$$

Thus $\partial T/\partial h$ has the sign of $f(w)$, where $f(w)$ is defined by the right-hand equation in (A51). From (A49) $0 < w < 1$ for any project undertaken. Calculate

$$f'(w) = -a - \ln(1 - a), \quad \lim_{w \to 0} f(w) = 0$$

$$f''(w) = 1/(1 - w) > 0, \quad \lim_{w \to 1} f(w) = 1 - a$$

(L'Hôpital's rule was used to find the limit as $w \to 1$.) These calculations show that f is a convex function, negative for values of w near zero, decreasing to a negative minimum at $w = 1 - e^{-a}$, and then rising toward $1 - a$ as $w \to 1$. Therefore $f(w) = 0$ has exactly one solution w^* between 0 and 1. For $w < w^*$, $f(w) < 0$; for $w > w^*$, $f(w) > 0$. From the definition of w, w and h are positively related. Let h^* be the unique value of h corresponding to w^*. Then our results can be stated equivalently as: for $h < h^*$, $\partial T/\partial h < 0$ and for $h > h^*$, $\partial T/\partial h > 0$. This means that T is a U-shaped function of h, attaining a minimum at $h = h^*$.

The minimizing h^* might be negative. If it is, then the firm's choice of development period increases with the degree of innovative rivalry for all $h \geq 0$. In this case the assurance of monopoly ($h = 0$) results in the minimum development period. On the other hand, a positive h^* corresponds to an innovation-maximizing degree of rivalry that is intermediate.

Two related questions remain. (1) Under what conditions is the innovation-maximizing degree of rivalry positive? (2) If positive, how does that degree of rivalry vary with the data? From (A50) with w held fixed at w^*, it is clear that h^* varies inversely with A and r and directly with $\bar{P}$. Thus the more attractive the project is, the larger the innovation-maximizing degree of rivalry and the more apt it is to be positive.

Under what conditions will development be undertaken? It is apparent that the expected net gain from innovation over staying with the current good must be positive; $B_2 > 0$ is a necessary condition. This follows because the left side of (A44) grows without bound in this case. If the market is stationary ($g = 0$) or declining ($g < 0$), there will be a solution only if the net benefit B_2 is sufficiently large relative to the effective effort required A. In particular, in case $g = 0$, development is optimally undertaken in those cases that (A47) is satisfied because the left side of (A44) has least upper bound with respect to T of 1 in that case. If $g < 0$, then the left side of (A44) is single peaked with respect to T, attaining a maximum value of less than one. This means that there is no solution to (A44) when $g < 0$ unless the right side is also less than this maximum. The condition for undertaking the project is then more stringent than (A47) and is increasingly stringent as g falls.

A range of innovations
Suppose that the value of the expected benefit stream to be received from the innovation is an increasing concave function of the amount of effective effort devoted to it. We suppose innovative rivalry can be described by an exponential probability function, use the same development function, and assume the market growth rate $g = 0$. Then we seek the innovation size A and introduction date T to

$$(A52) \quad \max \exp(-(i + h)T)sP(A)$$

$$- A^{1/a}((i + h)n/(\exp(n(i + h)T) - 1))^{1/n}$$

where $P' > 0$, $P'' < 0$, and s is a multiplicative shift parameter, reflecting the profitability of the class of potential inventions. It could, for instance, reflect the life of the patent to be awarded.

Set the first derivatives of (A52) with respect to T and A equal to zero. These two equations can be shown to be equivalent to the pair

$$aAP'(A)/P(A) + \exp(-n(i+h)T) = 1$$

$$(as)^n P'^{1/(1-a)}(1-a)/(i+h)P = 1$$

Differentiating this system totally gives

$$a(d(AP'/P)/dA)\,dA - n(i+h)\exp(-n(i+h)T)\,dT$$

$$= nT\exp(-n(i+h)T)\,dh$$

$$(P''/(1-a)P' - P'/P)\,dA = dh/(i+h) - nds/s$$

Solving this pair of linear equations, we find that

$$\partial A/\partial h < 0 \quad \text{and} \quad \partial A/\partial s > 0$$

The greater the intensity of innovational rivalry is, the smaller is the project attempted. The greater the rewards are (e.g., the longer the patent), the larger is the project.

Self-financing

We reconsider problem (A31) in which development ceases upon rival entry and assume there is a liquidity condition, as text constraint (25):

$$(A53) \quad \max \int_0^T \exp(-(i-g)t - hv(T))(r_0 + hu(t)r_1/(i-g))\,dt$$

$$+ \exp(-(i-g)T - hv(T))\bar{P}$$

$$- \int_0^T \exp(-it - hv(t))y(t)\,dt$$

subject to

$$x' = ix - e^{gt}r_0 - y, \quad x(0) = x_0, \quad x(T) \geq 0,$$

$$z' = y^a, \quad z(0) = 0, \quad z(T) = A$$

We require the cash balance to be nonnegative at T. This assures that the cash balance is nonnegative throughout because, as we shall see, if the balance were to become zero or negative, it could not rise later. The cash inflow grows no faster than rate g, whereas the outflow will be seen to grow faster than $i/(1-a) > g$. Thus for this problem the terminal nonnegativity restriction on the cash balance assures nonnegativity over the development period.

Let $\lambda_1(t)$ and $\lambda_2(t)$ be the multipliers associated with the cash equation and the development function, respectively. Then the Hamiltonian for (A53) can be written as

$$H = \exp(-it - hv(t))y(t) + \lambda_1(t)(ix(t)$$
$$+ e^{gt}r_0 - y(t)) + \lambda(t)y^a(t)$$

Necessary conditions for solution are that $x(t)$, $y(t)$, $z(t)$, $\lambda_1(t)$, and $\lambda_2(t)$ obey the constraints of (A53) and also that

(A54) $H_y = -\exp(-it - hv(t)) - \lambda_1 + a\lambda_2 y^{a-1} = 0$

(A55) $\lambda_1'(t) = -i\lambda_1(t), \quad \lambda_1(T) \geq 0, \quad \lambda_1(T)x(T) = 0$

(A56) $\lambda_2'(t) = 0$

(A57) $\lambda_1(T)(e^{gT}r_0 - y(T))$
$$+ \lambda_2 y^a(T) - \exp(-iT - hv(T))y(T)$$
$$= \exp(-(i-g)T - hv(T))$$
$$\times [(i - g + hu(T))\bar{P} - r_0 - hu(T)r_1/(i-g)]$$

where (A57) is the transversality condition for optimal choice of T.

If the cash constraint is never binding, then $\lambda_1(t) = 0$, $0 \leq t \leq T$. Setting $\lambda_1 = 0$ and using (A54) to eliminate λ_2 from the transversality condition (A57) gives

(A58) $y(T) = ne^{gT}[(i - g + hu(T))\bar{P} - r_0 - hu(T)r_1/(i-g)]$

if cash is not tight. The spending rate at terminal time will not exceed the contemporaneous revenue rate, provided that $y(T) \leq e^{gT} r_0$, that is,

(A59) $(i - g + hu(T)) \bar{P} \leq r_0/a + hu(T) r_1/(i - g)$

If spending can be financed out of current receipts at terminal time T, then it can be through the development period (because spending grows faster than receipts do). Therefore (A59) is a sufficient condition for the self-financing constraint to be nonbinding.

Condition (A59) is more apt to be satisfied when receipts from the current good are larger, expected rewards from the contemplated good are smaller and the intensity of innovational rivalry and parameter a are smaller. Thus self-financing is most readily achieved for products that are modest improvements, for situations where the threat of rival innovation is slight, and in cases where there are sharply diminishing returns to time compression of the development.

Cash needs of a newcomer. The amount of cash a newcomer needs to develop a new product at the optimal pace is most readily determined in the case of a stationary environment, $g = 0$, in which rival entry is thought to be governed by an exponential distribution ($u(t) = 1$). Needed cash is

(A60) $Y \equiv \int_0^T e^{-it} y(t)\, dt$

where, from (A54) and (A58), with $\lambda_1 = 0$, $g = 0$, $r_0 = r_1 = 0$, $u = 1$,

(A61) $y(t) = n(i + h) \bar{P} \exp[((i + h)/(1 - a))(t - T)]$

and the development period T satisfies

(A62) $e^{-(i+h)nT} = 1 - A(i + h)^{1-a} n^{1-a} / \bar{P}^a \equiv b < 1$

(This can also be obtained from (A46).) Substituting (A61) into (A60) and then using (A62) gives

$$\int_0^T e^{-it} y(t)\, dt$$
$$= (a(i+h)\bar{P}/(h+ai))(e^{-iT} - \exp(-(i+h)T/(1-a)))$$

Hence

(A63) $Y = (a(i+h)\bar{P}/(h+ai))(b^{i/(i+h)n} - b^{1/a})$

To show this needed cash increases with innovational rewards $\bar{P}$, we compute

$$\partial Y/\partial \bar{P} > 0$$

On the other hand, an increase in the required effective effort A may either increase or decrease cash required since

$$\partial Y/\partial A = ((i+h)\bar{P}/(h+ai))$$

$$\times [(i(1-a)/(i+h))b^{i/(i+h)n} - b^{1/a}](\partial b/\partial A)/b$$

Because $\partial b/\partial A < 0$, the sign of $\partial Y/\partial A$ is opposite to the sign of the square-bracketed term. Manipulation of that term reveals that $\partial Y/\partial A$ is positive when A is small and is negative when A is large relative to $\bar{P}$. Thus for a project with a relatively large benefit/cost, additional required effort increases the cash needed. But an increase in the effort required for a mediocre project prolongs the desired development period and reduces the total cash required for development at the optimal pace.

Tight cash. Now suppose the financing constraint is tight. Then $\lambda_1(t) = \lambda_1^0 e^{-it} > 0$ from (A55). Differentiating (A54), using (A55) to (A56) gives

$$(1-a)y'/y = i + hu(T)/(1 + e^{hv(T)}\lambda_1^0)$$

so that

(A64) $i/(1-a) \le y'/y \le (i + hu(T))/(1-a)$

The proportionate rate of spending growth is positive and bounded between the rates observed under contractual and noncontractual

R&D programs without a cash constraint. If there is no innovational rivalry, then $y'/y = i/(1 - a)$ as in the earlier cases and the proportionate spending rate is unaffected by the financing requirement. Then the effect of the constraint is to reduce the spending path proportionately throughout and to extend its duration so that financing is possible.

Finally, note that because the spending rate always grows at least as fast as $i/(1 - a)$, which exceeds the growth rate g of revenues, our earlier assertion about the cash balance is supported. It will be nonnegative throughout if it is nonnegative at completion time. Further, the balance will never be zero prior to completion time.

If the budget constraint is tight, completion time is determined as follows. Integrating the cash balance equation with $x(T) = 0$ gives

(A65) $$\int_0^T e^{-it} y(t)\, dt = x_0 + (1 - e^{-(i-g)T}) r_0 / (i - g)$$

The present value of the spending stream just equals the initial cash plus the present value of receipts over the development period. In addition, from the development function

(A66) $$\int_0^T y^a(t)\, dt = A$$

where, from (A54) and (A55),

(A67) $$y(t) = (a\lambda_2 e^{it} / (\lambda_1^0 + e^{-hv(t)}))^{1/(1-a)}$$

With $y(t)$ given by (A67), equations (A65), (A66), and (A57) determine λ_1^0, λ_2, and T. It is possible, though tedious, to perform a comparative statics analysis upon these three equations to determine the response of the optimal development period to a change in the data. It is easier to study the special case $h = 0$.

If $h = 0$ (but not otherwise), (A67) implies that

$$y(t) = \exp(i(t - T)/(1 - a)) y(T)$$

Putting this expression into (A66) gives

$$y^a(T) = inA/(1 - e^{-inT})$$

Then substituting into (A65) gives, after further manipulation,

(A68) $(in)^{1/n}A^{1/a}/(e^{inT}-1)^{1/n} = x_0 + (1-e^{-(i-g)T})r_0/(i-g)$

This implicitly defines the optimal introduction time T in the case of limited cash but no innovational rivalry. Implicit differentiation of (A68) shows that

$$\partial T/\partial x_0 < 0, \quad \partial T/\partial r_0 < 0, \quad \partial T/\partial A > 0$$

Innovation is hastened by a larger initial cash balance or larger cash flow from the current good and is retarded by a larger required total development effort when cash is tight. In the special case of no innovational rivalry the rewards from innovation have no impact on the speed of development, and the impact of the receipts from sale of the current good is solely as a means of financing. Analysis of (A65), (A66), and (A57) with h positive but small and $u(t) = 1$ shows that an increase in the innovational rewards will hasten development.

Tight cash, no rivalry. We show that a firm facing no innovational rivalry in a stationary environment will undertake an R&D project provided that

(A69) $B^a > A(in)^{1-a}$

where

(A70) $B \equiv \bar{P} - r_0/i$

Note that this assertion is not qualified with respect to whether the cash constraint is tight.

The firm will have adequate financing to develop at the unconstrained optimal pace, completing at T satisfying (from (A46) with $h = 0$)

(A71) $e^{-inT} = 1 - A(in)^{1-a}/B^a = b$

in case $b > 0$ (equivalent to (A69)) and in case needed cash does not exceed cash availability:

(A72) $Y = B(b^{1/n} - b^{1/a}) \le x_0 + (1 - b^{1/n})r_0/i$

(Use (A63) with $\bar{P}$ replaced by B and with $h = 0$ to get the left side of (A72). The right side is the cash availability $x_0 + (1 - e^{-(i-g)T})r_0/(i - g)$, with T replaced by its optimal value from (A71).) It can be verified that $b > 0$ is a sufficient condition for development to be worthwhile if the liquidity condition is not tight, because then the maximum value of the objective function is positive. (Put $h = 0$ in (A46) to (A48).) But it is less readily apparent that this is so if the development pace is retarded by a cash limitation. We provide the needed demonstration.

Suppose $g = 0$ and $h = 0$ and that the cash constraint is tight, so that (A72) does not hold. The project will be worthwhile if the value of the innovational reward upon completion exceeds the original cash plus all earnings from the current good. (These earnings are fully used for development until T under present hypotheses and disappear after T.) Thus development is worthwhile only if

(A73) $\bar{P}e^{-iT} > x_0 + r_0/i$

Because cash is tight, the optimal introduction time T^* satisfies (from (A68))

(A74) $f(T) \equiv x_0 + (1 - e^{-iT})r_0/i - (in)^{1/n}A^{1/a}/(e^{inT} - 1)^{1/n} = 0$

Note that $f(T)$ is an increasing function that is negative for T near zero and positive for T large.

Define T^0 by

(A75) $\exp(-iT^0) = (x_0 + r_0/i)/\bar{P}$

Then if $\exp(-iT^*) > \exp(-iT^0) = (x_0 + r_0/i)\bar{P}$, T^* will satisfy (A73) and the project will be worthwhile. We shall show that $T^* < T^0$, so these inequalities will be satisfied, by showing that $f(T^0) > f(T^*) = 0$.

Substituting from (A75) for T^0 into (A74) and manipulating the resulting expression, we can show that $f(T^0) > 0$ in those circumstances where

(A76) $1 - (1 - b)^{1/(1-a)} > (x_0 + r_0/i)^n/\bar{P}^n$

But because cash is tight, (A72) fails. It follows (after some manipulation) that if $b > 0$,

(A77) $\quad (x_0 + r_0/i)^n/\bar{P}^n < b[1 - b((\bar{P} - r_0/i)/\bar{P})]^n$

$$< b < 1 - (1 - b)^{1/(1-a)}$$

The first inequality follows from failure of (A76). The second follows because the coefficient of the leading b is less than one. The last inequality is due to the identity

$$1 - (1 - b)^{1/(1-a)} - b = (1 - b)(1 - (1 - b)^n) > 0$$

Therefore if $b > 0$ and cash is tight (so (A76) fails), then (A77) holds; (A77) implies (A76) holds, which in turn means that $f(T^0) > 0$ so $T^0 > T^*$ so (A73) holds. This implies that the project is worth developing despite the cash constraint. This completes the demonstration that $b > 0$ or, equivalently, (A69) is the condition for a project to be profitable in case $h = g = 0$.

Rival precedence need not halt R&D

If a rival appears at time t when effective development effort is $z(t) < A$, the firm may complete development according to an altered schedule. If it finishes at T_1, its profits from t forward will be (from text equation (28))

(A78) $\quad (1 - \exp(-i(T_1 - t)))r_1/i + \exp(-i(T_1 - t))P_2$

$$- (A - z(t))/m)^2 i/(\exp(i(T_1 - t)) - 1)$$

where the first two terms are the values of pre- and postintroduction receipts and the third term is the minimum cost of completion by T_1. Evidently, completion can be worthwhile only if it raises receipts: $p_2 \equiv iP_2 > r_1$. The cost was obtained from (A30), putting $a = 1/2$, $n = 1$, remaining effective effort equivalent to $(A - z(t))/m$, and completion period $T_1 - t$.

Set the derivative of (A78) equal to zero and rearrange to

(A79) $\quad 1 - \exp(-i(T_1 - v)) = i(A - z(t))/m(p_2 - r_1)^{1/2}$

which implicitly gives the optimal completion time T_1, if it exists. The right side of (A79) must be less than unity for completion to be worthwhile. If

(A80) $i(A - z(t))/m \geq (p_2 - r_1)^{1/2}$

the firm should abandon its development efforts upon rival precedence. Its maximum return from t forward will then be the larger of zero (if it leaves) and r_1/i (if it continues selling the old good).

If (A80) does not hold, then completion may be worthwhile and (A79) gives the optimal time span within which to do it. Substituting from (A79) into (A78) gives the maximum profit available from completion after rival precedence at t:

(A81) $P_2 - 2(p_2 - r_1)^{1/2}(A - z(t))/m + i(A - z(t))^2/m^2$

Viewed as a function of $z(t)$, (A81) has a minimum value of r_1/i. Thus if $r_1 > 0$, completion is worthwhile because it gives a larger net return than is available by stopping. But if rival precedence inflicts absolute losses, $r_1 < 0$, then when will the maximum profit from completion (A81) be positive? Analysis of the quadratic (A81) shows it will be positive in case $r_1 < 0$ whenever

(A82) $A - m((p_2 - r_1)^{1/2} - (-r_1)^{1/2})/i < z(t)$

Therefore the maximum profit available upon rival entry at $t < T_0$ is

(A83) $G(t, x(t), z(t)) = \begin{cases} r_1/i & \text{if } r_1 > 0 \text{ and (A80) holds} \\ \text{expression (A81)} & \text{if either} \\ \quad \text{(i) } r_1 > 0 \text{ and (A80) fails or} \\ \quad \text{(ii) } r_1 \leq 0 \text{ and (A82) holds} \\ 0 & \text{if } r_1 \leq 0 \text{ and (A82) fails} \end{cases}$

Note that G does not depend on t or x under our assumptions; it is a function of z alone. (If cash were tight or if $g \neq 0$, then x or t, respectively, would be nontrivial arguments of G.)

The firm's problem at time $t = 0$ is to find an original completion date T_0 and spending plan $y(t)$, $0 \leq t \leq T_0$ to follow until completion or rival precedence (whichever occurs first) that will maximize

(A84) $\int_0^{T_0} \exp(-(i+h)t)\,(hG(z(t)) - y(t))\,dt$

$+ \exp(-(i+h)T_0)\,(\bar{P} - r_0/(i+h))$

subject to

(A85) $z' = y^{1/2}, \quad z(0) = 0, \quad z(T_0) = A$

Using the constraint to eliminate y from the objective yields a free time, fixed end-point calculus of variations problem in z. The Euler equation is

(A86) $z''(t) - (i+h)z'(t) + hG'(z(t))/2 = 0$

and the transversality condition is

(A87) $hG(z(T_0)) + (z'(T_0))^2 + r_0 = (i+h)\bar{P}$

Case 1. In this situation $r_1 \geq p_2$ so the reward as follower is no more than is available from the old good. Development always stops upon rival precedence. This case has been adequately discussed. See especially (A46) to (A48).

Case 2. Development, once begun, will be completed regardless of when a rival appears if either

(A88) $p_2 > r_1 \geq 0 \quad$ and $\quad (p_2 - r_1)^{1/2} > iA/m$

or

(A89) $r_1 \leq 0 \quad$ and $\quad (p_2 - r_1)^{1/2} - (-r_1)^{1/2} \geq iA/m$

Suppose one of these two situations obtains, so the conditions of line 2 of (A83) are met. Substituting from (A81) into (A86) and (A87) gives, respectively,

(A90) $z'' - (i+h)z' + ihz/m^2 = (A - (p_2 - r_1)^{1/2}m/i)ih/m^2$

and

(A91) $(z'(T_0))^2 = (i+h)B_3$

where

(A92) $B_3 \equiv \bar{P} - P_2 + (p_2 - r_0)/(i + h)$

The solution of (A90) is

(A93) $z(t) = c_1 \exp(q_1 t) + c_2 \exp(q_2 t) + A - m(p_2 - r_1)^{1/2}/i$

where

(A94) $q_1, q_2 = i + h \pm ((i + h)^2 - 4ih/m^2)^{1/2}/2$

and where c_1 and c_2 are constants of integration. We assume $m > 2(ih)^{1/2}/(i + h)$ so the roots (A94) are real and distinct. Then $q_1 > q_2 \geq 0$.

The boundary conditions $z(0) = 0$ and $z(T_0) = A$ together with the transversality condition (A91) form a system of three equations to be solved for the constants of integration c_1 and c_2 and the completion date T_0:

$$c_1 + c_2 = m(p_2 - r_1)^{1/2}/i - A$$

(A95) $c_1 \exp(q_1 T) + c_2 \exp(q_2 T) = m(p_2 - r_1)^{1/2}/i$

$$c_1 q_1 \exp(q_1 T) + c_2 q_2 \exp(q_2 T) = (i + h)^{1/2} B_3^{1/2}$$

Solve the first two equations for c_1 and c_2 in terms of T. Substitute the result into the third and rearrange to

(A96) $f(T) \equiv a_2 \exp(-q_1 T) - a_1 \exp(-q_2 T)$

$$= (q_1 - q_2)(1 - iA/m(p_2 - r_1)^{1/2})$$

where $f(T)$ is defined as the expression on the left and

(A97) $a_j \equiv (i/m)((i + h)B_3/(p_2 - r_1))^{1/2} - q_j, \qquad j = 1, 2$

Then

$$\lim_{T \to \infty} f(T) = a_2 - a_1 = q_1 - q_2$$

$$> (q_1 - q_2)(1 - iA/m(p_2 - r_1)^{1/2})$$

$$> 0 = \lim_{T \to \infty} f(T)$$

Because $f(T)$ takes values both larger and smaller than the right side of (A96), there is a T that solves (A96). Uniqueness can be established as follows. If $a_1 \leq 0$, then $f(T)$ descends monotonically for all $T > 0$. On the other hand, if $a_1 > 0$, then $f(T)$ falls to a negative minimum and then rises toward zero with increasing T. In either case $F(T)$ is monotone when positive so (A96) has a unique solution T_0, the optimal planned introduction time in Case 2. Comparative statics analysis of this equation indicates how T_0 varies with the parameters of the problem.

To find the revised completion date in the event of rival appearance at some time v, substitute from (A93) for $z(v)$ into (A79), giving

$$(\text{A98}) \quad e^{-iL} = (1 - w)\exp(-q_1 D) + w\exp(-q_2 D)$$

where

$$D \equiv T_0 - v \quad \text{and} \quad L \equiv T_1 - v$$

and

$$(\text{A99}) \quad w \equiv (1 - iA/m(p_2 - r_1))^{1/2}$$

$$- \exp(-q_1 T_0))/(\exp(-q_2 T_0) - \exp(-q_1 T_0))$$

Note that the relation between the remaining time to completion D following the original plan and the remaining time to completion L according to the revised plan does not depend on the particular date of rival entry v.

Because the transversality condition (A91) can be written as

$$(\text{A100}) \quad (1 - w)q_1 + wq_2 = (i/m)((i + h)B_3/(p_2 - r_1))^{1/2}$$

the impact of rival introduction upon the firm's development schedule can be examined by combining (A98) and (A100), equating expressions for w from each:

$$w = [q_1 - (i/m)((i + h)B_3/(p_2 - r_1))^{1/2}]/(q_1 - q_2)$$

$$= (e^{-iL} - \exp(-q_1 D))/(\exp(-q_2 D) - \exp(-q_1 D))$$

Because the denominators are positive, the numerators' signs agree. Similarly, equating expressions for $1 - w$

$$\text{sign}[q_j/i - ((i+h)B_3/m^2(p_2-r_1))^{1/2}] = \text{sign}(q_j/i - L/D)$$

$$j = 1, 2$$

If $m = 1$, then either $q_1 = i$ or $q_2 = i$ so $L - D$ and $T_1 - T_0$ and $B_3 - (p_2 - r_1)/(i+h) = B_0$ all have the same sign. Development slackens upon rival entry in this case if $B_0 > 0$ but accelerates if $B_0 < 0$.

Case 3: Stop development upon early precedence. Suppose $r_1 \geq 0$ and $iA/m > (p_2 - r_1)^{1/2}$ so there will be profits on the old good after rival precedence and the advantage of being a follower is so small that the firm would not attempt development without the possibility of innovational rewards. Let v_0 be the latest date at which the firm would stop development upon rival entry. Then, from (A80)

(A101) $\quad z(v_0) = A - m(p_2 - r_1)^{1/2}/i$

For $0 \leq t < v_0$, $G(z(t)) = r_1/i$. Solving the Euler equation (A86) with $G = r_1/i$ and with boundary conditions $z(0) = 0$ and (A101) gives

(A102) $\quad z(t) = (A - m(p_2 - r_1)^{1/2}/i)(e^{(i+h)t} - 1)$

$$/(\exp((i+h)v_0) - 1), \qquad 0 \leq t \leq v_0$$

The solution to (A90) with end points (A101) and $z(T_0) = A$ is

(A103) $\quad z(t) = [\exp(q_1(t-v_0)) - \exp(q_2(t-v_0))]m(p_2-r_1)^{1/2}$

$$/i(\exp(q_1 S) - \exp(q_2 S))$$

$$+ A - m(p_2 - r_1)^{1/2}/i, \quad v_0 \leq t \leq T_0$$

where

$$S \equiv T_0 - v_0 = (q_1 - q_2)^{-1}\ln(a_2/a_1)$$

(on using the transversality condition), provided that

(A104) $\quad a_1 > 0$

and where a_1 and a_2 are as defined in (A97). If $a_1 \leq 0$, development is not undertaken. Continuity of z' at v_0 gives us

(A105) $\quad v_0 = -(i+h)^{-1}\ln(1-(i+h)(iA/m(p_2-r_1)^{1/2}-1)$

$$\times (a_2{}^{q_2}/a_1{}^{q_1})^{1/(q_1-q_2)})$$

from which it is clear that $v_0 > 0$ if and only if

(A106) $\quad (a_1{}^{q_1}/a_2{}^{q_2})^{1/(q_1-q_2)} > (i+h)(iA/m(p_2-r_1)^{1/2}-1)$

Thus if (A104) and (A106) both hold, development is undertaken and effective effort is accumulated according to (A102) and (A103). Otherwise development is not begun. The optimal development period $T_0 = v_0 + S$; parametric analysis of v_0, S, and T_0 can be performed.

Rival innovation before the critical time v_0 stops the firm's development. If a rival appears at some t, $v_0 \le t \le T_0$, the revised development plan is found on substituting from (A102) into (A79)

$$\exp(-i(T_1 - v)) = [\exp(q_1(v - v_0))$$

$$- \exp(q_2(v-v_0))]$$

$$/[\exp(q_1 S) - \exp(q_2 S)]$$

This equation can be rearranged to

$$\exp((q_1 - q_2)S) - 1 = (\exp(-q_2 D) - \exp(-q_1 D))$$

$$/(\exp(-q_1 D) - e^{-iL}) > 0$$

where

$$D = T_0 - v \quad \text{and} \quad L = T_1 - v$$

since $q_1 > q_2$, the left side and the numerator of the right side are each positive and so the denominator on the right must be positive also. This implies that

$$L/D = (T_1 - v)/(T_0 - v) > q_1/i$$

But from (A94), $q_1 \ge i$ if either $m \ge 1$ or $h > i$ or in other circumstances. Thus rival entry is apt to (but need not) delay the firm's new product introduction.

In Case 4 early rival entry forces the firm from the market, whereas the firm will complete its development if the rival appears late. Because the results of Case 4 are similar to those of Case 3, they are omitted.

5

Modern theories of market structure and innovation: the game theoretic approach

At the end of the last chapter we indicated how the decision theoretic formulation of the race to innovate can be used as the basis for the game theoretic formulation. The essential linkage is through technical uncertainty in the innovation process, which generates market uncertainty; without technical uncertainty, the game theoretic formulation suggests either no innovation or at most one innovator. This somewhat surprising result was independently recognized by Dasgupta and Stiglitz (1980b) and by Reinganum (1979). It is established through the following reasoning.

In the absence of technical uncertainty, each participant in the race knows exactly how much must be spent to develop the innovation in any specific length of time. Moreover, in the game theoretic formulation it is assumed that each firm knows how much each of its rivals intends to spend. The firm assumes that this amount is invariant to its own spending decision. Thus in order to win the race, it must spend slightly more than any of its rivals. If, as is commonly assumed in this formulation, the firms are identical, each would choose this strategy and the development period would be contracted to the point at which the cost of innovation to each firm just equals the reward. At this point each firm assures itself of tying for first. Because, however, the reward from the innovation is fixed or at least does not grow in proportion to the number of firms introducing it, each can realize only a fraction of the reward. Thus each firm would realize a net loss at this point, incurring costs equal to the total reward and receiving only a fraction of it. Now implicit in the game theoretic formulation is the assumption that all these calculations are carried out before any actual commitment of money. Thus none will choose to innovate.

Among the participants there may be a particularly clever one who realizes that all the others will have gone through these calculations and decided not to innovate and that therefore he will. Of course there can be only one such clever person, for if there are more, then we are back to the original situation, and no innovation takes place. But the presence of this one clever participant violates the assumption that the firms in the race are identical. Thus in the game theoretic formulation without technical uncertainty, we can have at most one innovator and that one must have some advantage over the other potential innovators. That advantage need not be simply that he is more clever. The innovator may enjoy a cost advantage in developing the innovation, be more foresighted and have recognized the merits of the innovation sooner and had a head start, or have financial or other resources not available to others.

Thus the game theoretic model under technical certainty is limited to explaining instances where there is only one innovator or when no innovation takes place even though it would appear to be attractive from the vantage point of a nonparticipant. The presence of technical uncertainty alone, however, is not enough to assure that a game theoretic formulation can explain several firms simultaneously seeking to innovate. As Dasgupta and Stiglitz (1980b) have observed, it is also necessary that the development activities of each of the firms be uncorrelated. That is, there are several paths to successful development of the innovation. If this is not true then each firm, by spending enough, can virtually assure itself a tie for being first and we are back to the situation in the absence of technical uncertainty. The key assumption needed for the game theoretic formulation to describe the race to innovate with several active participants is that no one can be assured of being first or at least tying for first. In order for this to hold, it is sufficient that there be more than one way of developing the innovation, with none of these alternatives assuring successful development by any specific date. Hence the models of this chapter all contain the assumption that there is technical uncertainty in development.

The game theoretic formulation that we shall describe is a generalized composite of the models developed by Loury (1979), Lee and Wilde (1980), Kami (1979), Kelley (1979), and Dasgupta and Stiglitz (1980b). We shall also describe a differential game formulation of market structure and innovation developed by Reinganum (1979). Olivera's (1973) analysis focuses on how to allocate the resources devoted to inventive activity so as to achieve the highest probability of success under decreasing, constant, or increasing returns to scale in the development process. He indicates that an allocation of resources resulting from the independent profit-maximizing behavior of individual firms need not yield an efficient allocation of resources. He does not, however, specify the nature of interaction among competitors.

Loury, Kami, Kelley, and Dasgupta and Stiglitz, assumed that development costs are contractual. That is, the same amount is spent whether or not the firm wins the race. In this situation development costs can be viewed as fixed costs. The merit or realism of this assumption has been discussed before. Lee and Wilde replace this assumption with the supposition that development costs are incurred through time, until the firm or a rival succeeds. As will be seen, this reverses some of the conclusions reached under the contractual development cost assumption.

All these formulations are essentially static in the sense that the firm chooses the amount it will spend on developing the innovation at the outset. In other words, the firm chooses a number. In Reinganum's formulation, on the other hand, the firm chooses how much to spend at each instant of time until successful development by it or a rival. Thus the firm chooses an entire expenditure path or function through time. In this sense Reinganum's formulation is dynamic.

Let us discuss the static model first. The assumptions are laid out, with the probability density of completion of the development at any time (given noncompletion to date) increasing with both time and the level of expenditure on development. There are two versions of the model, depending on whether the costs are taken to be contractual and fixed or noncontractual and stoppable upon innovation by a rival. A reward is received only by the innovator. The expected value of that reward is assumed known, although its exact value and pattern of receipt need not be known. The way that technical uncertainty in the development process leads to uncertainty about the entry time of rivals is displayed. Socially optimal levels of development spending are derived and shown to differ, depending on which of the two hypotheses about costs is adopted. The market solution also depends on that hypothesis but it is not efficient or socially optimal in either case. The amount of rivalry is endogenous and sensitive to the model employed. Finally, Reinganum's dynamic approach and her conclusions are reviewed.

Costs and the speed of development

Technical uncertainty can be represented by the assumption that devoting more resources to the development of an innovation increases the probability of completion by any given date (but does not assure it). For the static game theoretic formulation to be described here, it is simply assumed that the firm decides on the total level or rate of spending on development. This decision is made with no provision for revision later. The scenario conjured up is that the firm is confronted by a menu of probability distributions over the length of time until successful completion. The distributions with earlier expected completion times cost more than those with later ones. The contractual cost assumption is supposed to describe the real world situation in which development involves predominantly fixed costs.

The firm is to decide which of these distributions to buy in order to maximize its expected net profit. Assumptions regarding economies or diseconomies of scale are incorporated through specifying the cost of the distributions. Thus if there are economies of scale, by spending twice as much the firm can buy a probability distribution with expected completion time less than one-half as long.

Formally, in the contractual cost model, the probability that the innovation will be successfully developed on or before time t is given by

(1) $\qquad F(t;x) = 1 - e^{-h(x)v(t)}$

where x is the lump-sum amount of money invested in development and h and v are given functions to be characterized later. Specifically,

(2) $\qquad v(t) = \int_0^T u(s)\,ds$

where $u(s)$ is a given nondecreasing function. Equation (1) yields the exponential distribution used by Loury (1979), Dasgupta and Stiglitz (1980b), and others in case $u(t) = 1$ so $v(t) = t$.

The probability $F(t; x)$ is viewed as a function of t, with the spending level a parameter of the distribution. With this distribution, the expected development time is (see appendix)

(3) $\qquad E(t) = \int_0^\infty e^{-h(x)v(s)}\,ds$

(For the exponential case $E(t) = 1/h(x)$.)

The instantaneous conditional probability density that the innovation will be completed at t, given that it has not been completed by time t is

(4) $\qquad F'(t;x)/(1 - F(t;x)) = h(x)u(t)$

($F'(t; x)$ is the derivative of F with respect to t; the parameter x is held fixed.) This is analogous to the hazard rate in Chapter 4, except for the new appearance of the parameter x. Since $u(t)$ is a nondecreasing function, the conditional completion density stays constant or grows through time for any given resource investment x.

The more that is spent, the greater will be the conditional probability density of completion by any given time t; that is,

(5) $\qquad dh/dx = h'(x) > 0$

This implies that a greater expenditure will bring about an earlier expected completion date. In addition, we suppose that innovation is impossible without some investment of money:

(6) $h(0) = 0$

This is a "no free lunch" assumption; indicating that the firm has no prior experience or know-how that yields this innovation as a *costless* by-product. It also means that the firm cannot achieve the innovation by simply imitating others at no cost.

We assume further that the ability to foreshorten the expected completion time through more spending is limited, specifically, that

(7) $\lim_{x \to \infty} h'(x) = 0$

The impact of additional expenditures on shortening the expected development period eventually shrinks to zero. Finally, we suppose that there may be increasing returns to investment initially, but that as more money is added, returns to scale are eventually decreasing:

(8) $h'' \gtreqless 0$ as $x \lesseqgtr \bar{x}$

Decreasing returns to scale throughout the entire range is represented by $\bar{x} = 0$.

Thus far development costs have been assumed contractual, with the actual cost being x. If development costs are not contractual, however, then the firm can cease development after rival precedence and avoid incurring further cost. Hence the actual cost will be uncertain, depending on when the innovation appears.

Lee and Wilde assumed development costs are noncontractual. A fixed cost G is incurred as well as a fixed rate of spending q until the race to innovate has been won. Thus the firm spends a total amount with discounted value

$$G + \int_0^t e^{-is} q \, ds$$

if it or some rival innovates at time t. Of course t is unknown at the outset so the actual amount to be spent is likewise unknown.

The probability of successful completion on or before time t is assumed to be a function of the current flow cost. That is, $h(x)$ is replaced by $h(q)$ in (1) to (8). (Although we use h in both cases and make the same qualitative assumptions about it, the specific functions may differ in two cases.) Lee and Wilde (1980) studied the special exponential case ($u = 1$ so $v = t$). An interpretation of this formulation is that after the participant pays an entry fee of G to get into the race, he searches for a successful way of effecting the innovation. The magnitude of the search is determined by the level of q through $h(q)$.

Rewards

In the game theoretic formulations, the winner of the race to innovate receives the entire reward. The reward stream has expected capital value P at the moment of innovation. It may consist of a stream that is finite lived, as due to a patent of finite duration, or infinite lived. The stream may be constant or nonconstant through time; it is typically thought to rise for a time and then decline. What is important is the magnitude of the capital value P. Of course the value of the innovation P may not be known with certainty. Because the participants are risk-neutral and try to maximize the expected profits, it suffices to regard P as the expected reward for innovation, which is received only if the firm wins the race.

It is assumed further that there are no rewards from imitation. Each participant in the race is assumed to be a newcomer in the sense of having no currently profitable product that would be supplanted by the innovation. Presumably, these assumptions could be weakened along the lines followed in the preceding chapter but that has not been done.

Technical and market uncertainty

We indicated at the end of Chapter 4, expressions (34), (35), and (36), how technical uncertainty generates market uncertainty for a general class of probability distributions over the successful completion time. We shall, for notational convenience, assume that the analysis is being conducted from the perspective of the nth firm. Under the supposition that the efforts of all the firms are statistically independent, the probability that none of the other participants in the race succeed on or before time t is

$$(9) \qquad \prod_{1}^{n-1} [1 - F(t; x_j)] = \exp\left(- \sum_{1}^{n-1} h(x_j) v(t) \right)$$

where $F(t; x_j)$ reminds us that the probability that the jth participant will succeed on or before time t depends on its lump-sum investment x_j. The probability that one of its $n - 1$ rivals succeeds on or before time t, therefore, is

$$(10) \qquad 1 - \prod_{1}^{n-1} [(1 - F(t; x_j)] = 1 - \exp\left(- \sum_{1}^{n-1} h(x_j) v(t) \right)$$

If, as is commonly assumed in this formulation, the participants are identical, then each invests exactly the same amount, $x_j = x$ for all j, and (10) simplifies to

$$1 - (1 - F(t; x))^{n-1} = 1 - e^{-(n-1)h(x)v(t)}$$

The preceding expressions pertain to the behavior of a firm's $n - 1$ rivals. Analogous expressions pertaining to the behavior of all n firms are readily obtained by replacing $n - 1$ with n. For instance, the probability that the race is won by time t is, from (10) (replacing $n - 1$ by n),

$$1 - \exp\left(- \sum_{1}^{n} h(x_j) v(t) \right)$$

The corresponding probability density function associated with the race being won at t is the derivative with respect to t, namely,

$$(11) \qquad \sum_{1}^{n} h(x_j) u(t) \exp\left(- \sum_{1}^{n} h(x_j) v(t) \right)$$

The nth firm faces an instantaneous conditional probability density that one of its $n - 1$ rivals will successfully introduce the innovation momentarily, given that none has been introduced to date equal to

$$(12) \qquad \sum_{1}^{n-1} h(x_j) u(t)$$

The expected rival introduction time t as perceived by the nth firm is

$$(13) \qquad E(t) = \int_0^\infty \exp\left(- \sum_1^{n-1} h(x_j) v(t) \right) dt$$

Equations (12) and (13) express the nth firm's and by symmetry all the participants' perception of the intensity of rivalry it faces in the race to innovate. (Expression (12) is the counterpart of expression (3) in the last chapter describing the decision theoretic formulation. In that formulation, however, neither the number of rivals nor the amount each spent entered explicitly into the firm's perception of the intensity of rivalry.) Rivalry becomes more intense either because the number of rivals increases, or each rival spends more, or some combination of changes leading to an increase in the sum in (12). Thus even if each firm spent less as the number of firms increased, the aggregate effect might be to increase the intensity of rivalry. In terms of expression (13), more intense rivalry means that the expected rival introduction time decreases. Indeed, it is this result that supports identifying the magnitude of instantaneous conditional probability of rival introduction with the intensity of rivalry.

Associating the intensity of rivalry with the number of rivals in the race to innovate is very appealing because it coincides with the common assumption that numbers and competition are related, especially in a Cournot model. Whereas each rival takes the production level of each rival as given in the usual Cournot model, here each participant in the race takes the level of the others' expenditure as fixed. Moreover, he takes the number of rivals as fixed. In other words, each rival takes the hazard rate (12) as given and chooses his own level of expenditure on that assumption. The level of expenditure he chooses, he believes, will not cause the others to revise their choices. (This resembles the decision theoretic assumption.) Formally, this means that his conjectural variation $\partial x_j / \partial x_n = 0$ for all $j = 1, \ldots, n - 1$. This of course is the analog of the standard Cournot assumption.

The probability that the nth firm will win the race depends on how much it and each rival invests in development of the innovation. In order for the nth firm to win the race, it must succeed in completing the innovation while its rivals have not. Winning the race can occur at any time. It is verified in the appendix that if all n firms choose the same spending level x, then the probability that the nth firm (or any other specific firm) wins is just $1/n$; all have an equal chance to win.

Efficiency

Before going on to society's and to the firm's optimization problems, we address the question of the efficient allocation of resources to inventive activity in the preceding framework. That is, how many parallel projects should be conducted and how much should be spent on each to minimize the expected completion date, given a fixed amount of money to be spent on invention? The answers depend critically on the assumed properties of the function $h(x)$ and whether costs are contractual or noncontractual. We consider each case in turn.

Because the projects are symmetric, all funded projects may be of the same size. For a given total budget we seek the number of projects to make the expected development period as short as possible, that is, to minimize the expected development period. For the contractual cost situation the answer depends on the properties of the development function $h(x)$. (See appendix.) If there are diseconomies of scale in development throughout the entire range, then there should of course be a very large number of very small projects. Likewise, if there are economies of scale throughout, then it is best to allot the entire budget to a single project.

Finally, and typically (as we shall assume), development may be characterized by economies of scale, followed by eventual diseconomies of scale for large scale. Then (see appendix) the optimal size of project is x_0, where x_0 is defined by

(14) $h(x_0)/x_0 = h'(x_0)$ where $x = X/n$

$h''(x) \leq 0$

Note that the optimal project size depends *only* on the function $h(x)$. Under hypothesis (8) with $\bar{x}$ positive and finite, x_0 is uniquely determined by (14) and $h''(x_0) < 0$. For the optimally sized project the average contribution per dollar to the conditional completion probability density is maximized. With $x = x_0$, then $n = X/x_0$. A constant proportionate shift in the efficacy of R&D (realized by replacing $h(x)$ by $mh(x)$ where $m > 1$) will *not* affect the optimal scale of project.

Turning to the noncontractual cost case, we again seek the efficient number of projects and optimal level at which to fund them. That is, we seek the number and size of projects to minimize the expected development period for a given expenditure. (Recall the actual expenditure required for completion is unknown because spending continues until completion.) We find (see appendix) that the optimal project size q is characterized by

(15) $h(q) > qh'(q)$

This q necessarily exceeds q_0, where q_0 satisfies $h(q_0) = q_0 h(q_0)$. The exact value of q depends on properties of the function h, as well as on all the parameters. There will be a finite number of projects even if there are decreasing returns throughout, because the positive fixed cost G makes an indefinitely large number of projects unattractive. If there are increasing returns to scale throughout, it is optimal to have just one project.

In both the contractual and noncontractual formulations, it is tacitly assumed that development proceeds by running parallel independent projects. This derives from the behavioral assumption that each firm conducts its own development effort in isolation. The firm learns nothing about the efficacy of others' efforts nor does it reveal its experience to others. Thus in order to compare the resource allocation to innovation under the assumption of independent, expected profit-maximizing rivals with no spillover effects, with the efficient allocation of resources chosen by a social planner, one must restrict the latter to parallel projects. In reality of course neither the planner nor the firm, for that matter, need be restricted to parallel efforts. The most efficient development of the innovation might be through a sequential development strategy. One might begin with several parallel efforts that are narrowed down as it is learned which are the most promising. An elegant characterization of the optimal sequential search strategy for development of an innovation is presented by Weitzman (1979).

Social optimality

We have analyzed the efficient allocation of resources with a given expected budget. The next question is what size budget maximizes social welfare. The simple answer is the size at which the social benefit of marginally reducing the expected completion time equals the marginal social cost. The social cost of a marginal dollar in the research budget is the sacrificed social benefit attainable by devoting it to its next best use. This is the "simple answer," because it is difficult for several reasons to specify the social benefit from an innovation in practice.

First, the magnitude of the benefit of an innovation is uncertain. This is especially true for an entirely new product – one for which there are no close substitutes. (Television replaced radio as a source of home entertainment and was also supposed to be a substitute for movies. Yet it has attributes possessed by neither radio nor movies nor any combination of the two.) It is difficult both to assess the demand curve for a nonexistent product and to gauge the value of an entirely new product without knowing the demand for it.

Second, the value of an innovation often depends on the development of a complementary innovation. (The commercialization of lasers has been spurred by advances in computer technology.) Because the feasibility of the complementary innovation may not be known, it is difficult to assess the value of the original innovation. Moreover, if the innovations simultaneously benefit from each other's occurrence, it becomes hard to separate the benefits derived from each alone.

Third, it is difficult to determine the value of the innovation through time. The innovation may be supplanted by another at some unknown future date. On the other hand, it may lead to other innovations and they to others, indefinitely. (This is a theme of von Weizacker's (1979) theory of technical advance.) All these difficulties arise from uncertainties and therefore are beyond those posed only by problems of measurement.

Thus identification of the social benefit from a major innovation requires some very heroic assumptions. The simple assumption employed in these formulations is that the innovation gives rise to a benefit stream with expected discounted value of P^*. This benefit is taken to exceed the private benefit P. It often includes the consumers' surplus generated by the innovation. Further, the social benefit stream from the innovation exceeds its private stream in duration because its social benefit extends beyond the life of the patent. Indeed, that is one of the reasons for granting patents. The duration of the benefits of the innovation depends in part on how soon it is superseded. But note also that the superseding innovation may have been made possible by the original one.

The socially optimal number of projects and amount of money to devote to each will maximize the expected social benefit (taking into account the uncertainty in amount and the uncertainty in time of completion of development) less the cost of the parallel development efforts. We find in the contractual cost case (see appendix) that the efficiency condition is of course satisfied: $x = x_0$. Thus the optimum scale of project depends *only* on the development function $h(x)$, as expected from our study of efficient solutions. The optimal number of projects does depend on the other parameters. The gross benefit P^* must be sufficiently large to warrant undertaking development; this is made precise in the appendix (equation (A10)) for the exponential case. The larger the benefit P^* is, the larger is the optimal number of projects and the sooner is the expected completion. A uniform proportionate upward shift in the efficacy of development expenditures may raise or reduce the optimal number of projects, although it leaves the optimal scale per project unchanged. (See appendix.)

The socially optimal number and size of projects in the case that expenditures are noncontractual likewise satisfies the corresponding efficiency condition, with $q > q_0$. For further study of this case we have specialized the model to the exponential case in the appendix. We find that development will be worthwhile if the second-order conditions for a maximum are satisfied; this amounts to a condition that h be sufficiently concave (roughly). It can be shown (see appendix) that an increase in the fixed charge G causes the optimal number of projects to fall (so fewer fixed charges are incurred) and raises the spending rate on each project. An increase in the benefit P^* raises the optimal rate of spending per project but need *not* raise the optimal number of projects. Nonetheless, expected expenditure will rise and the expected completion time will fall with an increase in the benefit. A constant proportionate increase in the efficacy of R&D spending (an upward shift in the function h) will raise the optimal rate of spending per project. Finally, it is shown in the appendix that for the exponential case there is no solution unless the fixed cost G is strictly positive.

The market solution

Having described the technology of innovation, its rewards, the efficient allocation of resources for its development, and the socially optimal level of resources to be devoted to it, we turn to the analysis of how the market will allocate resources to this activity. The market setting, it will be recalled, is characterized by n independent participants in the race to innovate. The winner of the race receives the entire reward and the losers get nothing. We ask: Will the market allocate resources to development of the innovation efficiently? Will the total amount of resources that are devoted be socially optimal? How does the number of participants in the race depend on the characteristics of the development process and of the innovation? Recall that in the game theoretic formulation each participant in the race regards the level of investment by others in innovation as fixed and unresponsive to his decision about how much to invest.

Before proceeding further there is a conceptual issue to be faced. Shall we restrict each participant to a single project or allow each to conduct several parallel projects? The prevailing convention has been to restrict each firm to a single project except when analyzing the polar case of only one participant, a monopolist. The monopolist may run several parallel projects. Thus the monopolist's behavior is similar to that of a social planner in deciding how many parallel projects to run and at what intensity. He will, as would the social planner, make an efficient allocation of any fixed level of total resources.

The monopolist, however, chooses to spend less on development than would a social planner because his reward from innovation is smaller than the total social benefit. This is true for two reasons. First, the monopolist receives a reward stream only over the finite duration of the patent, whereas the benefits to society may continue into the indefinite future. However, even if the patent's life were infinite, the reward to the monopolist would be lower than to society as a whole. This brings us to the second reason, namely, the monopolist's inability to capture the entire consumers' surplus associated with the innovation. The monopolist's reward from innovation would coincide with society's only if the patent were of infinite duration *and* he had the power to discriminate perfectly.

A word of caution – the reward to the monopolist discussed here is the net reward after all income transfers have been taken into account. It does not include the gross benefits to the innovator that derive from, say, supplanting an existing product of others. A monopolist may of course reckon the entire profit gained from capturing the market of an existing product as the reward to innovation rather than just the net addition to profits. Under these circumstances, possibly the monopolist will regard the reward to an innovation larger than society's and devote more resources to its development than socially desirable.

Keeping in mind the definition of the reward to innovation by the monopolist, one can easily see that because its value to him is less than its social value, he will choose fewer parallel projects than society would if costs are contractual. This conclusion need not follow in case costs are noncontractual, however.

The other polar case is perfect competition, by which we mean that there is immediate imitation of any innovation. In the framework of this formulation, perfect competition corresponds to a patent life of zero duration, so there is no reward from innovation. It follows that under perfect competition there would be no innovation. Thus, under monopoly, innovation occurs but at a slower pace than is socially optimal, whereas under perfect competition there is none at all. This of course leads to consideration of the trade-off between perfect competition and its static efficiency properties and monopoly, which lacks static efficiency but allows for innovation.

The next question is whether we must sacrifice competition altogether in order to have innovation. In particular, must monopoly prevail both before and after the innovation or might we do better by permitting competition in the development of the innovation? Schumpeter (1975), as indicated in Chapter 2, appeared to believe that the best arrangement is competition in the development of the innovation with some monopoly profits to the winner of the race. The prospect of realizing monopoly profits would provide the incentive for innovation and innovative competition would hasten it.

We turn therefore to the case where there is a patent or other means for allowing the winner of the race to realize monopoly profits. Each firm runs just one development effort. We study the investment that maximizes its expected profit less cost. If the total number of participants in the race were an exogenous parameter, then the firm's expenditure level can be shown to fall in response to an increase in the number of rivals (see appendix). Increased rivalry, in this sense, implies a reduced incentive to innovate because the expected reward declines while the cost does not. This observation was first made by Loury (1979) for the special case of an exponential distribution over completion times.

For the market solution it is supposed that participants join or leave the race until the expected net profit to each participant is zero. Analysis of the resulting conditions that determine x and n (namely, the expected profit be maximal and equal to zero) indicates that if the development process exhibits increasing returns to scale at the outset, eventually followed by decreasing returns to additional investment, then the value x of resources devoted to innovation by each firm will be *less* than the efficient amount x_0, for any distribution function F. The amount chosen increases with the prospective reward, although it always stays below x_0. It is, however, unchanged by a proportionate increase in the efficiency of R&D spending. (See appendix.)

Since $x = X/n,$ it follows that there would be too many parallel efforts compared to the efficient number for any *given* level of total expenditure X. In other words, the efficient solution calls for fewer firms, each making a larger investment in development, ceteris paribus, than obtains under the market solution. This result is reminiscent of Chamberlain's (1933) conclusion that in a market with differentiated products, free entry results in too many firms with suboptimal plants. More recently, this situation has been analogized with the overexploitation of a common property resource through independent individual action. This does *not* mean that there is overinvestment in development of the innovation under *perfect* competition; our discussion pertains to free entry during the development stage with patent protection after development. Of course the level of expenditure that is socially optimal generally differs from the expenditure chosen by the expected profit maximizers collectively, so the applicability of the preceding ceteris paribus argument is quite limited.

The extent of rivalry in the free market setting described here is endogenous. It can be shown in the exponential case (see appendix) to increase with the rewards available. An increase in the benefits will thereby (since both x and n increase) raise total R&D spending and reduce the expected time to innovation. A uniform improvement in the efficiency of R&D will increase the number of rivals.

If decreasing returns in the development process prevail throughout, the zero profit condition can be satisfied only by $x = 0$, which means that $n \to \infty$. Thus in this case the market solution and the efficient solution coincide, with an indefinitely large number of participants in the race, each spending a very small amount. If there are increasing returns in the development process throughout, however, the efficient solution and the market solution need not coincide, with possibly too many firms, each investing too little compared with the efficient solution.

We turn now to the market solution in the noncontractual cost case. Again, each firm has just one development project and selects the rate of spending on it to maximize the expected net benefit. Each assumes its rivals' spending rates are constant and unaffected by its own choice. If the number of participants n is an exogenous parameter, then the firm's spending rate q *increases* with n as long as expected profits are positive and the probability distribution over completion times is exponential (see appendix). This result of Lee and Wilde (1980) is opposite to that obtained for the contractual cost case. Greater rivalry stimulates R&D in this noncontractual situation because expected costs as well as expected benefits decline with n, and because the latter is assumed to exceed the former.

As in the contractual cost case, in the market solution it is assumed that participants join or leave until the expected net profit of each is zero. The two conditions that firms choose q to maximize their net profits, and that these net profits will be zero, determine n and q. It turns out (see appendix) that the firm's choice of q exceeds q_0. In the efficient solution, q also exceeds q_0. It has not been possible to compare the social and market values of q, other than to note that these values both exceed q_0.

As in the contractual cost case, there is no solution unless the entry fee G is positive (see appendix).

The size of the project chosen by the expected profit-maximizing firm can be shown (see appendix) to increase with the prospective reward. It also increases with a rise in the efficiency of R&D. These directions of effect are the same as in the socially optimal solution. However, an increase in the fixed cost G will *reduce* the spending rate of the expected profit maximizer, even though the efficient, socially optimal solution calls for an increase.

The extent of rivalry – the number n of participants in the race – is endogenous and may generally increase or decrease in response to a change in any of the parameters. In particular, an increase in the prospective reward P need *not* call forth more participants. However, it can be shown that an increase in P will lead to a greater total expected spending by the participants collectively and to earlier expected innovation.

Summary

Two related static game theoretic models of the race to innovate have been studied in this chapter. They are generalizations of models proposed and developed recently by Loury, Lee and

Wilde, Kami, Kelley, and Dasgupta and Stiglitz. In one the cost of innovating is a single lump-sum fee subject to choice and paid at the outset. The conditional probability density of completion at any time rises and the expected completion period shrinks as the amount paid increases. In the second there is a fixed entry fee that must be positive for any solution to exist. In addition, a flow cost is paid until the race is won. The expected completion is hastened by a larger rate of spending.

If each firm selects its R&D spending to maximize its expected net profit and if the number of participants is exogenous, then the effect of increased rivalry upon spending depends on whether costs are contractual or noncontractual. In the former case increased rivalry reduces the desired spending rate, whereas in the latter case it raises the spending rate.

The socially optimal solution and the market solution, in which entry of rivals occurs until the expected profit of each is zero, have been described. If there are economies of scale in the development process for all scales, the efficient solution calls for no more than one project or participant. It is possible that the market solution will call forth more than one, however. On the other hand, if there are diseconomies in development at all scales, then the efficient solution calls for an indefinitely large number of minuscule projects if costs are entirely contractual and the market solution will have this property. But in the model with a fixed entry fee and noncontractual costs thereafter, there should be only a finite number of projects. The market solution likewise gives a finite number, usually different from the socially optimal one.

Typically, there are increasing returns to scale for small efforts, followed eventually be decreasing returns. This case received the bulk of our attention. The solution is always in the region of decreasing returns. For the case of a single lump-sum development cost the socially optimal expenditure x_0 maximizes $h(x)/x$ and the free market generates projects of suboptimal size $x < x_0$. In the model with an entry fee and noncontractual development costs thereafter both the socially optimal and free market rates of spending per project exceed the rate q_0 that maximizes $h(q)/q$ (Table 1).

Table 1.

	Project size	
	Socially optimal solution	Market solution
Contractual – lump-sum pay	$x = x_0^a$	$x < x_0^a$
Noncontractual – flow pay until innovation	$q > q_0^a$ where x_0 and q_0 satisfy $h(x) = xh'(x)$	$q > q_0^b$

[a]Verified for general distribution function F.
[b]Verified for exponential distribution function.

We find that in each case an increase in the reward for innovation will raise the total expected expenditure of the participants collectively and hasten the expected appearance of the innovation. We also find that, for both models, the market solution differs both quantitatively and qualitatively from the socially optimal solution. These latter findings are summarized in Table 2, which shows the direction of change of the project size and the number of projects or rivals with respect to a change in each of the parameters.

In the contractual model the efficient project size depends only on the characteristics of the R&D process and not on the rewards or the discount rate. The market solution is sensitive to these parameters but always generates projects that are smaller than the efficient size. In both the socially optimal solution and the market solution, an increase in the reward will raise the number of projects or participants.

In the model with R&D costs incurred only until the moment of innovation the efficient project size depends on all the parameters. The direction of sensitivity of the market solution is generally the same, except that an increase in the entry fee G leads to fewer, larger projects in the socially optimal solution, while it causes the market participants to reduce the size of their projects. The number of projects or rivals may either increase or decrease in response to

Table 2. *Direction of impact of parametric change upon endogenous variables*

	Socially optimal solution		Market solution	
	Project size x or q	Number of projects n	Project size x or q	Number of rivals n
Contractual — lump-sum payment				
Reward P^* or P	0^a	$+\,^a$	$+\,^b$	$+\,^b$
R&D efficiency m	0^a	$?\,^a$	0^b	$+\,^b$
Noncontractual — flow payment until innovation				
Reward P^* or P	$+\,^b$	$?\,^b$	$+\,^b$	$?\,^b$
R&D efficiency m	$+\,^b$	$?\,^b$	$+\,^b$	$?\,^b$
Entry fee G	$+\,^b$	$-\,^b$	$-\,^b$	$?\,^b$

[a]General distribution function.　　[b]Exponential distribution function.

changes in other parameters for both solutions. In particular, an increase in the reward for innovation need not lead to more participants in this model. Thus the effect of changes in the innovational development function or in the innovational rewards upon the number of rivals depends crucially upon the assumption about the nature of costs!

The contractual cost and noncontractual cost models are not strictly comparable. For example, it does not appear possible to say whether a participant spends more on development in the contractual case than in the noncontractual case. In the contractual case the probability density of developing the innovation at any given date depends on a single lump-sum investment. In the noncontractual case, on the other hand, the probability of success depends on the rate of investment at each point in time and is completely independent of the fixed cost incurred. This indicates the sensitivity of the conclusions about the efficacy of the market mechanism in eliciting innovation to the details of modeling. In those situations where commitments must be made in advance in the development of an innovation, the contractual formulation may be more appropriate; otherwise the noncontractual formulation would be better. An obvious generalization of these two formulations is one in which the probability of successful development depends on both fixed costs and variable costs.

A shortcoming of both the contractual formulation and the noncontractual one previously noted is the assumption that the participant chooses how much to invest or the single investment rate in development once and for all. That is, these are static models. In fact, of course it is more realistic to suppose that each participant in the race can adjust the investment level through time. Another shortcoming of these formulations is the absence of any learning in the development process. In the contractual version the probability of success by any date depends on the level of investment at the outset, thereby precluding any possibility of learning. In the noncontractual formulation the probability of success by any given date depends on the current level of spending. Past expenditures in this formulation have no effect on the current probability of success. Both these deficiencies are remedied in Reinganum's (1979) formulation.

A dynamic approach

In Reinganum's formulation the probability of successful completion of the innovation by any given date is a function of the accumulated effective effort by that time. This assumption and its implications are discussed in connection with expressions (34) to (37) of the last chapter. The probability of successful completion on or before time t is assumed to be exponential,

(16) $F(z) = 1 - e^{-kz(t)}$

where $z(t)$ denotes total accumulated effort by time t. Effort is assumed to accumulate directly with the amount of knowledge acquired per unit time, $y(t)$:

(17) $dz/dt = z'(t) = y(t), \qquad z(0) = 0$

and the increment to knowledge at any time is assumed to be bounded. Because effective effort is accumulated through time, the firm can determine the probability of successful completion by any date through its choice of the pace of accumulation of effort. The cost of an incremental unit of knowledge is assumed to equal the square of knowledge acquired. Development costs are assumed to cease the moment the race to innovate has been won.

Thus the nth participant seeks a plan $y_n(t)$, $0 \le t \le T$, to

(18) $\displaystyle \text{maximize} \int_0^T e^{-it} \left(P \prod_1^{n-1} (1 - F(z_j)) F'(z_n) y_n(t) \right.$

$\left. - \prod_1^n (1 - F(z_j)) y_n(t)^2 \right) dt$

subject to (17) where P denotes the reward for being first and T denotes the planning horizon.

This is a dynamic formulation of the optimal behavior of each participant in the race. Each participant takes into account the decisions of the others, assumed fixed, in formulating his best expenditure plan. This of course is similar to the behavioral assumptions employed in the other game theoretic formulations. The fact that this formulation calls for selection of an entire optimal plan classifies it as a differential game.

According to the Reinganum formulation, the optimal rate of expenditure on development increases through time. Only if the discount rate is zero and the planning horizon is infinite does the optimal plan call for a constant rate of investment, as was supposed by Lee and Wilde. She also finds that if the participants agree to share the rewards from innovation but are compelled to carry out its development independently, they will slacken the development pace relative to the winner-take-all situation. This follows from the fact that each faces a lower expected reward than in the absence of collusion. Likewise, she finds that an increase in the reward for innovation speeds up development. When costless imitation is incorporated into the formulation, it is found that as the reward from imitation increases, the development pace slackens. In the absence of possible imitation the rate of investment in development at each moment increases with the number of participants in the race. This conclusion is similar to Lee and Wilde's in the static formulation.

Reinganum's formulation represents the most sophisticated game theoretic formulation at present. It draws most heavily on the decision theoretic formulation and therefore brings these two formulations closer together. What still remains to be incorporated into the game theoretic formulation is the possibility that the participant in the race may be currently realizing a profit on a product that will be supplanted by the innovation; that there may be rewards from imitation that can be captured at a cost and therefore that the participant may decide to accelerate development after preemption by a rival; and that each participant may have to finance development of the innovation out of his own assets. Relaxation of the functional forms employed appears to be barred at present by analytical difficulties. Thus an alternative approach, relying on simulation techniques, has been proposed by Nelson and Winter (1977, 1978). We shall discuss their approach in the next chapter.

Appendix

Costs and speed of development

To derive the expected completion time of text equation (3), recall that by definition of expectation

$$E(t) = \int_0^\infty tF'(t)\, dt$$

Integrate by parts, using the identity

$$\int_a^b u\, dv = uv \Big|_a^b - \int_a^b v\, du$$

Let $u = t$ and $dv = F'(t)\, dt$ so that $du = dt$ and $v = -(1 - F(t))$. Making these substitutions yields

(A1) $E(t) = \int_0^\infty (1 - F(t))\, dt$

for any probability function with domain $t \geq 0$, as claimed.

Technical and market uncertainty

We verify that if all n firms choose the same spending level and are otherwise identical, then each firm is equally likely to win the innovational reward. The probability that the nth firm wins the race is given by the joint probability distribution

$$S = \int_0^\infty \sum_1^{n-1} (1 - F(t; x_i)) F'(t; x_n)\, dt$$

where the first term in the integrand is the probability that none of the other $n - 1$ firms complete the innovation on or before time t and the second term is the nth firm's probability density of successful completion of the innovation at t. Substitution from text equations (1) and (9) into S gives

$$S = \int_0^\infty u(t) h(x_n) \exp\left(- \sum_1^n h(x_j) v(t) \right) dt$$

If all the participants in the race spend the same amount, then the probability that the nth firm wins becomes

$$S = \int_0^\infty u(t) h(x) e^{-nh(x)v(t)}\, dt$$

$$= (1/n) \int_0^\infty nuhe^{-nhv}\, dt = 1/n$$

because the last integral is of the probability density the race is won at t if all spend the same amount (and a probability density must integrate to 1). Thus exactly as expected, if there are n rivals in the race and each spends exactly the same amount, then the probability that any specific one will win is $1/n$.

Efficiency

Contractual cost. In the contractual case we seek the number of projects n and the amount of money to devote to each,

$x_j, j = 1, \ldots, n$, to minimize the expected introduction time, given a fixed total budget X. Because the projects are mathematically identical, we may divide the total budget X equally among the funded projects. (Under text assumption (8) with $\bar{x}$ positive and finite, this is the unique efficient allocation.) Hence we seek the optimal number of projects to fund, with equal funding $x = X/n$ to each project. Using text equation (13), with $n - 1$ replaced by n, we find that the expected introduction time to be minimized by choice of n is

$$E(t) = \int_0^\infty \exp(-nh(X/n)v(s))\, ds \quad \text{subject to } n \geq 1$$

Treating n as a continuous variable and differentiating yields

$$dE(t)/dn = (xh'(x) - h(x)) \int_0^\infty v(s)\exp(-nh(x)v(s))\, ds \geq 0$$

with equality in case $n > 1$;

$$d^2E(t)/dn^2\big|_{dE/dn=0}$$

$$= -h''(X^2/n^3) \int_0^\infty v(s)\exp(-nh(x)v(s))\, ds \geq 0$$

in case $dE/dn = 0$.

From this we conclude that because the integrals are always positive, either

(A2a)　$n > 1, h(x)/x = h'(x)$　and　$h''(x) \leq 0$　where $x = X/n$

or

(A2b)　$n = 1$　and　$h(x)/x \leq h'(x)$

If $h'' < 0$ for all $x (\bar{x} = 0)$, there are diseconomies of scale throughout. Case (A2a) is satisfied only for $x = 0$. (Recall that $h(0) = 0$). This means we let $n \to \infty$. When there are diseconomies of scale in development, it is best to let the number of parallel projects approach infinity and to allocate an infinitesimal amount of money to each.

On the other hand, if there are economies of scale for all x, so $h'' > 0$ throughout ($\bar{x} = \infty$), case (A2b) holds. With economies of scale, it is best to allocate the entire budget to one project.

The third possibility is that the development process exhibits increasing returns to scale for small or modest size, but decreasing returns to scale are eventually realized ($0 < \bar{x} < \infty$). Then the optimal finite x satisfies (A2a) and $n = X/x$. The optimal project size depends only on the properties of the function h, and then the optimal number of projects is the number of projects of optimal size the budget can support.

Noncontractual cost. Next we consider the efficient project size and number under the alternative supposition of noncontractual costs, composed of a fixed entry fee G and a flow cost q per unit time until some project succeeds. As before, by symmetry we can fund all projects at the same rate q. But because the total cost is stochastic, the constraint will be a fixed expected expenditure rather than a known budget. We choose n and q to minimize the expected development period subject to a fixed expected discounted cost:

$$\min_{n,q} \int_0^\infty \exp(-nh(q)v(t))\, dt$$

subject to

$$nG + nq \int_0^\infty \exp(-it - nh(q)v(t))\,dt = K \qquad n \geq 1, \qquad q \geq 0$$

In the first constraint note that spending continues as long as no project has succeeded (probability $1 - F = e^{-nhv}$) and is discounted at rate i. To solve this constrained minimization problem in two variables, we assume $q > 0$, form the Lagrangian, and differentiate with respect to n and q:

$$L = \int_0^\infty \exp(-nh(q)v(t))\,dt$$

$$+ \lambda[nG + nq \int_0^\infty \exp(-it - nh(q)v(t))\,dt - K]$$

$$L_n \geq 0 \quad \text{implies} \quad h \int_0^\infty v e^{-nhv} \, dt$$

$$\leq \lambda \left(G + \int_0^\infty e^{-it - nhv} q (1 - nhv) \, dt \right)$$

$$L_q = 0 \quad \text{implies} \quad h' \int_0^\infty v e^{-nhv} \, dt$$

$$= \lambda \left(\int_0^\infty e^{-it - nhv} (1 - qnh'v) \, dt \right)$$

One can use the second condition to eliminate the multiplier from the first condition and rearrange the results to obtain

(A3) $\quad G \geq (h(q)/h'(q) - q) \int_0^\infty \exp(-it - nh(q)v(t)) \, dt$

with equality if $n > 1$.

The efficient n and q satisfy the problem constraint and (A3). Since G and the integral in (A3) are both always positive, whenever $n > 1$ the optimal project size q is characterized by

(A4) $\quad h(q) > qh'(q)$

The optimal $q > q_0$ where q_0 is defined by

(A5) $\quad h(q_0) = q_0 h'(q_0)$

It is apparent from (A3) that the optimal project size depends on properties of the development function h as well as on the other parameters of the problem.

Social optimality
Contractual cost. We seek the number of parallel projects and the amount of money to devote to each in order to maximize the net social benefit of the innovation:

(A6) $\quad \int_0^\infty P^* \exp(-it - nh(x)v(t)) nh(x) u(t) \, dt - nx$

This is the expected gross capital value to society of the innovation, discounted from the moment of innovation, multiplied by the probability density over completion times, less the cost of the n projects. We may take the parallel efforts to be of equal size by the symmetry argument suggested earlier. Setting the derivatives of (A6) with respect to x and n, respectively, equal to zero yields

(A7a) $\quad P^* n h' \int_0^\infty e^{-it-nhv} u(1-nhv)\, dt = n$

(A7b) $\quad P^* h \int_0^\infty e^{-it-nhv} u(1-nhv)\, dt = x$

Setting the ratio of left sides equal to the ratio of right sides leads to

(A8) $\quad h(x_0)/x_0 = h'(x_0)$

as is efficient. The number of projects is then determined implicitly from (A7b), say, on replacing x by x_0. In the exponential case $(u = 1,\ v = t)$, n can be found explicitly in this way to be

(A9) $\quad n = [(iP^* h'(x_0))^{1/2} - i]/h(x_0)$

For (A9) to be sensible (that is, $n \geq 1$), we must have

(A10) $\quad P^* \geq (h(x_0) + i)^2/ih'(x_0)$

That is, development is worthwhile only if the reward stream is sufficiently large. If (A9) holds, we can substitute for n from (A9) into (A6) and set $u = 1$, $v = t$ to get an expression for the maximum expected net benefit of the project in the exponential case:

$$nx_0((iP^* h'(x_0))^{1/2} - 1)$$

This is positive whenever (A10) is satisfied. If (A10) does not hold, then development should not be undertaken. A similar implicit restriction holds in the general case; (A7b) and (A8) implicitly define the optimal project size and number of projects in case the reward P^* is sufficiently large to warrant undertaking development.

The optimal scale of project x_0 depends only on the function h, as previously discussed. The optimal number of projects and hence the optimal amount of money to be spent are sensitive to other parameters. Putting $x = x_0$ in (A7b) and differentiating totally indicates that $\partial n / \partial P^* > 0$. Thus an increase in the benefit leads to more projects and therefore greater total spending and quicker expected completion (since project size is fixed at x_0). A uniform proportionate shift in the efficacy of development (realized by replacing h by mh, $m > 1$) may raise or reduce the optimal number of projects.

Noncontractual costs. The procedure for finding the socially optimal number of projects and the rate of spending on each in the noncontractual case is similar. The expected net benefit to society, to be maximized by choice of n and q is

$$(A11) \quad \int_0^\infty \exp(-it - nh(q)v(t))(P^*nh(q)u(t) - nq)\,dt - nG$$

subject to $n \geq 1$, $q \geq 0$

Setting the derivatives with respect to q and n, respectively, equal to zero (assuming the constraints are satisfied with strict inequality) yields

$$(A12a) \quad h'\int_0^\infty e^{-it-nhv}(Pu + nvq - Pnhuv)\,dt = \int_0^\infty e^{-it-nhv}\,dt$$

$$(A12b) \quad h\int_0^\infty e^{-it-nhv}(Pu + nvq - Pnuhv)\,dt = G + q\int_0^\infty e^{-it-nhv}\,dt$$

Combining these equations yields the efficiency condition (A3)

$$(A13) \quad h(q)/h'(q) - q = G/\int_0^\infty e^{-it-nhv}\,dt$$

Any two of the three equations (A12a), (A12b), and (A13) may be solved implicitly for n and q. So long as there is a positive fixed cost, the choices of optimal q and n are interdependent and both variables depend on all the parameters. Of course it follows from (A13) that $h(q) - qh'(q) > 0$ and the optimal $q > q_0$. The foregoing is applicable in case the innovation is sufficiently attractive to warrant pursuit.

To see circumstances under which innovation will be worthwhile and to perform comparative statics, we specialize to the exponential case ($u = 1$ so $v = t$). The objective (A11) specializes to

(A14) $V = n[P^*h(q) - q]/(i + nh(q)) - nG$

while (A12a), (A12b), and (A13) become, respectively,

(A15) $[h'(iP^* + nq) - (nh + i)]n/(nh + i)^2 = 0$

(A16) $i(hP^* - q)/(nh + i)^2 - G = 0$

(A17) $h - h'q - h'G(nh + i) = 0$

Using (A16) to eliminate $(P^*h - q)/(i + nh)$ from (A14) shows that the optimal expected value of the innovation is $V = n^2hG/i$, which is clearly positive. Thus development should be undertaken if the second-order conditions for a maximum are satisfied. At a stationary point satisfying (A15) to (A16) (and hence (A17)), we find $V_{qq} < 0$ so long as $h'' < 0$ but

$$V_{qq}V_{nn} - V_{qn}^2 \geq 0 \quad \text{if and only if}$$

(A18) $-2h''h/(h')^3 \geq nG$

R&D is not worthwhile unless (A18) holds. We assume (A18) holds and that the first-order conditions have positive solutions for n and q. We investigate the dependence of the optimal n and q upon the parameters of the problem. Any two of the three equations (A15) to (A17) may be used. We work with (A15) and (A17).

To study the effect of a constant proportionate upward shift in the function h, we replace h by mh, where m is a positive constant set equal to one at the point of interest.

Let

(A19) $f_1 = h'(iP^* + nq) - nh - i/m$

(A20) $f_2 = G(nmh + i) + q - h/h'$

Then $f_1 = 0$ when (A15) holds, while $f_2 = 0$ when (A17) holds. Setting the total differentials of (A19) and (A20) equal to zero gives at the equilibrium

(A21) $h''(iP^* + nq)\,dq - (h - h'q)\,dn = -ih'\,dP^* - i\,dm$

(A22) $(Gnh' + hh''/(h')^2)\,dq + Gh\,dn = -(nh + i)\,dG - nhG\,dm$

Cramer's rule may be applied to find the partial derivatives of the equilibrium n and q with respect to the parameters. The determinant of the coefficient matrix on the left is

(A23) $D_1 \equiv G(nh + i)(2hh''/h' + Gn(h')^2) \leq 0$

where the second-order condition (A18) has been used to sign D_1. We assume the strong inequality holds in (A18) and hence in (A23). We find that

(A24) $\partial q/\partial P^* = -D_1 h'hGi > 0$

$\partial q/\partial G = -D_1(nh + i)(h - h'q) > 0$

$\partial q/\partial m = -iGhD_1 - nhG(h - h'q)D_1 > 0$

$\partial n/\partial P^* = D_1 ih'(Gnh' + hh''/(h')^2)$

$\partial n/\partial G = -D_1 h''(iP^* + nq)(nh + i) < 0$

Thus the optimal project size increases as the reward or fixed cost rises. An upward shift in the conditional probability of completion likewise results in an increase in the optimal project size. Although the dependence of q on the parameters is clear, the way that n varies with the parameters is not. We can say that an increase in the fixed cost per project will reduce the number of projects. But note that an increase in the reward will *not* necessarily increase the number n of efforts; (A18) does not tell us the sign of $\partial n/\partial P^*$.

   The total expected expenditure is

(A25) $\bar{c} = nq/(nh(q) + i) + nG$

where n and q satisfy (A15) to (A18). The rate of change in expected spending with change in the benefits is

(A26) $\partial \bar{c}/\partial P^* = (\partial \bar{c}/\partial q)(\partial q/\partial P^*) + (\partial \bar{c}/\partial n)(\partial n/\partial P^*)$

The needed partial derivatives of $\bar{c}$ are readily computed from

(A25), whereas $\partial q/\partial P^*$ and $\partial n/\partial P^*$ are given in (A24). We find that

(A27) $\partial \bar{c}/\partial P^* = i(iq/(nh+i)^2 + G)hh''/D_1h' > 0$

Thus an increase in the benefits raises the expected total spending, even though it need not increase the optimal number of projects.

Finally, the expected completion time is the reciprocal of $nh(q)$. We find that, at the optimum,

(A28) $\partial(nh(q))/\partial P^* = nh'\partial q/\partial P^* + h\partial n/\partial P^*$

$$= ih^2h''/D_1h' > 0$$

so that the expected completion period shrinks as the reward grows.

One may inquire about the limiting case of zero fixed costs: $G = 0$. It appears from (A17) that the efficiency condition coincides with the efficiency condition in the contractual setting. But then (A16) would imply $P^* = q_0/h(q_0)$. There is no reason for this equation to be satisfied because it contains no variables. Thus there will be *no* solution to the noncontractual problem unless $G > 0$, as has been assumed.

The market solution

Contractual cost. Let P be the expected capital value to the firm upon innovation if it wins the race. Then the expected net benefit to the nth firm, to be maximized by choice of spending level x_n, is

(A29) $\int_0^\infty \exp\left(-it - \sum_1^n h(x_j)v(t)\right)Pu(t)h(x_n)\,dt - x_n$

This is the expected discounted reward, multiplied by the probability density that the nth firm succeeds at t and no others have succeeded by t, and integrated over all possible completion times, less the expenditure x_n. The levels of expenditure of the rivals, $x_1, \ldots, x_{n-1}$ are taken to be known parameters by the nth firm, assumed to be independent of the firm's choice x_n. Setting the first derivative of (A29) with respect to x_n equal to zero gives

(A30) $Ph' \int_0^\infty \exp(-it - \sum_1^n h(x_j)v)u(1 - hv)\, dt - 1 = 0$

The second derivative is assumed to be nonpositive; it will surely be nonpositive in the exponential case if $h'' < 0$.

Because all participants in the race are identical, each satisfies (A30) at the same level of investment x. In equilibrium, therefore, (A30) implies

(A31) $Ph' \int_0^\infty e^{-it-nhv}u(1 - hv)\, dt = 1$

One can integrate by parts to show that

(A32) $\int_0^\infty e^{-it-nhv}u\, dt = \int_0^\infty e^{-it-nhv}v(i + nhu)\, dt$

It then follows from (A31) and (A32) that

(A33) $\int_0^\infty e^{-it-nhv}u(1 - vh)\, dt = \int_0^\infty e^{-it-nhv}v(i + (n-1)hu)\, dt$

This shows that the left side of (A31) is always positive. Equation (A33) will be of use later as well.

If the number of firms were exogenous, then it would be of interest to see how the firm's R&D effort is related to the number of rivals. The left side of (A30) is decreasing in x_n by our hypothesis that the second-order condition for a maximum of (A29) is satisfied. With all firms identical, (A30) becomes (A31). The partial derivative of (A31) with respect to the number of rivals n is

(A34) $-Ph'h \int_0^\infty e^{-it-nhv}uv(1 - hv)\, dt$

To sign this, we note the identity

(A35) $\int_0^\infty e^{-it-nhv}uv\, dt = (\tfrac{1}{2}) \int_0^\infty e^{-it-nhv}(i + nhu)v^2\, dt$

which may be verified by integration by parts on the left. Substituting (A35) into (A34) and collecting terms gives an expression equivalent to (A34), namely,

(A36) $-Ph'h \int_0^\infty e^{-it-nhv}((i + (n-2)hu)v^2/2)\, dt < 0,$ $n \geq 2$

This shows that the left side of (A30) is decreasing in n (with all firms identical) as well as in x_n. It follows that if firms adjust their expenditures to maintain (A29) at its maximum, and hence to maintain equality in (A30), then an increase in the number n of rivals will *reduce* each firm's equilibrium R&D expenditure level.

    The number n of firms in the market solution is determined by the condition that the expected profit to each firm is zero. This means, from (A29),

(A37) $Ph \int_0^\infty e^{-it-nhv}u\, dt = x$

The equilibrium n and x are determined as the simultaneous solution to (A31) and (A37).

    Combining (A31) and (A37) by eliminating P between them leads to

(A38) $(h' - h/x) \int_0^\infty e^{-it-nhv}u\, dt = h'h \int_0^\infty e^{-it-nhv}uv\, dt$

Because the integrals are positive, it follows that

(A39) $h' > h/x$

and therefore that the value of x chosen by the firm satisfies

(A40) $x < x_0$

where x_0 is the efficient size, defined by $h(x)/x = h'(x)$. (Inequality (A40) is implied by (A39) since $h - xh'$ is an increasing function of x that is zero at x_0 and negative at the market solution, by (A38).)

    For our parametric analysis we use the exponential distribution. Putting $u = 1$, $v = t$, we find that (A37) and (A38) are equivalent to

(A41) $Ph - x(nh + i) = 0$

(A42) $h(nh + i) - xh'((n-1)h + i) = 0$

respectively. Replace $h(x)$ by $mh(x)$, where m is a positive constant and define

(A43) $\quad f_1 = Ph - x(nh + i/m)$

$\qquad f_2 = h(nh + i/m) - xh'[(n-1)h + i/m]$

Then at the optimum, with $m = 1$, we have $f_1 = f_2 = 0$. Computing the total differentials gives at the optimum

(A44) $\quad -xh'(n-1)\,dx - xh\,dn = -h\,dP - xi\,dm$

$\qquad [hh'((n-1)h + 2i)$

$\qquad\qquad /(n-1)h + i - xh''((n-1)h + i)]\,dx$

$\qquad\qquad -h(xh' - h)\,dn$

$\qquad\qquad = -i(xh' - h)\,dm$

Recalling (A39), analysis of the pattern of signs in the coefficient matrix on the left in (A44) shows that the determinant $D_2 = \begin{vmatrix} - & - \\ + & - \end{vmatrix} > 0$. We compute

(A45) $\quad \partial x/\partial P = D_2 h^2(xh' - h)i > 0$

$\qquad \partial x/\partial m = 0$

and check the sign patterns for

(A46) $\quad \partial n/\partial P = D_2 \begin{vmatrix} - & - \\ + & 0 \end{vmatrix} > 0$

$\qquad \partial n/\partial m = D_2 \begin{vmatrix} - & - \\ + & - \end{vmatrix} > 0$

Noncontractual cost. If costs are noncontractual, then they are incurred only so long as the innovation has not appeared. Thus the nth participant in the race chooses the rate of spending q_n to maximize the expected net benefit

(A47) $\quad \int_0^\infty \exp\left(-it - \sum_1^n h(q_j)v(t)\right)(Pu(t)h(q_n) - q_n)\,dt - G$

This is the discounted value of the innovation, multiplied by the probability density that the firm wins the race at t, less the variable cost incurred until the race is won, and less the fixed charge. Setting the first derivative with respect to q_n equal to zero yields

$$(A48) \quad \int_0^\infty \exp\left(-it - \sum_1^n h(q_j)v(t)\right)(Puh'(q_n)(1 - vh(q_n))$$
$$-1 + q_n h'(q_n)v) \, dt = 0$$

We assume the second derivative of (A47) with respect to x_n is negative for an interior maximum.

By symmetry of the firms, (A48) becomes in equilibrium

$$(A49) \quad \int_0^\infty e^{-it-nhv}(Puh'(1 - vh) - 1 + qh'v) \, dt = 0$$

If participants continue to join the race until expected profits are zero, then, from (A47),

$$(A50) \quad \int_0^\infty e^{-it-nhv}(Puh - q) \, dt = G$$

The equilibrium number of participants n and their common expenditure rate q are the solution to the simultaneous equations (A49) and (A50).

One can eliminate P between (A49) and (A50) to find that

$$(A51) \quad (h - qh') \int_0^\infty e^{-it-nhv} \, dt \int_0^\infty e^{-it-nhv}u \, dt$$

$$= Gh' \int_0^\infty e^{-it-nhv}u(1 - vh) \, dt$$

$$+ qhh'\left[\int_0^\infty e^{-it-nhv}v \, dt \int_0^\infty e^{-it-nhv}u \, dt\right.$$

$$\left. - \int_0^\infty e^{-it-nhv} \, dt \int_0^\infty e^{-it-nhv}uv \, dt\right]$$

Since the coefficient of $h - qh'$ on the left is positive, $h - qh'$ has the sign of the right side. The coefficient of G is positive by identity (A33) (on replacing x by q in that demonstration). We have been unable to sign the last square-bracketed term on the right in the general case, but it is equal to zero if $u \equiv 1$. Thus if the probability distribution over completion time is exponential, then

(A52) $h > qh'$ so $q > q_0$

For further analysis we restrict attention to the exponential case. With $u = 1$, $v = t$, the first-order condition specializes to

(A53) $(Ph' - 1)/(i + nh) - h'(Ph - q)/(i + nh)^2 = 0$

If the number of participants n were exogenous, then q would be determined by (A53). We know that the left side of (A48) and hence of (A53) is decreasing in q_n by our hypothesis of an interior maximum. The partial derivative of the left side of (A53) with respect to n is

$$-(Ph' - 1)h/(i + nh)^2 + 2hh'(Ph - q)/(i + nh)^3$$

$$= h(Ph' - 1)/(i - nh)^2 > 0$$

The second line was obtained by using (A53) and collecting terms. Positivity follows from (A53), since $Ph - q > 0$ for a project that is expected not to generate a loss. Therefore $\partial q/\partial n > 0$; the spending rate q increases with the number of participants. This result of Lee and Wilde (1980) is opposite to that obtained for the case of contractual costs.

With $u = 1$, $v = t$, the zero profit condition (A50) specializes to

(A54) $Ph - q = G(i + nh)$

Substituting for $Ph - q$ from (A53) into (A54) gives

(A55) $P - 1/h' - G = 0$

which must also be obeyed.

The earlier finding that no optimum exists if $G = 0$ also obtains here; setting $G = 0$ in (A54) and (A55) yields

$$h(q_0) = q_0 h'(q_0) \quad \text{and} \quad P = 1/h'(q_0)$$

The former equation determines q_0 and the second contains no variables so it is unlikely to hold. Thus there is no market solution unless $G = 0$, as we assume.

Any two of the three equations (A53) to (A55) can be used to determine n and q. For our parametric analysis we use (A55) and (A54). Replace h by mh and let

(A56) $g_1 = P - 1/mh' - G$

(A57) $g_2 = Ph - q/m - G(nh + i/m)$

Then $g_1 = 0$ when (A55) holds, whereas $g_2 = 0$ when (A54) holds. Setting the total differentials equal to zero and $m = 1$ gives

(A58) $(h'' / (h')^2)dq = -dP + dG - dm/h'$

(A59) $-h'G(n - 1)\, dq - Gh\, dn = -h\, dP + (nh + i)\, dG$

$$- (q + iG)\, dm$$

The determinant of the coefficients on the left side of (A58) to (A59) is

(A60) $D_3 = -Ghh'' / (h')^2 > 0$

Using Cramer's rule, we find that

(A61) $\partial q/\partial P = D_3 Gh > 0$

$$\partial q/\partial G = -GhD_3 < 0$$

$$\partial q/\partial m = D_3 Gh/h' > 0$$

The signs agree with those found in the case of social optimality except in the case of the fixed cost G. An increase in the fixed cost per project causes the spending rate per project to go down in the market solution, although it called for an increase in the socially optimal rate of spending. We were unable to determine the direction of response of n to any parametric change. For instance,

(A62) $\partial n/\partial P = -D_3(h''h/(h')^3 + G(n - 1))h'$

Because (A62) may have any sign, an increase in the reward from innovation may either increase or decrease the number of innovational rivals!

The total expected spending is

(A63) $c = nq/(nh + i) + nG$

Its rate of change with respect to the reward is

$$\partial c/\partial P = (\partial c/\partial q)(\partial q/\partial P) + (\partial c/\partial n)(\partial n/\partial P) > 0$$

The expected development period is $1/nh(q)$. Since

(A64) $\partial(nh(q))/\partial P = h\,\partial n/\partial P + nh'\,\partial q/\partial P > 0$

a larger reward leads to quicker innovation on average.

6

Summary and prospectus

According to Paul Samuelson (1973), "even children learn in growing up that 'both' is not an admissible answer to a choice of 'which one'." It is a lesson, however, that is rarely appreciated. Individually and collectively we seek to deny it. We want higher incomes and more leisure, a better environment and a cheap source of energy, a cure for cancer and a good five cent cigar.

Having to choose between desired alternatives is not a trick, it is a necessity; avoiding the choice and getting both is the trick. Contemplation that such a trick is possible verges on belief in magic, on the plausibility of drawing rabbits out of an empty hat. And yet, bizarre as it may seem, the trick has been performed, to paraphrase the TV commercial, through the magic of technology. The studies we have reported on, theoretical and empirical, are in the final analysis meant to remove the magical quality of technical advance. We want to know which forces contribute to technical advances and which retard. With that knowledge we could promote the former and suppress the latter.

The Schumpeterian hypothesis, which has stimulated much of the work surveyed in this book, is that the presence of some monopoly power and the opportunity to realize some monopoly profits contribute to technical advance, whereas perfect competition now and in the future retards it. This contention poses a dilemma, because the cornerstone of Western economic doctrine is that competition is good – and the more the better. The efficiency of the price system in allocating resources is the first theorem of modern welfare economics. Departure from perfect competition leads to an inferior allocation of resources. Thus technical advance appears to require the sacrifice of some allocative efficiency at each moment in time for the purpose of greater efficiency in the long run. Obviously, the question of how much sacrifice of static efficiency is worthwhile is one of balance. Ideally, the marginal short-run sacrifice should equal the marginal long-run gain. At present, we have no precise way of making such a calculation; and, concomitantly, we cannot say how great a departure from perfect competition is ideal in general. To the extent that current antitrust policy is to be modified to take into account the possible salutary effects of monopoly power on technical advance, it must still do so on a case-by-case basis. Our present knowledge is inadequate to allow for sweeping generalizations or universal formulas.

On a perhaps more modest level, our understanding of the process of technical advance is a little better. Empirical studies tend to reveal the absence of economies of scale in the research and development process beyond a minimum scale. Constant returns appear to prevail over a substantial range. Large firms do tend to spend more on research and development than small firms do. But this increase in spending tends to be less than proportionate to firm size. Fisher and Temin (1973, 1979) have claimed that the empirical studies attempting to test the Schumpeterian hypotheses are methodologically flawed. Scherer (1973) claims they are okay.

At present, the conventional wisdom appears to be that demand-pull or economic opportunity is more important than technological opportunity as a spur to invention. It is difficult to argue that the opportunity to profit creates no incentive to invent. This knowledge, however, does not go very far in indicating when, and even if, an invention will be forthcoming. Perhaps the most important insight emerging from this debate is that both forces are important and interactive. Advances in basic knowledge make possible exploitation of opportunities for profit while profit opportunities stimulate research.

Markets affording some opportunity for realizing monopoly profits through invention, and in which incumbent firms' profits are vulnerable to erosion through innovation by others, appear to be the ones with the greatest level of innovative activity. If this is what Schumpeter was claiming, then the empirical studies of market structure and innovation appear to support him. A conceptual difficulty with these studies is that they ignore the interaction between market structure and innovation. That is, although the current market structure may influence the level of innovative activity, the results of innovative activity feed back to the market structure. Successful innovators grow and prosper while the unsuccessful shrink or even leave the market. Entrants may be attracted by the success of some and repelled by the failure of others. Thus the structure of the market is constantly changing as a consequence of the process of technical advance. This interaction between market structure and the process of technical advance should be kept distinct from the interaction between market structure and the substance of technical advance. As an example of the latter, technical advance may increase the efficient scale of production of an item, thereby leading to a reduction in the number of firms producing it.

A literature is emerging on the simultaneity between market structure and the process of technical advance. Levin (1978) has described how incumbent firms may attempt to maintain their existing market position through continuous innovation. A similar theme is taken up by Dasgupta and Stiglitz (1980a). In these formulations, however, the focus is on an equilibrium market structure that, once achieved, continues on. Moreover, these formulations do not deal with the approach to equilibrium, which may be the more interesting question. For if a market structure that is supportive of technical advance leads to one inimical to it, then technical advance is not self-sustaining in a market environment.

The self-sustainability of technical advance in a market environment is, we believe, the most important outstanding issue in this field. Our analysis in Chapter 4 of the inventive behavior of the firm indicated that those that succeed in the race to innovate and realize a monopoly profit have, ceteris paribus, less of an incentive to innovate on the next round than those who lost and are therefore earning only normal profits. All other things, however, need not be equal. If innovation involves reduction in the unit cost of producing an item, then the firm that succeeds may expand its market share relative to its rivals. This in turn may make further cost-reducing innovations more attractive to it than to its rivals because the benefits of such inventions increase with the scale of production to which they are applied. On the other hand, a firm with substantial market share may be more aware of the downward-sloping nature of the demand curve than its smaller rivals and therefore recognize that its efforts to expand output involve a decline in the market price. This awareness and the concomitant knowledge of the possible reduction in the value of the innovation may inhibit the large firm from innovating. Still another factor in the interaction between the process of innovation and evolution of market structure is that successful innovators are in a better position than their unsuccessful rivals to finance further innovation internally.

Ideally, we would like to construct a model of the interaction between the process of technical advance and market structure that incorporates all these features and others as well. Firms should be able to revise their development plans in response to the successes or failures of rivals. Rewards might accrue to imitation as well as to innovation. There should be possibilities for strategic behavior both with respect to identifiable existing rivals and unidentifiable potential entrants. Firms should be allowed to learn from their past innovation experience. Exogenous shocks representing technological breakthroughs complementary to the particular market under study might also be incorporated. The main question to be addressed in this framework is how market structure evolves through time. Does an industry initially composed of firms of comparable size and strength remain that way through time or does it evolve into an industry with only a few, or only one, dominant firm and many small rivals? And, most importantly, what happens to the pace of innovation in this industry through time? If it turns out that the industry becomes more concentrated through time and the pace of invention declines, then technical advance is not self-sustaining. The process of "creative destruction" described by Schumpeter may turn on itself and destroy the foundation on which it is based. From an empirical standpoint the slackened pace of innovation observed in some industries, which is presently ascribed to shrinkage of technological opportunities or exhaustion of the underlying scientific base, may instead be the result of the evolution of market structure.

Formulation and analysis of a comprehensive model of inter-action between market structure and the process of innovation poses formidable technical difficulties, involving methods and concepts (for example, the theory of repeated games), which are themselves in the process of development and refinement. Despite these obstacles, work in this direction has begun. Futia (1980) formulated a dynamic stochastic model in which a firm's market share in the current period depends on whether it won the race to innovate in the previous period. A firm's success in the race depends on how much it spends and on its rivals' spending. Successful innovation by any of the rivals ends a period and starts a new race. In each race rivals regard each other along the game theoretic lines described in the last chapter. The long-term evolution of the industry is viewed as a Markov process with endogenous transition prob-abilities. Futia also permits imitation and entry into the industry and changes in technological opportunity. The long-run equilibrium of the industry is associated with the steady state of this Markov process. This model is not amenable to complete analytic solution and Futia turns to numerical examples to exhibit some of its prop-erties, showing that his formulation leads to results consistent with empirical findings. Specifically, his model is consistent with the claim that innovative activity increases with industry concentration but less so in industries with extensive opportunities for innovation than in those with few opportunities. Industries with moderate concentration or barriers to entry tend to foster a higher level of innovative activity than either those with high or low concentration.

Flaherty (1980) formulates a model in which each firm in an industry chooses an investment sequence through time, designed to lower its unit production costs. The relation between investment and cost reduction is assumed to be deterministic. The firms in the industry behave noncooperatively and each takes the investment sequence of the others as fixed and unresponsive to its own choices. Each firm also selects an output level at each point in time based on its production costs. The output decision is carried out in a standard Cournot oligopoly framework. In her formulation, symmetric equilibria, those with equal market shares, tend to be unstable, whereas equilibria with unequal market shares tend to be stable.

Certainly, the most ambitious effort to study the interaction between market structure and the process of innovation has been undertaken by Nelson and Winter (1977, 1978). They simulate an industry composed of firms that may either innovate or imitate and follow prespecified rules in choosing from these alternatives and the level of investment. A firm's investment in innovation is proportional to its capital stock. Expansion of its capital stock occurs when the firm realizes profits above a target level. Large firms have a higher target profit rate than small firms. A firm's output is proportional to its capital stock and innovation consists of improvement of the productivity of capital. The result of investment in research and development is uncertain but the more that is spent, the higher is the probability of coming up with a new technology superior to the present one. The opportunities for finding a superior technology with a given level of expenditure improve through time exogenously. Research and development is financed internally so large firms spend more than small firms. Because large firms have higher target profits, they expand their capital stock less than small firms.

Firms plan only one period ahead and are not directly racing against their rivals in the industry. That is, their planned expenditures on innovation are not based on the actual or anticipated expenditures of their rivals. Using different values for such parameters as aggressiveness in research and development (aggressive firms tend to be innovators, whereas passive ones are imitators), ease of imitation, the exogenous rate of improvement in the underlying technology base, and the variability of the industry over a twenty-five-year period, they find that the industry becomes more concentrated in all cases. (Entry of new firms into the industry is not allowed.) The level of concentration, however, increases less in an industry that is initially highly concentrated than in one that is less concentrated. Technological opportunity that is rapidly improving appears to lead to greater concentration than if it is growing modestly.

Simulation enables Nelson and Winter to explore properties of their model that do not at present appear to be susceptible to study by purely analytic techniques. This of course is an important virtue of the simulation approach. The results obtained through this approach, however, carry less weight than those reached by formal methods, for they appear to be more suggestive of general patterns than conclusive. Ideally, the simulation approach and the analytic approach complement each other – each guiding what to look for when the other is employed.

Perhaps the more controversial feature of the Nelson and Winter approach is their ascribing decision rules to firms that are not derived from optimization of any criterion function. They do so because the problems faced by the firm in a changing environment are not amenable to analytic solution. Thus firms in the real world adopt rules of thumb based on their past experience and possibly the experiences of others. These rules may change over time as a consequence of learning or revision of aspirations. All this is part of what has come to be known as the "behavioral theory of the firm" to which Nelson and Winter have been major contributors. Indeed, their attempt to employ this theory to explain the inter-action between market structure and the process of innovation may be the most important test of its explanatory power. Further work employing the behavioral approach has been conducted by Kay (1979).

A new and potentially very important source of explanation of difference in R&D intensity among firms has been offered by McEachern and Romeo (1978). They reason that a firm faces two types of risk: (1) the loss of resources associated with a failed R&D effort and (2) the loss of the market share from failure to invest in R&D while rivals are doing so. Which of these risks dominates the behavior of a firm, McEachern and Romeo theorize, depends on the relationship between its owners and its managers. If there is no single dominant stockholder, defined as one owning at least 4 percent of the outstanding stock, then the managers will behave conservatively and the first source of risk will dominate. On the other hand, if there is a dominant stockholder, then managers will fear the loss of market share more and will engage in R&D activity more intensively. A firm that is wholly owned and managed by a single stockholder should not exhibit either bias.

In a study of forty firms in the chemicals, drugs, and petroleum refining industries with R&D intensity measured by the ratio of R&D employees to total employment, McEachern and Romeo found support for their hypothesis in the chemicals and drug industries. The R&D intensity appears to be twice as high among firms with a dominant stockholder relative to firms that are either owner managed or have no dominant stockholder. This is especially true in the two industries with considerable R&D activity. The importance of this hypothesis will become clearer after it has been tested more extensively.

Regardless of which approach is employed, static or dynamic, deterministic or stochastic, decision theoretic or game theoretic, optimizing or behavioral, the quest is for a more complete understanding of the economics of technical advance. As this survey of our present state of knowledge discloses, there is still a long way to go before we can rest. And go on we must, for whether technical advance is regarded as a blessing or an evil, we cannot ignore it. Indeed, it is arguably the most important determinant of our past, present, and future.

REFERENCES

Abramovitz, M. 1956. Resource and Output Trends in the United States Since 1870. *American Economic Review,* 46, 5–23.

Adams, W. J. 1970. Firm Size and Research Activity: France and the United States. *Quarterly Journal of Economics,* 84, 386–409.

Aislabie, C. 1972. The Economic Efficiency of Information Producing Activities. *Economic Record,* 48, 575–83.

Allen, Bruce T. 1969. Concentration and Economic Progress: Note. *American Economic Review,* 59, 600–4.

Ames, E. 1961. Research, Invention, Development and Innovation. *American Economic Review,* 51, 370–81.

Angilley, Alan S. 1973. Returns to Scale in Research in the Ethical Pharmaceutical Industry: Some Further Empirical Evidence. *Journal of Industrial Economics,* 22, 81–93.

Arrow, K. 1962. Economic Welfare and the Allocation of Resources for Inventions. In R. R. Nelson (ed.), *The Rate and Direction of Inventive Activity.* Princeton, N.J.: Princeton University Press.

Arvidsson, G. 1970. A Note on Optimal Allocation of Resources for R and D. *Swedish Journal of Economics,* 72, 171–95.

Baily, M. N. 1972. Research and Development Costs and Returns: The U.S. Pharmaceutical Industry. *Journal of Political Economy,* 80, 70–85.

Bain, J. S. 1956. *Barriers to New Competition.* Cambridge, Mass.: Harvard University Press.

Baldwin, W. L. and G. L. Childs. 1969. The Fast Second and Rivalry in Research and Development. *Southern Economic Journal,* XXXVI, 18–24.

Barzel, Y. 1968. Optimal Timing of Innovations. *Review of Economics and Statistics,* 50, 348–55.

Beer, J. J. 1964. Coal Tar Dye Manufacture and the Origin of the Modern Industrial Research Laboratory. In Thomas Parke Hughes (ed.), *The Development of Western Technology Since 1500.* New York: Macmillan.

Bhattacharya, S. and J. R. Ritter. 1979. Innovation and Communication: Signal-

224

ling with Partial Disclosure. Graduate School of Business, University of Chicago (mimeo).

Biname, J. P. and A. Jacquemin. 1973. Structures industrielles des regions belges et grandes entreprises: quelques elements d'analyse. *Recherches Economiques de Louvain,* XXXIX, 437–58.

Binswanger, H. P., V. W. Ruttan, et al. 1978. *Induced Innovation.* Baltimore, Md.: John Hopkins University Press.

Blair, J. M. 1972. *Economic Concentration: Structure, Behavior and Public Policy.* New York: Harcourt Brace Jovanovich.

Bock, B. and J. Farkas. 1969. Concentration and Productivity. The Conference Board, Studies in Business Economics No. 103.

Bosworth, D. L. 1978. The Rate of Obsolescence of Technical Knowledge. *Journal of Industrial Economics,* XXVI, 273–9.

Branch, B. 1973. Research and Development and Its Relation to Sales Growth. *Journal of Economics and Business,* 25, 107–11.

Brown M. 1966. *On the Theory and Measurement of Technological Change.* Cambridge University Press.

Brozen, Y. 1951. Invention, Innovation, and Imitation. *American Economic Review,* 41, 239–57.

Carter, C. F. and B. R. Williams. 1957. *Industry and Technical Progress: Factors Governing the Speed of Application of Science.* London: Oxford University Press.

Chamberlain, E. 1933. *The Theory of Monopolistic Competition.* Cambridge, Mass.: Harvard University Press.

Cheung, S. N. S. 1977. Property Rights and Inventions: An Economic Inquiry (mimeo). University of Washington.

Comanor, W. S. 1964. Research and Competitive Product Differentiation in the Pharmaceutical Industry in the United States. *Economica,* N.S., 31, 372–84.

1965. Research and Technical Change in the Pharmaceutical Industry. *Review of Economics and Statistics,* 47, 182–90.

1967. Market Structure, Product Differentiation, and Industrial Research. *Quarterly Journal of Economics,* 81, 639–57.

and F. M. Scherer. 1969. Patent Statistics as a Measure of Technical Change. *Journal of Political Economy,* 77, 392–8.

Cooper, A. C. 1964. R & D Is More Efficient in Small Companies. *Harvard Business Review,* 3, 75–83.

Dansby, R. E. and R. D. Willig. 1979. Industry Performance Gradient Indexes. *American Economic Review,* 11, 249–60.

Dasgupta, P. and J. Stiglitz. 1980a. Industrial Structure and the Nature of Innovative Activity. *Economic Journal,* 90, 266–93.

1980b. Uncertainty, Industrial Structure and the Speed of R&D. *Bell Journal of Economics,* 11, 1–28.

Davis, K. 1975. Competition, Monopoly and the Incentive to Invent: Comment. *Australian Economic Papers,* 14, 128–31.

DeBondt, R. R. 1977. Innovative Activity and Barriers to Entry. *European Economic Review,* 10, 95–109.

Defay, J. 1973. Recherche et croissance economique. 3, *S.P.P.S.*, Brussels.

Delaney, J. B. and T. C. Honeycutt. 1976. Determinants of Research and Development Activity by Electric Utilities: Comment. *Bell Journal of Economics,* 7, 722–5.

Demsetz, H. 1969. Information and Efficiency: Another Viewpoint. *Journal of Law and Economics,* 12, 1–22.

Denison, E. F. 1962. The Source of Economic Growth in the United States and the Alternatives Before Us. CED Supplementary Paper No. 13.

Descartes, R. 1956. *Discourse on Method.* New York: Liberal Arts Press.

Deshmukh, S. D. and S. D. Chikte. 1977. Dynamic Investment Strategies for a Risky R&D Project. *Journal of Applied Probability,* 14, 144–52.

Duetsch, L. L. 1973. Research Performance in the Ethical Drug Industry. *Marquette Business Review,* 17, 129–43.

Elliott, J. E. 1980. Marx and Schumpeter on Capitalism's Creative Destruction: A Comparative Restatement. *Quarterly Journal of Economics,* 95, 45–68.

Elliott, J. W. 1971. Funds Flow vs. Expectational Theories of Research and Development Expenditures in the Firm. *Southern Economic Journal,* 37, 409–22.

Enos, J. L. 1962. Invention and Innovation in the Petroleum Refining Industry. In R. R. Nelson (ed.), *The Rate and Direction of Inventive Activity: Economic and Social Factors.* Princeton, N.J.: Princeton University Press, pp. 299–321.

Fellner, W. 1951. The Influence of Market Structure on Technological Progress. *Quarterly Journal of Economics,* 65, 650–67.

1961. Two Propositions in the Theory of Induced Innovations. *Economic Journal,* LXXI, 305–8.

Finet, P. 1975. Determinants de la recherche-developpement industrielle en Belgique. *Recherches Economiques de Louvain,* 41, 51–61.

Fisher, F. M. and P. Temin. 1973. Returns to Scale in Research and Development: What Does the Schumpeterian Hypothesis Imply? *Journal of Political Economy,* 81, 56–70.

1979. The Schumpeterian Hypothesis: Reply. *Journal of Political Economy,* 87, 386–9.

Fixler, D. 1979. Market Structure and the Incentive to Invent (mimeo). University of Wisconsin–Milwaukee, School of Business Administration.

Flaherty, M. T. 1980. Industry Structure and Cost-Reducing Investment. *Econometrica,* 48, 1187–209.

Freeman, C. 1965. Research and Development in Electronic Capital Goods. *National Institute Economic Review,* 34, 40–91.

1968. Chemical Process Plant: Innovation and the World Market. *National Institute Economic Review,* 45, 29–57.

1971. The Role of Small Firms in Innovation in the United Kingdom since 1945. Committee of Inquiry on Small Firms, Research Report No. 6, London.

1973. A Study of Success and Failure in Industrial Innovation. In B. R. Williams (ed.), *Science and Technology in Economic Growth.* New York: Wiley, pp. 227–45.

John Fritz Medal Board Award. 1917. *The John Fritz Medal.* New York: Bartlett Orr Press, 1917.

References   227

Futia, C. A. 1980. Schumpeterian Competition. *Quarterly Journal of Economics,* 94, 675–95.

Galbraith, J. K. 1952. *American Capitalism.* Boston: Houghton Mifflin.

Gerstenfeld, A. 1976. A Study of Successful Projects, Unsuccessful Projects, and Projects in Process in West Germany. *IEEE Transactions on Engineering Management,* EM-23, 116–23.

Gharrity, N. J. 1965. *The Use and Non-Use of Patented Inventions.* Ph.D. Dissertation, John Hopkins University.

Globerman, S. 1973. Market Structure and R&D in Canadian Manufacturing Industries. *Quarterly Review of Economics and Business,* 13, 59–67.

Gold, B., ed. 1975. *Technological Change: Economics, Management and the Environment.* Oxford: Pergamon Press.

Gort, M. 1962. *Diversification and Integration in American Industry.* Princeton, N.J.: Princeton University Press.

Grabowski, H. G. 1968. The Determinants of Industrial Research and Development: A Study of the Chemical, Drug and Petroleum Industries. *Journal of Political Economy,* 76, 292–306.

and N. D. Baxter. 1973. Rivalry in Industrial Research and Development. *Journal of Industrial Economics,* 21, 209–35.

and Dennis C. Mueller. 1978. Industrial Research and Development, Intangible Capital Stocks, and Firm Profit Rates. *Bell Journal of Economics,* 9, 328–43.

, J. M. Vernon, and L. C. Thomas. 1978. Estimating the Effects of Regulation on Innovation: An International Comparative Analysis of the Pharmaceutical Industry. *Journal of Law and Economics,* 21, 133–63.

Griliches, Z. 1957. Hybrid Corn: An Exploration of the Economics of Technological Change. *Econometrica,* 25, 501–22.

1973. Research Expenditures and Growth Accounting. In B. R. Williams (ed.), *Science and Technology in Economic Growth.* New York: Wiley, pp. 59–83.

1979. Issues in Assessing the Contribution of Research and Developments to Productivity Growth. *Bell Journal of Economics,* 10, 92–116.

(in press). Returns to Research and Development Expenditures in the Private Sector. In J. W. Kendrick and B. Vaccara (eds.), *New Developments in Productivity Measurement.*

Hamberg, D. 1966. *R&D: Essays on the Economics of Research and Development.* New York: Random House.

1967. Size of Enterprise and Technical Change. *Antitrust Law and Economics Review,* 1, 43–51.

Harberger, A. C. 1954. Monopoly and Resource Allocation. *American Economic Review,* 44, 77–87.

Harris, M. and A. Raviv. 1978. Some Results on Incentive Contracts. *American Economic Review,* 68, 20–30.

Heertje, A. 1978. *Economics and Technical Change.* New York: Halsted Press.

Hennipman, P. 1954. Monopoly: Impediment or Stimulus to Economic Progress? In E. H. Chamberlin (ed.), *Monopoly and Competition and Their Regulation.* London: Macmillan, pp. 421–56.

Hicks, J. R. 1932. *The Theory of Wages.* London: Macmillan.

Hirshleifer, J. 1971. The Private and Social Value of Information and the Reward to Inventive Activity. *American Economic Review,* 61, 561–74.

Holmstrom, B. 1979. Moral Hazard and Observability. *Bell Journal of Economics,* 10, 74–91.

Hope, E. 1973. The Effects of Firms Size and Market Structure on Innovation: A Survey. Discussion Paper, Norwegian School of Economics and Business Administration.

Horowitz, I. 1962. Firm Size and Research Activity. *Southern Economic Journal,* 28, 298–301.

    1963. Research Inclinations of a Cournot Oligopolist. *Review of Economic Studies,* 30, 128–31.

Howe, J. D. and D. G. McFetridge. 1976. The Determinants of R&D Expenditures. *Canadian Journal of Economics,* IX, 57–71.

Hu, S. H. 1973. On the Incentive to Invent: A Clarifactory Note. *Journal of Law and Economics,* XVI, 169–78.

Jackson, R. 1972. Market Structure and the Rewards for Patented Inventions. *Antitrust Bulletin,* 17, 911–26.

Jacquemin, A. P. and H. W. De Jong. 1977. *European Industrial Organization.* London: Macmillan.

Jewkes, J., D. Sawers, and R. Stillerman. 1969. *The Sources of Invention.* New York: Norton, 2nd ed.

Johannisson, B. and C. Lindstrom. 1971. Firm Size and Inventive Activity. *Swedish Journal of Economics,* 73, 427–42.

Johnston, R. E. 1966. Technical Progress and Innovation. *Oxford Economic Papers,* 18, 158–76.

Jorgenson, D. W. 1966. The Embodiment Hypothesis. *Journal of Political Economy,* 74, 1–17.

Kami, T. 1979. The Activity of the Firm Under Technological Rivalry (mimeo). Northwestern University.

Kamien, M. I. and N. L. Schwartz. 1968. Optimal Induced Technical Change. *Econometrica,* 36, 1–17.

    1969. Induced Factor Augmenting Technical Progress from a Microeconomic Viewpoint. *Econometrica,* 37, 668–84.

    1970. Market Structure, Elasticity of Demand, and Incentive to Invent. *Journal of Law and Economics,* XIII, 241–52.

    1971. Expenditure Patterns for Risky R and D Projects. *Journal of Applied Probability,* 8, 60–73.

    1972a. Timing of Innovations Under Rivalry. *Econometrica,* 40, 43–60.

    1972b. Market Structure, Rival's Response, and the Firm's Rate of Product Improvement. *Journal of Industrial Economics,* XX, 159–72.

    1972c. Some Economic Consequences of Anticipating Technical Advance. *Western Economic Journal,* 10, 123–38.

    1974a. Risky R&D with Rivalry. *Annals of Economic and Social Measurement,* 3, 276–7.

    1974b. Patent Life and R&D Rivalry. *American Economic Review,* 64, 183–7.

    1975. Market Structure and Innovative Activity: A Survey. *Journal of Economic Literature,* 13, 1–37.

    1976a. Technology: More for Less? In S. Weintraub (ed.), *Modern Economic*

Thought. Philadelphia, University of Pennsylvania Press.

1976b. On the Degree of Rivalry for Maximum Innovative Activity. *Quarterly Journal of Economics*, XC, 245–60.

1978a. Self-Financing of an R&D Project. *American Economic Review*, 68, 252–61.

1978b. Potential Rivalry, Monopoly Profits and the Pace of Inventive Activity. *Review of Economic Studies*, XLV, 547–57.

1980a. Conjectural Variations. *Center for Mathematical Studies in Economics and Management Science*, Northwestern University.

1980b. A Generalized Hazard Rate. *Economics Letters*, 5, 245–9.

1981. *Dynamic Optimization: The Calculus of Variations and Optimal Control in Economics and Management*. New York: Elsevier North Holland.

Kay, N. M. 1979. *The Innovating Firm*. New York: St. Martin's Press.

Kelley, K. H. 1979. *The Economics of Risky Innovation*, Ph.D. Dissertation, SUNY at Stony Brook.

Kelley, P. and M. Kranzberg. 1978. *Technological Innovation: A Critical Review of Current Knowledge*. San Francisco: San Francisco Press.

Kelly, T. M. 1970. *The Influences of Firm Size and Market Structure on the Research Efforts of Large Multiple-Product Firms*. Ph.D. Dissertation, Oklahoma State University.

Kendrick, J. W. 1977. *Understanding Productivity*. Baltimore, Md.: Johns Hopkins University Press.

Kennedy, C. 1964. Induced Bias in Innovation and the Theory of Distribution. *Economic Journal*, 74, 541–7.

and A. P. Thirlwall. 1972. Surveys in Applied Economics: Technical Progress. *Economic Journal*, 82, 11–72.

Koenig, M. E. D. and D. J. Gans. 1975. The Productivity of Research Effort in the U.S. Pharmaceutical Industry: A Statistical Approach. *Research Policy*, 4, 330–49.

Lange, O. 1943. A Note on Innovations. *Review of Economics and Statistics*, 25, 19–25.

Langrish, J., M. Gibbons, W. G. Evans, and R. F. Jevons. 1972. *Wealth from Knowledge: Studies of Innovation in Industry*. London: Macmillan.

Lave, L. B. 1966. *Technical Change: Its Conception and Measurement*. Englewood Cliffs: Prentice-Hall.

Layton, C. with C. Harlow and C. De Hoghton. 1972. *Ten Innovations: An International Study on Technological Development and the Use of Qualified Scientists and Engineers in Ten Industries*. London: Allen & Unwin.

Lazarcik, G. 1962. Scientific Research and Its Relation to Earnings and Stock Prices. *Financial Analysts Journal*, 18, 49–53 (reprinted in E. B. Fredrikson, (ed.), *Frontiers of Investment Analysis*, Scranton, Pa.: International Textbook, 1965).

Lee, T. and L. Wilde. 1980. Market Structure and Innovation: A Reformulation. *Quarterly Journal of Economics*, 194, 429–36.

Leibenstein, H. 1966. Allocative Efficiency vs. "X-Efficiency." *American Economic Review*, 56, 392–415.

Leonard, W. N. 1971. Research and Development in Industrial Growth. *Journal* of Political Economy, 79, 232–56.

Levin, R. C. 1978. Technical Change, Barriers to Entry and Market Structure. *Economica,* 45, 347–61.

Lilienthal, D. 1953. *Big Business: A New Era.* New York, Harper.

Link, A. N. 1978. Rates of Induced Technology from Investment in Research and Development. *Southern Economic Journal,* 45, 370–9.

1978. Optimal Firm Size for R&D Innovations in Electric Utilities. *Journal of Economics and Business,* 31, 52–6.

1980. Firm Size and Efficient Entrepreneurial Activity: A Reformulation of the Schumpeter Hypothesis. *Journal of Political Economy,* 88, 771–82.

Loeb, Peter D. and V. Lin. 1977. Research & Development in the Pharmaceutical Industry – A Specification Error Approach. *Journal of Industrial Economics,* 26, 45–51.

Loury, G. C. 1979. Market Structure and Innovation. *Quarterly Journal of Economics,* XCIII, 395–410.

Machlup, F. 1962. *The Production and Distribution of Knowledge in the U.S.* Princeton, N.J.: Princeton University Press.

Maclaurin, W. R. 1954. Technological Progress in Some American Industries. *American Economic Review,* 44 Sup., 178–89.

Mansfield, E. 1968a. *Industrial Research and Technological Innovation – An Econometric Analysis.* New York: Norton.

1968b. *The Economics of Technological Change.* New York: Norton.

, J. Rapoport, J. Schnee, S. Wagner, and M. Hamburger. 1971. *Research and Innovation in the Modern Corporation.* New York: Norton.

, J. Rapoport, A. Romeo, E. Villani, S. Wagner, and F. Husic. 1977. *The Production and Application of New Industrial Technology.* New York: Norton.

Markham, J. W. 1965. Market Structure, Business Conduct, and Innovation. *American Economic Review,* 55, 323–32.

1974. Concentration: A Stimulus or Retardant to Innovation. In H. J. Goldschmid (ed.), *Industrial Concentration: The New Learning.* Boston: Little Brown.

Marx, K. 1919. *Capital.* Chicago: Charles H. Kerr.

Mason, E. 1951. Schumpeter on Monopoly and the Large Firm. *Review of Economics and Statistics.* XXXIII, 139–44.

McEachern, W. A. and A. Romeo. 1978. Stockholder Control, Uncertainty and the Allocation of Resources to Research and Development. *Journal of Industrial Economics,* XXVI, 349–61.

McGee, J. S. 1966. Patent Exploitation: Some Economic and Legal Problems. *Journal of Law and Economics,* IX, 135–62.

McLean, I. W. and D. K. Round. 1978. Research and Product Innovation in Australian Manufacturing Industries. *Journal of Industrial Economics,* XXVII, 1–12.

Meadows, D. H., D. L. Meadows, J. Randers, and W. W. Behrens III. 1972. *The Limits to Growth.* New York: Universe Books.

Merton, R. K. 1973. *The Sociology of Science.* Chicago: University of Chicago Press.

Mill, J. S. 1965. *Principles of Political Economy.* London: Routledge & Kegan Paul.

Mowery, D. and N. Rosenberg. 1979. The Influence of Market Demand Upon Innovation: A Critical Review of Some Recent Empirical Studies. *Research Policy,* 8, 102–53.

Mueller, D. C. 1967. The Firm's Decision Process: An Econometric Investigation. *Quarterly Journal of Economics,* 81, 58–87.

and J. E. Tilton. 1969. Research and Development Costs as a Barrier to Entry. *Canadian Journal of Economics,* 2, 570–9.

Mueller, W. F. 1962. The Origins of the Basic Inventions Underlying Du Pont's Major Product and Process Innovations, 1920–1950. In R. R. Nelson (ed.), *The Rate and Direction of Inventive Activity: Economic and Social Factors.* Princeton, N.J.: Princeton University Press, pp. 323–53.

Myers, S. and D. G. Marquis. 1969. Successful Industrial Innovations: A Study of Factors Underlying Innovation in Selected Firms. National Science Foundation, NSF 69-17.

Nadiri, M. I. 1970. Some Approaches to the Theory and Measurement of Total Factor Productivity: A Survey. *Journal of Economic Literature,* VIII, 1137–77.

Nelson, R. R. 1959. The Simple Economics of Basic Scientific Research. *Journal of Political Economy,* 67, 297–306.

, M. J. Peck, and E. D. Kalachek. 1967. *Technology Economic Growth and Public Policy.* Washington, D.C.: The Brookings Institution.

and S. G. Winter. 1977. Dynamic Competition and Technical Progress. In B. Balassa and R. Nelson (eds.), *Economic Progress, Private Values and Public Policy: Essays in Honor of William Fellner.* Amsterdam: North-Holland.

1978. Forces Generating and Limiting Concentration Under Schumpeterian Competition. *Bell Journal of Economics,* 9, 524–48.

1980. *An Evolutionary Theory of Economic Capabilities and Behavior.* Unpublished manuscript.

Ng, Y. K. 1971. Competition, Monopoly, and the Incentive to Invent. *Australian Economic Papers,* 10, 45–9.

Nordhaus, W. D. 1969. *Invention, Growth, and Welfare.* Cambridge, Mass.: M.I.T. Press.

Norris, K. and J. Vaizey. 1973. *The Economics of Research and Technology.* London: Allen & Unwin.

Nutter, C. W. 1956. Monopoly, Bigness and Progress. *Journal of Political Economy,* 54, 520–7.

Olivera, J. H. G. 1973. On Bernoullian Production Sets. *Quarterly Journal of Economics,* 87, 112–20.

Parker, J. E. S. 1978. *The Economics of Innovation.* London: Longman, 2nd ed.

Pavitt, K. and S. Wald. 1971. The Conditions for Success in Technological Innovation. OECD, Paris.

Peck, M. J. 1962. Inventions in the Post-War American Aluminum Industry. In R. R. Nelson (ed.), *The Rate and Direction of Inventive Activity: Economic and Social Factors*. Princeton, N.J.: Princeton University Press, pp. 279–98.

Phillips, A. 1956. Concentration, Scale, and Technological Change in Selected Manufacturing Industries, 1899–1939. *Journal of Industrial Economics,* 4, 179–93.

1965. Market Structure, Innovation and Investment. In W. Alderson, V. Terpstra, S. J. Shapiro (eds.), *Patents and Progress: The Sources and Impact of Advancing Technology*. Homewood, Ill.: Irwin, pp. 37–58.

1966. Patents, Potential Competition, and Technical Progress. *American Economic Review,* 56, 301–10.

1971. *Technology and Market Structure: A Study of the Aircraft Industry*. Lexington, Mass.: Heath, Lexington Books.

Phlips, L. 1971. Research. Chapter 5 in *Effects of Industrial Concentration: a Cross-Section Analysis for the Common Market*. Amsterdam: North-Holland, pp. 119–42.

Reinganum, J. F. 1979. *Dynamic Games with R&D Rivalry*. Ph.D. Dissertation, Northwestern University.

Rescher, N. 1978. *Scientific Progress*. Pittsburgh, Pa.: University of Pittsburgh Press.

Roberts, B. and H. Holdren. 1972. *Theory of Social Process: An Economic Analysis*. Ames, Iowa: Iowa State University Press.

Rodriquez, C. A. 1979. A Comment on Fisher and Temin on the Schumpeterian Hypothesis. *Journal of Political Economy,* 87, 383–5.

Rogers, E. M. and F. F. Shoemaker. 1971. *Communication of Innovations: A Cross-Cultural Approach*. New York: Free Press.

Romeo, A. A. 1977. The Rate of Imitation of a Capital-Embodied Process Innovation. *Economica,* 44, 63–9.

Rosenberg, J. B. 1976. Research and Market Share: A Reappraisal of the Schumpeter Hypothesis. *Journal of Industrial Economics,* XXV, 110–12.

Rosenberg, N. 1965. Adam Smith on the Division of Labor: Two Views or One? *Economica,* 32, 127–40.

1972. *Technology and American Economic Growth,* New York: Harper & Row.

1976. *Perspectives on Technology,* New York: Cambridge University Press.

Ruff, L. E. 1969. Research and Technological Progress in a Cournot Economy. *Journal of Economic Theory,* 1, 397–415.

Ruttan, V. W. 1959. Usher and Schumpeter on Invention, Innovation and Technological Change. *Quarterly Journal of Economics,* LXXIII, 596–606.

Salop, S. C. 1979. Strategic Entry Deterrence. *American Economic Review,* 69, 335–8.

Salter, W. E. G. 1960. *Productivity and Technical Change*. Cambridge University Press.

Samuelson, P. A. 1964. The Pure Theory of Public Expenditure. *Review of Economics and Statistics,* 36, 387–9.

1965. A Theory of Induced Innovation Along Kennedy-Weisacker Lines. *Review of Economics and Statistics,* XLVII, 343–56.

1973. *Economics,* New York: McGraw-Hill, 7th ed.

Scherer, F. M. 1965a. Size of Firm, Oligopoly, and Research: A Comment. *Canadian Journal of Economics and Political Science,* 31, 256–66.

1965b. Firm Size, Market Structure, Opportunity, and the Output of Patented Inventions. *American Economic Review,* 55, 1097–125.

1967a. Market Structure and the Employment of Scientists and Engineers. *American Economic Review,* 57, 524–31.

1967b. Research and Development Resource Allocation Under Rivalry. *Quarterly Journal of Economics,* 81, 359–94.

1973. Research and Development Returns to Scale and the Schumpeterian Hypothesis: Comment. Preprint of the International Institute of Management, Berlin.

1980. *Industrial Market Structure and Economic Performance.* Chicago: Rand McNally, 2nd ed.

Schmalensee, R. 1978. Entry Deterrence in the Ready-to-Eat Breakfast Cereal Industry. *Bell Journal of Economics,* 9, 305–27.

Schmookler, J. 1965. Technological Change and the Law of Industrial Growth. In W. Alderson et al. (eds.), *Patents and Progress.* Homewood, Ill.: Irwin.

1966. *Invention and Economic Growth.* Cambridge, Mass.: Harvard University Press.

1972. The Size of Firm and the Growth of Knowledge. In J. Schmookler (ed.), *Patents, Invention, and Economic Change.* Cambridge, Mass.: Harvard University Press.

Schumpeter, J. A. 1961. *Theory of Economic Development.* New York: Oxford University Press.

1964. *Business Cycles.* New York: McGraw-Hill.

1975. *Capitalism, Socialism and Democracy.* New York: Harper & Row, Harper Colophon Ed.

Schwartzman, D. 1976. *Innovation in the Pharmaceutical Industry.* Baltimore, Md.: Johns Hopkins University Press.

Shanks, M. 1967. *The Innovators.* Baltimore, Md.: Penguin Books.

Shavell, S. 1979. Risk Sharing and Incentives in the Principal and Agent Relationship. *Bell Journal of Economics,* 10, 55–73.

Shell, K. 1973. Inventive Activity, Industrial Organization and Economic Growth. In J. A. Mirrlees and N. H. Stern (eds.), *Models of Economic Growth.* New York: Wiley.

Shrieves, R. 1976. Firm Size and Innovation: Further Evidence. *Industrial Organization Review,* 4, 26–33.

1978. Market Structure and Innovation: A New Perspective. *Journal of Industrial Economics,* 26, 329–47.

Silk, L. L. 1960. *The Research Revolution.* New York: McGraw-Hill.

Sivazlian, B. D. and L. E. Stanfel. 1975. *Analysis of Systems in Operations Research.* Englewood Cliffs, N.J.: Prentice-Hall.

Smith, A. 1937. *The Wealth of Nations.* New York: Modern Library.

Smith, B. A. 1974. Technological Innovation in Electric Power Generation: 1950–1970. *Land Economics,* 50, 336–47.

Smith, V. K. 1973. A Review of Models of Technological Change with Reference to the Role of Environmental Resources. *Socio-Economic Plan. Sci.,* 7, 489–509.

Smith, W. J. J. and D. Creamer. 1968. R&D and Small Company Growth: A

Statistical Review and Company Case Studies. The Conference Board, Studies in Business Economics No. 102.

Smyth, D. J., W. J. Boyes, D. E. Peseau. 1975. The Measurement of Firm Size: Theory and Evidence for the United States and the United Kingdom. *Review of Economics and Statistics,* 57, 111–14.

, J. M. Samuels, and J. Tzoannos. 1972. Patents, Profitability, Liquidity and Firm Size. *Applied Economics,* 4, 77–86.

Solo, C. S. 1951. Innovation in the Capitalist Process: A Critique of the Schumpeterian Theory. *Quarterly Journal of Economics,* 65, 417–28.

Solow, R. 1957. Technical Change and the Aggregate Production Function. *Review of Economics and Statistics,* 39, 312–30.

Stekler, H. O. 1967. Technological Progress in the Aerospace Industry. *Journal of Industrial Economics,* 15, 226–36.

Stigler, G. J. 1956. Industrial Organization and Economic Progress. In L. D. White (ed.), *The State of the Social Sciences.* Chicago: University of Chicago Press, pp. 269–82.

1957. Perfect Competition, Historically Contemplated. *Journal of Political Economy,* 65, 1–16.

Stonebra. er, R. J. 1976. Corporate Profits and the Risk of Entry. *Review of Economics and Statistics,* 58, 33–9.

Stoneman, P. L. 1979. Patenting Activity: A Re-evaluation of the Influence of Demand Pressures. *Journal of Industrial Economics,* 27, 385–401.

Sweezy, P. W. 1943. Professor Schumpeter's Theory of Innovation. *Review of Economics and Statistics,* 25, 93–6.

Taussig, F. W. 1915. *Inventors and Money-Makers.* New York: MacMillan.

Terleckyji, N. 1977. Recent Findings Regarding the Contribution of Industrial R&D to Economic Growth (Mimeo). National Planning Association.

Uhlmann, L. 1978. The Innovation Process in West European Industrial Countries. *ifo-digest,* 1, 15–20.

Usher, D. 1964. The Welfare Economics of Invention. *Economica N.S.,* 31, 279–87.

Utterback, J. M. 1974. Innovation in Industry and the Diffusion of Technology. *Science,* 183, 620–6.

Vernon, J. M. 1972. *Market Structure and Industrial Performance.* Boston: Allyn & Bacon.

and P. Gusen. 1974. Technical Change and Firm Size: The Pharmaceutical Industry. *Review of Economics and Statistics,* 56, 294–302.

Villard, H. H. 1958. Competition, Oligopoly and Research. *Journal of Political Economy,* LXVI, 483–97.

von Weizacker, C. C. Forthcoming. *Barriers to Entry: A Theoretical Treatment.* New York: Springer-Verlag.

Wall Street Journal Staff. 1968. *The Innovators.* Princeton, N.J.: Dow Jones Books.

Weiss, L. 1963. Average Concentration Ratios and Industrial Performance. *Journal of Industrial Economics,* 11, 237–54.

1971. Quantitative Studies of Industrial Organization. In M. D. Intriligator (ed.), *Frontiers of Quantitative Economics.* Amsterdam: North-Holland.

Weitzman, M. L. 1979. Optimal Search for the Best Alternative. *Econometrica*, 47, 641–54.

Wilder, R. P. and S. R. Stansell. 1974. Determinants of Research and Development Activity by Electric Utilities. *Bell Journal of Economics and Management Science*, 5, 646–50.

Williamson, O. E. 1965. Innovation and Market Structure. *Journal of Political Economy*, 73, 67–73.

  1975. *Markets and Hierarchies: Analysis and Antitrust Implications.* New York: Free Press.

Wilson, R. W. 1977. The Effect of Technological Environment and Product Rivalry on R&D Effort and Licensing of Inventions. *Review of Economics and Statistics*, LIX, 171–8.

Wood, A. 1971. Diversification, Merger and Research Expenditures: A Review of Empirical Studies. In R. Marris and A. Wood (eds.), *The Corporate Economy: Growth, Competition and Innovative Potential.* Cambridge, Mass.: Harvard University Press.

Worley, J. S. 1961. Industrial Research and the New Competition. *Journal of Political Economy*, 69, 183–6.

Yamey, B. S. 1970. Monopoly, Competition and the Incentive to Invent: A Comment. *Journal of Law and Economics*, XIII, 253–6.

AUTHOR INDEX

237

SUBJECT INDEX